THE ORDINARY SPACEMAN

THE ORDINARY SPACEMAN

From Boyhood Dreams to Astronaut

CLAYTON C. ANDERSON

Foreword by NEVADA BARR

University of Nebraska Press
Lincoln & London

Library of Congress Cataloging-in-Publication Data

Anderson, Clayton C., 1959–
The ordinary spaceman: from boyhood dreams
to astronaut / Clayton C. Anderson; foreword by
Nevada Barr.

pages   cm
ISBN 978-0-8032-6282-9 (cloth: alk. paper)
ISBN 978-0-8032-7731-1 (ePub)
ISBN 978-0-8032-7732-8 (mobi)
ISBN 978-0-8032-7733-5 (pdf).
1. Anderson, Clayton C., 1959–. 2. Astronauts—
United States—Biography. 3. United States—
National Aeronautics and Space Administration—
Biography. 4. International Space Station.
5. Extravehicular activity (Manned space
flight). I. Title.
TL789.85.A53A3 2015
629.450092—dc23
[B]
2014048858

Set in Minion Pro by Lindsey Auten.

To Dex, a true and honest leader of men and women, whose time both on and off this Earth was far too short.

To all my crewmates:

C.J., Bru, Swany, Pat, Danny, and J.R. of STS-117

Fyodor, Oleg, and Suni of Expedition 15

Scott, Scorch, Rick, Davyd, T.C., Babs, and B. Alvin of STS-118

Yuri, Peggy, and Sheikh of Expedition 16

Pambo, Zambo, Flambo, Longbow, Robo, Rocky, and Bo-ichi of STS-120

Dex, Mash, Rick, Dottie (Cheese!), Naoko, and Stephanie of STS-131

You have shared your lives on terra firma and in outer space with me, and I am forever grateful to you for allowing me that wonderful opportunity.

To my Group 17 "Penguin" classmates of 1998: while I may not have flown with all of you, I was always honored to be one of you.

For my mother and father and my brother and sister, who taught me that giving up is never an option . . .

. . . and for my wife, son, and daughter, who taught me why.

CONTENTS

Foreword
   by Nevada Barr ix
Acknowledgments xi
Introduction xiii

1. First Flight 1
2. Beginnings 17
3. Freshman Fifteen 35
4. Hey, There's an App for That! 47
5. Answer the Phone, Will Ya? 63
6. Baby Astronauts 81
7. Hail *Columbia*! 89
8. Age of Aquarius 113
9. From Russia with Love 131
10. Survival of the Fittest 159
11. Sign of the Times 181
12. Sixty-Two and Counting 193
13. Dark Days of Summer 205
14. Crime and Punishment 217
15. The "Void" of Outer Space 235
16. The Doctor Is In 243
17. The Hard Thump of Reality 259
18. The Serendipity of Chance 277
19. Walking Tall 289
20. Fame and Fortune 299
21. Find Us Faithful 311
22. Impacts 331
23. The End Becomes the Beginning 343

FOREWORD

Nevada Barr

I have known Clay Anderson for many years. We met at a National Education Association conference shortly after his daughter was born. He sang at my wedding and called me from outer space so I could yell "Love you!" into the black reaches of the universe. Since meeting Clay, I have met several presidents and first ladies and a handful of celebrities, but he remains the only astronaut I know. They are rare, these individuals who orbit around our world, and Clay is everything one could want in a hero: tall, well built, well married, honest, forthright, and, ironically for an astronaut, down-to-earth.

In reading Clay's *The Ordinary Spaceman* you get no sense of separation between the reader and the event; it is as if your best friend is taking you with him under the sea, to Russia, freezing and floating and trying to find a way to eat and pee without gravity. The trip is personal and fun. Reading this book is the next best thing to becoming an astronaut yourself. Maybe the best thing, since you can share all the wild adventures Clay had without ever having to spend hours curled up like a fetus getting fitted for a space suit or slogging through a Russian winter to prove you have the Right Stuff.

Prepare to launch.

ACKNOWLEDGMENTS

Literally thousands of individuals, and surely an equal number of organizations, have been responsible, in part, for the stories contained in this book. From the time I entered elementary school until I hung up my astronaut boots, I have felt the impact of caring people doing their damnedest to help me succeed. While it is imprudent for me to attempt to thank each one individually, there are some who do deserve a special shout-out of thanks.

First and foremost are my wife and family. Susan, Cole, and Sutton, you bring me great joy, and I thank you for accompanying me on this glorious journey. I love you with all my heart and soul.

Notable is my longtime friend and referee colleague John Milstead. A steadfast supplier of daily morale-boosting emails while I lived in space, John provided guidance in the development of the book's introduction. I thank him for his help, his wit, and his friendship.

While I served as an Aquarius aquanaut, the National Oceanic and Atmospheric Administration, the University of North Carolina Wilmington, and the Key Largo Office of the National Undersea Research Center stood out. Owners and operators of the habitat, with their high level of training competency, professionalism, and adherence to safety at all costs, gave us the confidence we needed to succeed. Thanks to Kea, Birnsey, Coop, Otter, Jim, Dominique, Dr. Jay, Dr. Steve, Kim, Billy, Kendall, Otto, Smitty, Roger, Byron, Hal, and Thor. You were my "watchdogs" and my friends.

Pilots Andy Roberts and Ray "Governor" Heineman, flying under the radar (but at very high speed), were willing to assist my waning memory on the technical aspects of the T-38. I thank you for your efforts, which will (I hope) keep others with flying expertise from pointing out any errors I made.

A hearty *cnacebo* (thank you) is provided for Dr. Anthony Vanchu. One of a cadre of outstanding Russian language instructors assigned to me during my astronaut career, Dr. Vanchu graciously reviewed the manuscript to ensure that I had minimal *ошибки* (mistakes). I am grateful for his multilingual expertise.

To all the spacefarers of our world—those who came before me and those still to come—I offer my thanks for dedicating your lives to the premise that we are explorers and that what we do is important to the future of our world.

Significantly, I extend the greatest of thank-yous to my dear friend and writing coach, author, actor, and artist Nevada Barr. The patience and confidence you showed in this neophyte author allowed me to grow as a writer and more effectively share my once-in-a-lifetime experience. Without your help, this book would be just a collection of random stories, made up of painfully long sentences and laced with multiple adjectives.

Finally, I would be remiss if I did not say thank you to NASA, her centers, and her employees. Twice you took a chance on this small-town boy from Nebraska. Thank you for hiring me in 1981 and for choosing me to represent the United States of America as an astronaut. I am forever grateful for your trust and confidence and hope that you consider it a risk that paid off.

Many incredible books have been written about the wonders of space, by and about astronauts more famous than I: fantastic rocket journeys through a paper-thin atmosphere, initiated on virgin, unproven towers of explosive fuel, and resulting in stunning views of our beautifully fragile and breathtaking home planet, Earth. Those literary gems each told their stories using thousands of NASA photographs; they spoke of individual death-defying forays into the vacuum of space on the end of a single frail steel-cable tether. They related life stories and battles against the temptation to always want more.

I want this book to be free of the mundane and politically correct. I want to convey to readers what life was truly like on this incredible journey, from the beginning, when I applied to become an astronaut, to my selection and training, and finally, to my assignment to and execution of a mission. I want you to know the highs and lows that occurred along the way as I lived my dream performing the ultimate "work abroad."

My father used to relate a classic joke about me to anyone who would listen. He would smile at them and say, "I told my son, don't just take up space in school." Well, Dad, I did take up space in school, and I have chosen to write this book for a very simple reason: to share the tremendous experience of becoming an astronaut. I want as many people as humanly possible to know the wonder and glory of that place we call outer space . . . and I want them to know it on my terms.

There are a lot of things I approach with reverence. I'm reverent about my relationship with God. I'm reverent about my love for my family and my responsibilities and obligations to each of them. I'm reverent about being the best man I can possibly be: the best husband, the best father, the best brother, the best friend, the best astronaut. I can't begin to explain the reverence I felt while encapsulated in a space suit with just a few layers of fabric and Kevlar between me and the great vacuum of space, standing on the end of the fifty-eight-foot Canadian-built robotic arm of the International Space Station, or while looking at the Earth and the heavens. But I approach other things from an altogether different direction. I once heard of an overly pompous gentleman who was admonished that he had broken the "Third Rule." When he asked what the Third Rule was, he received the reply, "You've taken yourself too seriously." He then asked what the other rules were. "There are no other rules," was the answer.

I have done some pretty serious things, and I have taken them very seriously. I've respected my parents and family, my teachers, my education, my religion, my friends, my job, my coworkers, and myself. But I have never broken the Third Rule. I'm pretty irreverent about Clay.

I am forever grateful to the wonderful folks at the University of Nebraska Press for agreeing to publish this book. While Rob T., Courtney, Ann, Martyn, Emily, Rob B., Rosemary, Erica, Thomas, Tish, and Lona performed flawlessly as my closeout crew—getting ready for this analogous launch of a "bound paper rocket"—the full list of mission objectives would not have been accomplished without the dedication and yeoman efforts of the entire press staff.

Some spectacularly wonderful things have happened to me during my short time here on Earth, but I've always considered myself to be just a small-town boy from Nebraska—nothing special, just an ordinary American. I'm even a bit embarrassed to think that you might find me interesting enough to have picked up this book. But since you have, I'll try to tell you about some of the truly extraordinary things that have happened in my life, and I'll try to keep it interesting . . . and irreverent. Live long and prosper!

First Flight

Life is filled with firsts: first word, first step, first date, first kiss, first tax audit . . . well, you get the picture. The life of a brand-new astronaut is filled with firsts as well. From the day you report to the Johnson Space Center (JSC) in Houston and journey up the six flights of stairs in Building 4 South to the hallowed halls of the Astronaut Corps, you are destined for experiences that, while fully expected, are certainly not inconsequential: your first staff meeting, first trip to the men's restroom, first run-in with a veteran astronaut who thinks you might be taking over his next spacewalk. All are a part of the rite of passage so crucial to becoming an accepted member of perhaps the most elite group of men and women on (and off) the planet.

Perhaps *the* most significant of these firsts should also be defined as a perk . . . a perk that occurs at over 850 miles an hour! The day was November 4, 1998, only two short months after I had reported for duty as an astronaut candidate (ASCAN) at JSC. The weather was bright and sunny with the temperature in the low eighties: a beautiful fall day in southeast Texas, the time of year Texans long for and then lament when it passes quickly and the first of December arrives.

I had arrived at Ellington Field plenty early, with a healthy amount of nervous anxiety. A former air force base in southeast Houston, Ellington Field has been repurposed as the home to NASA's fleet of T-38 training jets. I was anticipating an experience that would stick in my memory forever. I tentatively climbed the narrow internal stairwell on the southeast side of Hangar 276 while casting longing, worshipful glances at the beautifully sleek white-and-blue jet aircraft on the floor below. Within this massive building all the jets rested quietly and majestically, each an individual piece of a well-designed jigsaw puzzle nested together so the entire fleet could avoid exposure to the brutal windstorms, rain, hail, and searing heat of south Texas. Feeling every bit the rookie in this unfamiliar place, I carefully opened the blue door to the "ready room"—the sacred area where pilots and astronauts execute their individual flight preparations. Inside, I quickly made my way toward the far hallway, silently hoping that I wouldn't be stopped and questioned.

My presence was announced with each creaking step, as the floor of the World War II–era hangar squealed in distress under the pressure of my highly polished black leather military boots. I searched for the office adorned with the right nameplate. A third of the way down the hall I found myself at the door of Col. Andy Roberts (U.S. Air Force, Reserve), whose title was astronaut instructor pilot (IP). I was here for a baptism of sorts, to fly for the first time in one of NASA's T-38s. (The T-38s—"T" for "trainer"—are a fleet of twin-engine jets maintained by NASA specifically for astronauts to fly.)

Wearing my new royal blue astronaut flight suit, complete with a nametag declaring that Clayton C. Anderson, JSC, had made it this far, I stood as tall as I could while I waited patiently for Andy's acknowledgment that it was okay to enter the room. Beckoned with a warm smile and a welcoming wave, I entered, then paused for a moment to survey the lair of the former U.S. Air Force fighter pilot.

Andy's workspace was shared with three other IPs and adorned with the unceremonious trappings one might expect at a U.S. government facility. The drab gray government-issue office furniture and cubicles were arranged as if to barricade themselves from the outside world and anyone or anything that might ruin their day. Bookshelves and file cabinets were set up the way kids might build forts in their grandma's front room. As my eyes scanned this cacophony of paper and personal mementos, gathered through years of career service and family milestones, I noticed that my treasured rookie flight suit—so crisp, blue, and stiff—now felt like a rough piece of cardboard freshly removed from a three-pack of new t-shirts. Nerves and anxiety alerted every pore, causing me to break into a nice preflight sweat, as I realized how well worn my veteran-fighter-pilot-turned-instructor's garb was compared to mine.

His flight suit, once the same brilliant hue and crispness of the one I so proudly wore, had the look of a comfortable denim shirt, soft to the touch and conforming to each contour in the wearer's upper torso. The one-time bright royal blue had become a faded blue pastel, reminding me a bit of a favorite old bathrobe. Yet his appearance was one of total confidence. On each of his sleeves, near his biceps, were the classic military-type patches—a U.S. flag on the left and the circular flight instructor patch of the NASA Aircraft Operations Directorate on the right. Even these patches had faded, beaten down by hours upon hours of the relentless sun shining through the clear glass cockpit of the T-38, testifying to flight hours so numerous that they require a computer to track. Each thread had been hammered by ultraviolet radiation, every flight pushing the fabric further toward the yellow end of the spectrum.

My flight instructor's suit was repeatedly an inanimate passenger in a jet as it ascends through the atmosphere to pierce cotton-like clouds the way a needle drives through a piece of fabric. Yet for all the abuse that suit got, its ultimate reward was to be touched by beams of high-energy radiation emanating at the speed of light from our very own star, poised majestically ninety-three million miles away at the center of our solar system.

I looked at Andy's nametag framing his name and rank. Though tarnished from wear, the time-honored air force silver border still shone proudly as the emblem of the service for which he risked his life. Oh sure, he could have gotten a new flight suit—all it took was a short walk across the hangar floor and up another flight of stairs to reach the equipment shop. He could have been wearing one just as stiff and uncomfortable as mine. But as I would quickly come to learn, he wore his "gently used" flight suit with as much honor as any of the others who have so proudly served; he wore it to commemorate how he had bravely challenged the skies for his country and had come out a winner every single time.

Andy was on the phone finishing a call with his wife. I was not eavesdropping, but just before he hung up I heard him say something like, "Honey, I've got to go. I've got one of the new ASCANS here for his 'Zoom and Boom' ride." I was already nervous enough, and hearing those words certainly got my attention. I feared that I would quickly be coming to grips with the real meaning of the phrase "baptism under fire."

I knew Andy from one of our previous T-38 training lectures when he had described to our class the nuances of the T-38's hydraulic system. We reintroduced ourselves, and after five minutes of chatting about life in general, he stopped the small talk. His tone of voice changed to that of an air force pilot, and he started to pepper me with technical details relating to our upcoming "sortie." This training flight would take place in the area designated as W-147C (or *whiskey* one-four-seven *charlie*). W-147C, a practice area covering the northern Gulf of Mexico, was artistically depicted on our flight control avionics screen as a huge triangle of bright green. Our preflight briefing covered each and every detail, from the tail number of our jet to the high-threat areas we would encounter along the way (birds near the runway, small planes in the area of Ellington Field), as well as the visual signals we would use to communicate with each other in the event of an emergency and possible ejection from the aircraft. When we came to the subject of communication and the situation known as "nordo" (no radio), Andy calmly asked, "Do you think you can operate the radio system, Clay?"

"Yes, sir, I believe I can," was my confident reply. Every ASCAN new to flying receives classroom ground school training in all aspects of the T-38 and its systems, including communication and the radios. With that, Andy handed me a small sheet of paper complete with the list of frequencies we would need for our one-hour-and-fifteen-minute flight—a flight that would fully (and finally) expose me to the high-speed world of jet aircraft.

After a quick bathroom break we reconnoitered in the parachute room, where more than one hundred green military parachutes hung from symmetrical racks of simple wooden poles, having been prepared meticulously by the aircrew equipment staff. There they waited for the next astronaut or pilot to slide into one, cinch the straps tightly, and silently pray that it wouldn't be needed that day. Andy and I each chose a parachute matching our size (extra large for me), threw it over our right shoulder, grabbed our helmet bags from our designated cubbies, and headed to the flight line.

As we strode to the jet, I held myself tall and proud. Inside, my nerves tingled with anticipation. After quickly stuffing foam earplugs into my ears, I solemnly followed Andy around the aircraft, watching with rapt attention as he performed and narrated a detailed preflight check of the jet and her high-tech appendages.

As our "bird" was in the expected pristine condition, I climbed the blue ladder that hung from the sill of the rear cockpit and settled into the back seat of this vintage two-seater. As I wasn't accustomed to the process of sitting down and strapping in, a longtime member of the flight line crew helped me jostle into all of my flight gear: gloves, helmet, pub bag (as in "publications"—maps and charts), then verified that I had gotten the myriad of connections, buckles, and straps in the proper configuration for a safe trip. With a pat on my shoulder and a smile that more closely resembled a smirk, he looked me straight in the eye and bid me a safe flight. I got the distinct impression that he was well aware of my rookie status.

Moving with what I thought was the speed of a tortoise wallowing in molasses, I checked my rear cockpit gauges, dials, and displays to make sure they resembled the configuration I had been taught to expect for takeoff. Strapped tightly into my seat, with my helmet's chin strap locked in place, I cast my eyes to the lower center of the cockpit, just slightly above the control stick, to double-check the radio management system display. Comparing the five LED segments to those on the handwritten card that was clipped to my kneeboard, I relaxed just a bit, confident that I had entered the correct numbers into the various frequency slots.

Andy's voice was cool and calm: "Ready to start on the right." He pushed the corresponding start button located in his front cockpit. Then, watching to see that the RPM gauge reached the required level of 12 to 14 percent, he called out, "Start the clock," verbally acknowledging that the ignition circuit would be armed for only thirty seconds. As he began to gently ease the right engine throttle forward, the quiet inside the cockpit was instantly filled with the powerful roar of a jet turbine. With the engine spinning at more than 2,000 RPMs and drinking fuel by the second, the variable-area nozzle was now spitting out the hot pungent exhaust of Jet A fuel. A massive thirty-six hundred pounds of thrust are produced at sea level by this General Electric–built, eight-stage turbo jet engine. Andy repeated the process for the left engine. My earplugs were already paying huge dividends as the thunder of the two axial-flow engines hummed in near-simultaneous rhythm.

With an easygoing style born of years of military jet experience, Andy contacted the control tower for clearance: "Ellington Tower, this is NASA niner-one-seven, I-F-R to *whiskey* one-four-seven *charlie*, clearance on request."

After a wait of ten to fifteen seconds, the tower operator at Ellington keyed his microphone and sent his voice crackling across the airwaves: "NASA niner-one-seven, cleared to *whiskey* one-four-seven *charlie*, radar vectors, then via EFD radial two-zero-six at fifty. Call ready for taxi."

Not really understanding all of what the tower operator had just said, I was frantically trying to manipulate my ballpoint pen. My ability to legibly "copy clearance" in this foreign language was severely compromised by the Nomex flight gloves covering my shaking hands. Plus, I had to capture this critical information on a sheet of paper strapped to a kneeboard wrapped tightly around my right thigh. Frustrated and overwhelmed, I gave up. My pilot provided me with a second chance by calmly repeating the clearance exactly as it was dictated by the tower: "Ellington Tower, NASA niner-one-seven, cleared to *whiskey* one-four-seven *charlie* via radar vectors to EFD radial two-zero-six at fifty. We are ready for taxi and we have 'echo.'"

"NASA niner-one-seven, Ellington Tower. Taxi to runway one-seven right, via *hotel*," said the faceless voice in the tower.

In the front cockpit, Andy simultaneously pushed the engine throttles slowly forward with his gloved left hand. The jet patiently roared to life, inching forward from its parking spot on the tarmac, as we initiated the long trip from the T-38 hangar on the field's south end, down the intersecting taxiway "*hotel*," to runway one-seven right at the north end of Ellington Field almost eleven thousand feet away.

The taxi to runway one-seven right, at the far end of the vast expanse of concrete, takes slightly longer than to the neighboring strips. This was a good thing for me. It gave me ample time to do the necessary pretakeoff checks and to get one last briefing on what I was to watch for as we barreled down the runway.

Even early in November the Texas winds come predominantly from the south. Using runway one-seven right—taking off into the wind—gives a nice added lift for the T-38's short stubby wings. Another call to the tower from Andy, letting them know we were ready for takeoff, resulted in a standard call-back phrase from our Ellington Field air traffic controller (ATC): "NASA niner-one-seven, turn left heading zero-niner-zero [090], maintain two thousand [feet altitude], cleared for takeoff, runway one-seven right."

Andy repeated the call back to the tower, then smoothly muscled the two side-by-side thrust levers forward, gently pushing our twelve-thousand-pound aircraft onto the runway. With his toes pushing hard and forward against the jet's brake pedals, he drove the throttle quadrant levers all the way to their initial stops, the position known as "military power." The engines, producing near the thrust level required for takeoff, were trying to drive the jet down the runway. Andy's strong legs on the brakes were the only force keeping us stationary. "Clay, you ready to go?" Andy asked.

My meek "yes" surely must have sounded to him like a timid little third grader.

Andy pulled his feet back from the brake pedals and tightened his grip on the throttles. He added just enough force to push the handles through the detent and then slammed them full forward past the military stops into the afterburner position. With the engines whining at their highest thrust level, the jet leaped forward down the runway with the horsepower of more than twenty-five thousand metallic stallions.

The thrust force increased against my chest as the needle on the rear cockpit speedometer began a steady crawl clockwise. (Its original at-rest position is 60 knots.) Andy, appearing to be in total control (remember, I only knew how to work the radio), made the requisite calls that would one day emanate from my vocal chords: "Off the peg—60 knots, 100 hundred knots, go speed." The scenery outside began to blur.

"SETOS [single engine takeoff speed, pronounced SEE-*tose*]. SETOS plus ten," came the call that indicated we were now traveling just fast enough to take off even if we were to lose one of our engines.

We were flying down the runway at a velocity of over 155 knots, a speed that I had never before experienced. Using his feet on the rudder pedals like a surfer riding a surfboard, Andy held the jet's nose directly on the runway's center line. A slight backward pull on the control stick lifted the nose just five degrees and we were airborne. Buildings on the ground rapidly began to resemble little dollhouses.

Andy called me on the intercom frequency. With an impish tone in his voice that undoubtedly matched a face I couldn't see, he suggested I take a look out the window and tell him what I saw. "The Johnson Space Center and Clear Lake City," was my reply.

Laughing, Andy said: "Look again."

Not knowing what he was trying to get me to say, I once again scanned the shrinking scene below in a vain effort to find the clue to this game we apparently were playing.

I choked out another ill-fated reply: "Uh . . . NASA?"

He laughed a second time, then told me to check the angle of flight. A scant minute since clearing the ground and we were screaming into the sky in a position that almost approached vertical!

When we reached our destination—41,000 feet in altitude, high above the Gulf of Mexico—I was calmed by the fact that we had slowed to a more leisurely rate of speed, with a correspondingly lower angle of climb (the angle that the jet's nose makes with the horizon). I began to engage Andy in light chatter as if I were a veteran of high-speed aircraft. But this brief period of confidence began to erode when Andy asked a very strange question.

"Clay, can you hear me?" was the call from the front cockpit.

"Yes, I can hear you," I answered without reservation.

"Clay, can you hear me?" came back again through my helmet's headset, causing me to think that maybe I needed to speak louder.

"Yes!" I nearly bellowed into my oxygen mask, beginning to grasp the fact that perhaps something important was going on.

In the next second the jet began to rock violently. Something had gone terribly wrong. My dearth of experience was becoming more apparent with every passing second. Forcing myself to stay calm, I began racking my brain to recall any portion of my miniscule training. Almost as if by accident, an idea started to kick in. I glanced to the forward cockpit and watched the back of Andy's head, steady in front of the thick scratched glass.

Apparently our communication system was malfunctioning. I tapped my right ear with my royal blue gloved hand, then followed with the universally understood thumbs-up signal where Andy could see it in the rearview mirror mounted above the right side of his instrument panel. Next, with renewed hope that I had actually figured out what was going on, I tapped my oxygen mask, then motioned thumbs-down to indicate that perhaps I could hear him but he couldn't hear me.

His calm reply over the limping intercom put my fears at ease. "Looks like the intercom is intermittent. We're gonna have to head for home," he said. A second thumbs-up from me and we turned back for Ellington. My thoughts turned from dealing with a brewing disaster to "Oh my God, what did I do wrong?!"

We pulled back into the chocks at the line and completed the shutdown checklist. As we raised our cockpit canopies, I heard the flight line lead, Bob Mullen, ask Andy the question that all rookie astronauts fear: "What did he screw up?"

I was too new at this to have known I should begin the flight with the famous "astronaut prayer": "Dear Lord, please don't let me f*** this up!"

As I had done during our taxi to the hangar, I once again checked and rechecked every connection and pushbutton in that cockpit that I could find. Still not seeing anything out of order, I grew more and more confident that I had set up the radio panel correctly and that my helmet and communication connections had been made without error. Then the jet technician appeared, moving one of the blue metal ladders into place and climbing up slowly to my level. He cast a careful eye over the switches and dials of the rear cockpit. His skilled eyes and hands checked the exact same pushbuttons and connections that I had evaluated multiple times.

His resulting conclusion, that the radio management system (RMS) box had failed, vindicated me. A wave of relief allowed a huge sigh to push forth from my lungs. Without missing a beat, and without us even having to climb down from the jet, a new RMS box was swapped with the faulty culprit.

Back on the runway, we were once again screaming for the sky. This time the trip out to the Gulf was uneventful, except for the fact that Andy asked the ATC for a "block altitude" from twenty-eight thousand to forty-one thousand feet. When the ATC responded affirmatively, Andy asked if I would like to break the sound barrier. Thinking "Hell, yes!" I responded "Sure." In my mind I pictured us flying straight and level, screaming through the sky high above the water. I couldn't have been more wrong.

After we finally reached our target altitude of forty-one thousand feet, Andy easily leveled the T-38 until the digital readout from the altimeter began to steady itself, displaying forty-one followed by three zeroes. Within seconds, Andy rolled the aircraft upside down while pulling the stick back as far as he could, sending the jet's sleek nose pointing to the Gulf of Mexico. He continued to pull back until the stick nearly contacted the front edge of his seat. The plane seemed to flip over backward and plunge straight down toward Earth!

Flipped over on our backs, as if we were performing a half-gainer from the diving board of the community swimming pool, we sped directly for the white-capped waves below—which were growing larger with each passing second. "Check our velocity," Andy called to me as he gave the jet another half-rotation to place us rightside up again.

My head still spinning from my first backflip in a supersonic jet, I zeroed in on the velocity indicator (called a tape) and struggled to focus on it. Velocity: 0.88, 0.90, 0.92. I watched the numbers climb steadily, its pace dictated by the constant pull of Earth's gravity, coupled with the drive from two spinning eight-stage turbo jet engines. The numbers passed the digital value of Mach 1.0. We were traveling at the speed of sound!

Like a Tour de France biker fighting to reach the top of the highest hill, the numbers climbed slowly while the rate of increase started to level off. Finally, the value stayed steady at 1.27. We were now traveling *faster* than the speed of sound!

My newbie astronaut brain told me that I should be hearing a sonic boom. Seconds later, the only sound I heard was a voice inside my head saying "Duh!" We were *causing* the sonic boom. We were moving so fast that there was no way we would be able to hear it. The sonic boom was already far behind us.

The culmination of my first time breaking the sound barrier was as unexpected as its initiation. As we neared the bottom of our block altitude at twenty-eight thousand feet, once again subsonic on the normal side of the invisible barrier, Andy pulled back hard on the stick again and arrested our plummet toward terra firma. The resulting pullout felt like the jet's steel frame was bending, resisting that force of physics Newton discovered when an apple fell on his head. My weight of 195 pounds doubled in an instant and I sank deeper into my rear cockpit seat, feeling the pull from the force of Earth's gravity on my backside.

Falling back on memories of the Tom Cruise movie *Top Gun*, I began to make loud, serious grunting noises from the rear cockpit, with teeth clenched, pushing hard against my abdominal muscles as if engaged in a timely bowel movement. This vain attempt to force blood back to my head was only minimally successful. My peripheral vision began to go black like curtains being closed on a stage.

With renewed vigor and forceful abdominal thrusting brought on by my sudden fear of going blind and passing out, my vision eventually returned to normal. I was beginning to relish the excitement of this awesome experience when a guttural chuckle came through the jet's intercom system. Then Andy said, "You don't have to make so much noise when you're doing that." My pilot had been listening to my efforts. This pulled me out of my fighter pilot vision and returned me to the reality of a rookie flying his first flight.

Humming through the sky on a straight and level trajectory, doing about 350 knots, Andy suggested that I try an aileron roll. "You bet," I said. "What do I do?"

Andy's quick reply was, "You just have to push the stick to the right and hold it there for a few seconds. Let the jet roll, then bring the stick back to its normal position."

It sounded simple enough, so I gave it a try. I moved hard right on the stick, and held it for all I was worth. When the timing felt right (how would I know?), I slammed the stick back into the neutral position and looked up through the clear glass cockpit expecting the cloudless blue sky I had been enjoying since take-off. Water was all that I could see. We were upside down! Andy was laughing again. Assuming the role of instructor, he suggested that I "roll it just a bit further." A quick movement of the stick to a hard stop on the right, and then a return to its vertical neutral position, produced a glorious vision of blue sky over my head that made me right with the world again.

During our T-38 ground school training, we had been warned many times about the phenomenon known as the dreaded "stomach awareness." You are probably quite familiar with it—that feeling you get on a roller coaster ride for the third time, after having just downed a deluxe bacon cheeseburger and fries with a chocolate shake. Where you break into a cold sweat and your stomach starts to remind you that, yes, it's still there. Perhaps you pop a peppermint to help alleviate the cotton mouth that has taken over your tongue. Well, our next maneuver, the loop to loop, brought it all to the forefront of my consciousness.

Andy's plan was that he would first demonstrate this maneuver, which began with another hard pull full aft on the control stick, and then give me a chance to show if I'd been paying close attention. For the second time in our sortie we flipped over on our back, with the nose of the jet eventually pointing downward. But this time we continued through the bottom of the loop, and my body was subjected to another serious episode from the pull of gravity. Now a full-fledged veteran of these physiological effects, I was confident that this time would not present much of a challenge. It wasn't until sweat began to pour from the top of my head down the front of my face—it felt like a rain shower gushing down inside my visor—and my vision started to go black again that I understood I didn't really have any idea how to combat what was going on. I resumed my intercom-audible grunting and groaning, prompting an additional hearty laugh from my partner in the front cockpit. Embarrassed again (this was becoming too routine), I pressed on, undaunted. Desperately hoping for regained vision, I pushed so hard against my abdomen that this time I thought I was going to need a diaper. It was apparent that stomach awareness training—part 2—had kicked in. I extended my Nomex-gloved right hand toward the oxygen system controls.

I pushed the 100 percent oxygen (O2) and emergency levers hard forward to "gang load" the regulator, just as I had been taught in training class. Then I raised my helmet visor and rotated the air conditioning vent to blow frigid air directly on my face. It was helping, but the second loop was already in progress. While my heart wanted to stay aloft, my vestibular system was telling me that if we didn't land pretty soon, I was going to have a nasty mess riding with me in the cockpit.

The pullout of loop 2 brought Andy's glance to the depleting fuel gauges and resulted in his call that we needed to "RTB [return to base] to Ellington." While my glance could extend not much farther than the end of my nose, I thought that I had died and gone to heaven. Only a few more minutes for me to hang on until landing at NASA OPS and I would have achieved a critical milestone from among my many astronaut goals: not to puke on my first T-38 flight.

"Driving" the jet back to Ellington Field meant we were in a continual descent from about thirty-five thousand feet. The more we descended the hotter the inside of the aircraft became, since the jet's air conditioning system functions much better at higher altitudes (where the air is already cold and thus easier to keep that way). I was getting uncomfortably warm and beginning to sweat all over again. In perfect neurovestibular fashion, the warmer I got, the queasier my stomach became. Out of habit, I continually checked the oxygen and AC levels just to make sure it was still in position as "100%" and "Emergency" (full fan). Unfortunately, each time ended with the realization that nothing had changed, and it wasn't going to get any better until we were able to pop open the canopies and climb back down to the ground.

All was silent in the jet for the final uneventful minutes, each of us preoccupied with our own thoughts. Andy's could have been about heading home to his family or teeing up for eighteen holes of golf. Mine were focused on keeping all vomit contained within. Until we pulled to a stop on the tarmac adjacent to the NASA hangar, I was fighting with everything I had to keep it down.

With a final firm push on the brake pedals, a run through the shutdown checklist, and a nod from the flight line personnel, Andy punched off the engines and unstrapped himself from his seat harness—almost simultaneously, it seemed. I fumbled with my connections and gathered up all my gear while Andy hopped from his seat to the ladder and gave me what I figured was his obligatory "attaboy"—telling me how well I had done and that he had to bolt to his youngest son's soccer game.

Offering a sincere thanks to Andy and a not nearly so sincere shout of "I really enjoyed it," I was left to my own devices. I walked slowly from the jet back to the chute room. As I hung up my parachute and placed my helmet bag back into my cubby, the thought occurred to me that for the first time in my life, I had cheated death during a jaunt at jet speed!

I entered the locker room and sat down in front of my locker. I was not feeling too chipper. The combination of nausea and temperature was doing a number on me. I decided maybe a cold shower would be the ticket to recovery. After about twenty minutes of cold water pulsating and pouring down my exhausted body, which leaned ever so gently against the side of the fiberglass shower stall, I felt rejuvenated enough to return to my locker. Striking a pose like Rodin's *Thinker*, including being stark naked as I sat on the bench, I mustered enough energy to begin to slowly put my clothes back on. Once fully dressed, and with a few minutes of rest under my belt, I was feeling pretty good . . . and a little cocky. I was ready to face the world again, no longer a rookie with zero flight time!

Weaving through the two sets of double doors that led to the open hangar, I stood again on the hangar floor where this flying adventure had begun a few short hours ago. Admiring the sleek beauty of these fantastic airplanes, standing mere inches apart on the shiny gray floor, I took in the sounds . . . there were none (it was past quitting time) . . . and the smells . . . there were plenty, ranging from jet fuel to that familiar smell of new rubber tires.

Turning my head to verify there were no obstacles in my path to the exit door at the hangar's north end, I saw a quiet sentinel, its identity revealed by the label "trash" stenciled on the metal lid. I am not exactly sure what happened in that next instant, but I think it was the power of suggestion taking over deep within my cerebral cortex. A force welled up and instructed me to remove the trash can lid, thereby allowing the entire contents of my stomach to fly out at roughly the speed of our T-38 takeoff some minutes before.

Yep, it is true. As much as I hate to admit it, this steely-eyed astronaut's first "Zoom and Boom" had become nothing more than a "Whirl and Hurl."

2

Beginnings

My life began in earnest on February 23, 1959, sometime around 0530 (military time for early in the morning). I was the second of three children, growing up in a small town in southeastern Nebraska. Ashland, named in the 1800s by Henry Clay, who thought it reminded him of his hometown of Ashland, Kentucky, is nearly the midpoint between the two largest cities of the Cornhusker State (Lincoln and Omaha for the uninitiated). This quiet bedroom community lies on the south bend of the Platte River and is home to between eighteen hundred or twenty-two hundred (depending on the census date) good solid midwestern folk. It was a fine place to grow up, a typical community of the central plains, and there was plenty of stuff to keep us youngsters occupied.

I consider myself as having been a normal kid (though you might hear differently from others, so please don't ask around—I'm afraid of what they might say). I did all those things most kids of my generation did. I played almost every sport—football, basketball, baseball. I ran track and later in my high school career I took up golf.

I was active in my church, singing in the choir, participating in youth groups, Sunday school, and I even (along with my brother, Kirby, and sister, Lorie) played the piano and organ for the services.

Kirby and I, along with several of our close friends, built wooden forts on the banks of Salt Creek, wandered the trails provided by the miles of railroad tracks for the Burlington Northern and Union Pacific Railroads, and by the way, we rode skateboards on our bellies through Ashland's city storm sewers. We sat for hours in our neighbor's apple tree, munching on the fine at-the-ready fruit, following the superhuman exploits of our heroes Superman, Batman, and Robin, reading DC and Marvel comic books to our heart's content.

I was a member of our local Boy Scout troop, reaching the rank of First Class and getting inducted into the exclusive Order of the Arrow, scouting's honor society. Attending summer camp and spending overnights at the local camping area known as Crystal Springs were common occurrences in my younger days.

Yep, I was pretty normal.

My father, John Thomas Anderson, or "Jack" as he was known, was a highway engineer and project manager for the Nebraska State Department of Roads. A Korean War veteran and navy gunner's mate second class, he had a grand sense of humor and was one of those guys everybody knew and liked. Everyone was his friend.

A native of Ashland and a graduate of the local high school, my dad never attended college. He worked his way up through the maintenance ranks within the Department of Roads (where I would one day follow in his footsteps, for a couple of summers, anyway) to reach the position of project manager.

Dad had a heart of gold and did whatever he could to help his fellow man. He served on committees of every shape and size, was tremendously active in our church, and loved the world of sports.

Yet, tragically, he would never get to see me fly in space. As a matter of fact, he barely got to see me work for NASA. Fighting heart disease since his early thirties, and constantly battling the demons of alcohol, he died from a massive stroke in 1984, barely fifty-four years old.

My mom, Alice, also had a very kind heart. She was intelligent—an intellectual and a bookworm—but she also displayed a tendency toward naiveté, like Edith Bunker with brains. A devoted wife and mother, she always placed the needs of her kids and her husband first. She was an absolutely voracious reader, constantly curling up in her favorite chair with a paperback book in the early days of romance novels. It was indeed a rare occasion to find her without a book in her hand.

The love between my mother and father, and the willingness of each to sacrifice for the other, were always evident to me growing up. The fact that my father, a tremendously intelligent and capable man, had passed up an opportunity for a free college education was a favorite story of mine, as told to me by my mom.

Battling severe arteriosclerosis and a weak heart, Dad experienced three heart attacks by the time he was thirty-two years old. His uncertainty regarding his health made him anxious to provide for his family. Working for the state included a solid insurance benefit package, so he stayed, toiling in a job he didn't care for at all so his wife and family would be taken care of.

Dad displayed a rare selflessness, reflected by his decision to allow Mom to return to the University of Nebraska to complete her master's degree in speech pathology. Dad knew full well that upon graduation, she would head into the workforce and likely make more money than he did. According to Mom, this was something many men of that era would not tolerate.

For quite some time my mother's love of family was something I understood without question and took for granted. Only through happenstance, well after becoming an astronaut, did I learn of a particular story illustrating her personal sacrifice for our well-being.

While Mom and I were traveling to a public appearance I was to make in Beatrice, Nebraska, we began to talk of family matters. We ended up in conversation about Dad's final stroke and what I thought was his unexpected death. With a little prodding, I learned for the first time that Mom had asked the doctors to turn off my father's life support system. Our family physician, Dr. Richard Johnson, informed Mom that Dad had no brain activity whatsoever, but since he was breathing on his own, the only way for him to pass would be to disconnect his feeding tube. She had to make that horrible choice all by herself. For years, she carried tremendous guilt over this decision and never built up the courage to tell me what happened.

Perhaps due to the thousand-mile distance separating us, she chose to share this news only with my brother and sister, who continued to live in Nebraska.

Just like a mother, she was always trying to protect me.

As budding young "engineers," just skirting the edges of juvenile delinquency, my buddies and I planned and executed projects within our neighborhoods that often didn't meet the standards of conduct set forth by our parents and neighbors. For example, there was the time we decided to dig a tunnel from the middle of our backyard to the local establishment affectionately known as "the dime store on Silver Street."

Our grand plan was to tunnel all the way there (about ten city blocks) and up through the floor, thereby giving us unlimited access to the dime store's candy and comic books for the rest of our days. A flawed plan, to be sure, it was quickly disapproved by management (my father) the first night he came home from work and found a hole measuring six feet in diameter and three feet deep in the center of his backyard. Oh man, if we just wouldn't have taken that union work break.

Cutting down a half city block of the neighbor's blackberry bushes because their thorny stems ruined our backyard football games also didn't fare well with the management department.

My brother, Kirby, and I were not necessarily inseparable, but we had some good times together. As the big brother, I tried to maintain the image of being in charge. We enjoyed acting out our own comic-book-fueled scenarios, playing games of Batman and Robin. Adorned with old bath towels tied around our necks, just as our heroes from Gotham did as they slid down their bat pole, we adopted their crime-fighting personas for days at a time.

Once clad in our superhero outfits, we jumped from our garage roof in an effort to surprise those who would eventually bear the brunt of our crime-fighting talents. Kirby was always Robin, and Robin *always* wore the faded yellow towel. As Bruce Wayne, the ultimate Caped Crusader, I was clad in blue, ready to lead my young sidekick out of (or into) harm's way.

As youngsters, we were definitely a thorn in our sister's side. When one of her junior high beaus dropped over unannounced, my stalwart leadership and skills of persuasion convinced my kid brother to join me in a naked post-bath romp straight through the living room, prematurely and abruptly ending my sister's hand-holding session.

With Kirby and me sharing a tiny bedroom, many bedtimes began with sibling fisticuffs over some minor detail, usually leading to my brother's escalation of FPMs (fists per minute), followed by my excessive laughter, followed by another escalation of FPMs, only to end with both of us sound asleep in our double bed, the lights still blazing at sunrise.

Kirby and I were hugely into sports. We would come home from church on Sundays to watch the NBA game of the week (back then there was only *one* game a week on TV), and as soon as the game was over, we were out in the driveway shooting baskets, playing one on one and having a grand old time.

It was the same with football on Saturdays. Saturday was "game day." Husker football was almost as close to a religion in Nebraska as Catholicism and Protestantism. When we were kids, only the really *big* games were televised, meaning the Nebraska versus Oklahoma contest and a postseason bowl game. There was none of this every-game, every-night stuff so prevalent on sports channels today.

So we glued ourselves to the radio. Dad would crank up the volume on KFAB in Omaha and we would revel in the voice of Lyle Bremser, arguably one of the finest announcers of his era.

"Man, woman, and child, he's gone!" Lyle would yell into the microphone as Johnny "The Jet" Rodgers zigzagged his way to the goal line and fans across the state went crazy.

"He gave 'em a hip and took it away," cried the voice of the man who personified Husker football.

Kids were so Husker-crazy in Nebraska that during all-day band competitions, fully dressed high school band members would conceal a transistor radio in their tall fuzzy marching-band hats, with the earbud so cleverly placed that they could catch all the action while doing eight-count pinwheels on the turf of some high school football field.

After listening to the game, more often than not a Husker victory (those days, many were total wipeouts of the opposing squad), Kirby and I would grab our football and head onto the concrete pavement of Euclid Street to begin tossing the ball back and forth, eventually culminating our contest with punting and kicking, something we would both become adept at performing on the high school and college level.

My sister, Lorie, didn't share my passion for sports, but we had other things in common. Her forte was music, which was something I also enjoyed. For us, it was practice sessions at Mrs. Virginia Parks's house, waiting in her den watching TV or reading (but never doing homework) while the other sibling finished an organ or piano lesson.

When I joined the high school band as an eighth grader, I had to mind my p's and q's because sis was not going to let me get away with anything (although a properly placed spit valve discharge from my beat-up tenor trombone went a long way toward evening the score).

In school I did well without putting in too much effort. Academically speaking, things came easily for me. The crisis of homework didn't really set in until high school, which simply meant that I hauled my books home, set them on top of the TV, enjoyed the evening's activities and TV programming (while falling asleep on the floor), followed by carrying the damn books back to school the next morning.

Perhaps the story of how I came to be an astronaut is typical of those told by other astronauts throughout NASA's storied history. Yet, in order to put the details of my journey into perspective, it is useful to know that perhaps I was luckier than most. Because my childhood spanned the glory days of NASA and her triumphs, I was fortunate to be both young enough and old enough to understand and relish what was taking place around me. And I had pretty smart parents, too.

It was Christmas Eve 1968 when I first recall the spacefaring seed being planted in my soul. Mom and Dad woke up Lorie, Kirby, and me at what seemed to be an ungodly hour to "witness history," they would say.

In my mind, my parents were geniuses when it came to knowing something special was happening on the world stage. From the assassination of brothers John F. and Bobby Kennedy, to the equally repulsive slaying of Martin Luther King Jr., to the revelry of spaceflight and color TV, they were adamant that we kids be exposed to history, enabling us to better understand the dynamic world around us. On this holiday eve, Apollo 8 was to be the second human flight in the fledgling program and the first to orbit *humans* around the Moon.

Sitting "crisscross applesauce" style on the oval throw rug on the wood floor of our living room, I paid rapt attention. My head cocked slightly to one side, staring at our aging black-and-white Zenith television, I was mesmerized as Commander Frank Borman, command module pilot Jim Lovell, and lunar module pilot William Anders made history, and the United States one-upped the dreaded Soviets.

Together, my family and I witnessed one of the greatest feats in all of history. On their fourth day of flight, Christmas Eve, after a call from the capsule communicator (CAPCOM), "All systems are GO, Apollo 8," communications were interrupted as the capsule passed behind the moon, and the astronauts became the first men to see firsthand the moon's crater-bombarded far side.

Being only nine years old at the time, I was almost panicked by the astronauts' loss of communication with the leaders in Mission Control. All I could think of during the excruciatingly long ten to fifteen minutes of silence was that some disaster had befallen the brave crew. Imagination took over my youthful brain and I wondered if a lunar volcano had erupted into their orbit and burned them to bits. Or perhaps an evil space dragon had awakened from its slumber on the dark side and had blasted the spaceship with its fiery breath!

Tension mounted with the continuously droning static of the airwaves between Earth and the chunk of rock we call the Moon. Then the CAPCOM renewed his attempt to contact the crew, repeating "Apollo 8, Houston, over." Not until radio silence was broken by Houston, with the recognizable Quindar tone (the beep heard before and after any voice transmission between Mission Control and the orbiting spacecraft), did a response from Commander Borman crackle back from lunar orbit, a distance of some 240,000 miles:

"Apollo 8, over!"

"Hello, Apollo 8, loud and clear!"

"Roger. Please be informed, there is a Santa Claus!"

"That's affirmative!"

With that brief, almost casual exchange, I was finally able to relax and take a breath. I was hooked. That was what I wanted to do with my life. As far as I was concerned, my lifetime dream had begun.

It would just take me a while to get there.

Later that day, during the evening hours in the United States, the crew read the first ten verses from the Book of Genesis to television viewers on Earth and wished them "Goodnight, good luck, a Merry Christmas, and God bless all of you, all of you on the good Earth." Subsequently, the TV Guide for the week of May 10–16, 1969, claimed that one out of every four persons on Earth—nearly one billion people in sixty-four countries—heard the astronauts' reading that night, either on radio or on TV. Delayed broadcasts that same day reached thirty additional countries, according to official NASA accounts in the 1979 book *Chariots for Apollo: A History of Manned Lunar Spacecraft.*

The recollection of those events, viewed from my mother's eyes, is entirely different. She would adamantly state that I was only five or six when I decided that I wanted to be an astronaut. Apparently, it was the astronauts from the Mercury and Gemini programs that had captured my youthful imagination. She related to anyone who was interested that I always talked of becoming an astronaut. We would "discuss it," she would say.

The culmination of my dream at that early age was the Kiddie Parade of the Ashland "Stir-Up." A summer street carnival offering a wonderful assortment of activities for young and old alike, the Stir-Up took place over one weekend each July, with a highlight event being the parade.

Lasting only a few short city blocks, the parade involved children from throughout the municipality in a costume contest. Dressed in costumes of all shapes and sizes, we competed for the coveted first-, second-, and third-prize awards. And prizes they were! Perfectly shaped ribbons, embossed with gold lettering, differing only in their colors of blue, red, and white, they symbolized triumph over everyone in their age group. Probably ordered from the Sears and Roebuck catalog, their patriotic colors graced the hands and complemented the smiles of the winners.

Costumes were always original. Back then there were no Target stores, no Walmarts or Costcos where parents could run and drop twenty bucks to pick up the latest in attire for superheroes or princesses.

My mother's ingenuity prevailed. Working with scissors, tape, and a roll of Reynolds Wrap aluminum foil, she secured one of her huge round hatboxes from her bedroom closet and proceeded to turn me into her very own silver-clad Mercury astronaut. Everything wrapped in foil, my costume came complete with my hatbox helmet and Styrofoam-ball-tipped pipe-cleaner antennae, perfect for contacting space aliens.

During an interview on the Pat (Safford) and JT (Jill Hull) radio show in Omaha just prior to my first launch, Mom was asked about my dream to fly in space and the Kiddie Parade endeavor. She pointed out that our family lived a life of modest means: "You had to be creative. And in those days, most people didn't go out and buy a costume. Well, I don't know that they could; I don't know that they were available."

She continued relating her story to the radio audience. "Clay never wanted to be a fireman or a policeman or a cowboy. He talked about it, but he always wanted to be an astronaut, and so that's what we decided on. I would ask him, and he would ask me, and we'd kind of discuss it."

"I made him an astronaut with Reynolds Wrap. I wrapped him all up in it, his whole body. Then I used to wear a lot of hats and I had a lot of hatboxes. I had a round hatbox and I cut a rectangular place on the side so he could see, and then I wrapped the box in aluminum foil."

With exasperation evident in her voice, she concluded the interview, "And he didn't win first place! He was robbed." When Pat and JT questioned whether she remembered who won first place, she couldn't. But she remembered that I didn't.

I marched proudly that day, of that I am sure. And with regard to me being robbed, you know, I think Mom was right.

Dreaming of becoming an astronaut is one thing. Being fortunate enough to wear the coveted blue flight suit is another. So how exactly does one go about turning a childhood dream into a reality?

Throughout high school, and during my time at Hastings College, I made my intention to become an astronaut fairly well known. Whether it was in casual conversation with students in the cafeteria or on the practice field during football season, I was never hesitant to state what I dreamed I could become. But it took an entirely fortuitous set of circumstances to put me in Houston, Texas.

Approximately twenty-five miles southeast of Houston, on Interstate Highway 45, is a place called Clear Lake City, Texas. Engulfed by Houston's massive metropolitan area, Clear Lake City is not a city at all. It's a parcel of land annexed by the city of Houston to enable the "mother ship" to suck tax revenue from the area where the human space flight program was taking root. The growth and opportunities within the space program were proving to be a huge source of income for the Houston city council and their friends in Harris County.

It was here in Clear Lake City, at the dawn of the space shuttle program, that a very intelligent gentleman named Maynard Huntley toiled quietly as a data and software engineer for the National Aeronautics and Space Administration.

My journey really began when he entered the story.

Within his tiny government office on the administrative side of the building known as Mission Control, Huntley had no idea of the role he would play in my lifetime dream. Maynard's desk sat on the second floor at the south end of what was designated as Building 30 on the Johnson Space Center schematic found on the back cover of the JSC phonebook . He had worked there since graduating from Hastings College in 1961.

Maynard—a fellow Hastings College Bronco—was also an avid hunter, especially when it came to pheasants. Like clockwork, Maynard journeyed home to Nebraska every fall to enjoy the fresh air and outdoor beauty of pheasant hunting in the Midwest. The hunt scheduled during my senior year in the fall of 1980 would turn out to be quite significant for me *and* the pheasants.

That fall, his annual trip north led him to pair up with another gentleman with close ties to Hastings College. Dr. Gary Musgrave, the director of career development, counseling, and placement for the college, also happened to have a fondness for the taste of a good game bird.

How it came to pass, I do not know, but shotguns in hand, they would traipse together through the rugged wilderness of south-central Nebraska in search of game birds with regal plumage and a fear of shotguns. As they plodded across the rutted cornfields that months earlier had been the scene of a midwestern harvest, the conversation turned to their occupations and was said to have gone something like this:

"So, what do you do for a living, Maynard?" came the icebreaking question from the guidance counselor.

"I'm an engineer with NASA, down in Houston," the short, follicle-challenged engineer replied.

"That's very interesting, Maynard. We have a physics student here at Hastings College who is quite interested in NASA."

"Oh, really?" Maynard's eyes surely must have raised from where they were hidden behind his thick black plastic eyeglass frames. "Does he know that NASA has a great summer intern program down at Johnson where students may be selected to work various engineering support jobs during the summer? They return back to their schools at the start of the fall semester. I can send you an application form if you'd like."

With that chance conversation and my subsequent filling out and mailing of a multitude of NASA forms, I found myself seated at the desk of the Physics Department chair, Professor Clyde Sachtleben, in Steinhart Hall of Science on the campus of Hastings College. It was a beautiful spring afternoon as I sat just waiting for his jet black rotary phone to ring. "Doc S" watched nervously from one corner of his office packed with papers and books. It was so tense that I nearly jumped from the chair when the telephone rang.

Robert "Bob" Jones, coordinator of the JSC Summer Intern Program, and I spent thirty minutes or so chatting on the telephone, reminiscing as if we were old friends. That phone call, coupled with my successfully completed application, led me to join a small group of forty summer interns at JSC in June 1981, an event that kick-started my NASA career.

A twenty-two-year-old college graduate turned NASA summer intern, I found myself working in the Data Systems and Analysis Division within the Mission Support Directorate at NASA's Johnson Space Center. Occupying a desk in Building 5, wondering how in the heck I got there, would turn out to be a life-shaping time for me. But it didn't necessarily start out that way.

It was fortunate for me that Kirby, still a Hastings College junior and a track-and-field star, had qualified to participate in the National Association of Intercollegiate Athletics (NAIA) National Track and Field Championships in the four-hundred-meter intermediate hurdles. That track meet was to be held at Robertson Stadium, near the campuses of the University of Houston and Texas Southern University. Dad and I decided we should attend. We figured it was a great way to see Kirby participate (my brother would jokingly label himself as the second-fastest white guy in the nation after he finished seventh out of nine in the finals) and to scout out the area to see if I could find housing. Dad, always the planner, had scoped out the route from Ashland to Houston in his small spiral graph-paper notebook. A highway engineer, he had meticulously calculated the entire distance, including the subordinate distances to preplanned stopping points. I can still see in my mind the page that showed the final distance at the bottom—971 miles.

The trip was uneventful until our arrival. Following sketchy directions on how to get to the stadium, we came to Yates High School in Houston's Third Ward. This was not a nice part of town. As we slowly drove past the high school, Dad told me to lock the doors. This was our first exposure to an urban lifestyle in an economically challenged environment.

The school was surrounded by a ten-foot-high chain-link fence with barbed wire at the top. Everywhere, kids stood in small groups. Most were leaning back against the fence, balancing a boom box on their shoulder, blaring the latest music.

It was intimidating and a bit scary for us, especially for me. We continued our cruise through this "tough" neighborhood, scouting for a decent hotel for our two days in Houston. The accommodations were so destitute, we didn't stop.

When we finally found Robertson Stadium and a maroon-clad contingent of athletes from Hastings College (including my triple-jump partner and fellow senior, Jeff Edwards), we relaxed a bit and began to enjoy the sights and sounds of an athletic event held on a national scale.

Dad, frugalness being one of his strong suits, soon learned there was ample space in the dormitory where the Hastings athletes were staying. The next thing I knew we were stomping through a local Target, buying towels to use when showering in the dorm.

After Kirby's preliminary we had ample time to explore the area before the late-night finale. Dad and I decided it would be a good time to find out where this NASA place was, and whether we might be able to find somewhere for me to live for the summer.

We had some information that NASA provided, including the names of the other summer interns and NASA co-operative education students (co-ops) who might also be looking for housing. From that, we knew there was no form of public transportation far south of the city (about twenty-five miles) where the Johnson Space Center was located, so I would need my own vehicle. We checked out a couple of apartment complexes, starting at one near the Gulf Freeway (Interstate 45) and NASA Road One.

I'm still amazed to remember how naive we were. The folks who showed Dad and me their furnished one-bedroom "model" apartment neglected to tell us the furniture was not included. Yep, another hick from the Midwest, they must have thought. Somehow, though, my steel-trap engineering brain began to figure out that I was also going to have to furnish my summer home. Thank goodness for a company called Aaron Rents!

Using the orientation data package, we were able to tag up with another young man heading for a NASA summer slot. His name was Mark Jenkins and he hailed from Austin, Texas. We set up a meeting with Mark and his father at the now-defunct Quail Walk apartment complex, across the street from the (also defunct) Clear Lake public golf course and the Clear Lake United Methodist Church of then-Pastor Buddy Miller. Mark and I decided we could be roommates for the summer, saving us both some money and providing us with the ability to carpool to and from work in our non-air-conditioned cars. Another engineer, Sean Anderson, a student at the University of Illinois, would complete our all-male version of *Three's Company*.

The preliminary arrangements completed, my next trip to Houston would be on my own. I would drive the 971 miles solo, this time in my mother's maroon Mercury Bobcat hatchback (again no air conditioning). The sixteen-hour drive would take me the better part of two days, with a stop in Dallas. My official arrival in Clear Lake and our second-floor apartment put me less than three miles from the facility leased by the U.S. government from Rice University for the paltry sum of one dollar per year. I was on my way.

My first morning at work was spent in the offices of Human Resources filling out paperwork required for my temporary employment. Health insurance, life insurance, security clearances: it was a headache all its own and I hadn't even started my job yet. After I cleared HR, I headed to my new office in Building 5 at the Johnson Space Center.

Wayne Williams was my supervisor. Humberto "Bert" Davila was my lead and mentor for the summer. I would be working with software engineers Bob Brekke, Mark Jernigan, Larry Grisson, Darrell Boyd, Roger Burke, and Maury Minette. Our job was to develop and test the software that would drive the shuttle mission simulator (SMS). The simulator sat on the first floor of Building 5, tucked in the back of the southeast corner, perched high above the floor on hydraulic actuators that allowed it to move, turn, and "shake, rattle and roll." The mechanical monstrosity, similar to those used to train airline pilots, produced a lifelike simulation paralleling the ascent and entry of a shuttle I would one day experience for real. The SMS was the preeminent workhorse training facility for astronauts throughout the embryonic shuttle program.

My desk was one of seven. All were big, metal, gray, and ugly, and they sat in a large room known as the astronaut quarantine office space. I chose the desk in the far back corner of this bleak undecorated room. It was here NASA shuttle astronauts came the week before launch, while in their quarantine period, to do their desk jobs away from the threat of germs and illness. A far cry from what I would later experience in the plush astronaut crew quarters erected during my time in the Astronaut Office.

My fellow section members shared offices down the hall from mine. From my corner desk I could easily see my boss, Mr. Williams, when almost daily he nodded off to sleep with his hands quietly clasped and held over his belly near the tie clasp of his skinny black necktie.

Throughout that summer I was on the lookout for astronauts. I wasn't too knowledgeable about the space center and its layout, or where the astronauts did most of their training and spent the majority of their time. I did know, however, that they lived in Building 4 North, just behind our Building 5. Sequentially numbered buildings weren't always situated next to each other; the NASA JSC building numbering system is quite random. This would make for some interesting and time-wasting excursions in my career.

The astronauts had the entire third story in Building 4, with the shuttle flight directors and flight controllers having their digs on the second and first floors, respectively. My goal was to personally meet and shake the hand of a real shuttle astronaut before I returned to Nebraska.

The summer passed quickly and my internship was ending. I would be heading off to Nebraska to get ready for graduate school at Iowa State University in Ames, and I had yet to meet an astronaut. I had seen several. But as a small-town kid, dazzled by where I was and what I was doing, I simply couldn't muster the courage to introduce myself to these national heroes. Yet I knew that I must do it. I *had* to meet one. I could not go home to Nebraska where the first question from my friends and family would be "Well, did you meet any astronauts?" and not be able to answer with an honest "Yes!"

It became my all-consuming mission . . . to find one and to meet one before I left town, possibly forever.

I formulated my plan early Monday morning on my last week in Houston. I checked the SMS schedule to see which astronauts would be working in the simulator (the only thing I had "flown" at that point) in the upcoming days.

Friday at 0730, Richard "Dick" Truly and Joe Engle were scheduled for a four-hour period of ascent-and-entry runs in the SMS motion base. Truly and Engle were the STS-2 mission crew, Truly taking the forward cockpit's left seat as the commander and Engle flying in the right seat. I knew what I had to do. I would rise earlier than normal on Friday and head to work so I would be seated on the lower stairs of the motion base when Truly and Engle arrived. They would not be able to get to the cockpit without passing by me.

I made it through the entire week without letting anyone else know of my plan. I wasn't sure I would have the courage to play it out. At that time in my life I was not exactly the kind of person who took the bull by the horns and made things happen.

The few times I had seen astronauts emerging from the simulator, there was usually a gaggle of those pesky co-ops hanging around. There were many more co-ops than summer interns, and they tended to move in packs. Safety in numbers appeared to give them confidence when it came to approaching these local celebrities.

As Friday approached, I rehearsed over and over in my mind the words I would use when making my move at the introduction. A high school thespian, I figured memorizing my short speech would give me a leg up. I'd start talking before they ever knew what hit them. I would make eye contact, get them each to shake my hand, and give them a very hearty midwestern greeting: "Hello, my name is Clayton Anderson, and I just wanted to say 'hi' and wish you well in your training and upcoming mission."

Simple, straightforward, and nonintrusive. My biggest fear was that they would be so busy that my introduction would keep them from starting their session on time, which in the world of NASA, where launches and landings occurred to the exact second of the countdown clocks, would be a faux pas from which my reputation might never recover.

Friday arrived and found me seated exactly per my plan, waiting for 0730. I chose my seat carefully, a step about halfway up, where I could see over the barricade that separated the lobby from the business end of the simulator. My strategically chosen seat would allow me to see the astronauts approach down the hallway past the ops desk. They would stop at their gray standard-issue lockers (ahead of me and slightly to my left). Then I would hop up from my seat and meet them at the bottom of the stairway as they swung open the small gate of the barricade. I was ready!

As planned, at 0745, dressed in short-sleeved polo shirts, they came down the hallway. They emerged through the door and paused at the lockers to place their loose items inside. (During the simulator rides, anything not tied down falls to the back wall of the simulator.)

They turned toward the stairs, Mr. Truly in the lead. There I was, JSC summer intern from Nebraska, eyes bright and wide, hand extended, and bearing down on them at Mach 2.

Dick Truly was obviously in a hurry. He said a cordial hello, grasped my hand briefly, and then headed up the stairs. Joe Engle, however, was different. When I shook his hand and went through my prepared remarks, he paused, stopped, and asked me where I went to school. Learning that I was at a small liberal arts institution in midwestern Nebraska, and having come from a similar background, he chatted with me about his experiences in college before he entered into the military.

I was *chatting* with a United States astronaut! It was as if we had been friends for years and were having a relaxed, open, honest conversation. It was the greatest moment in my entire life so far. I was in heaven. I could now go home with confidence.

My dream of one day flying in space—only a dream for the first twenty-two years of my life—was now cemented deeply in my soul.

3

Freshman Fifteen

It was the fall semester of my second year at Iowa State University when the unexpected offer of full-time employment came—from Bob Brown of the Mission Planning and Analysis Division (MPAD). Prior to my second consecutive tour as an intern, which I had been fortunate to secure in the summer of 1982 (only thirty were selected that year), I asked NASA to place me with an organization that dealt with spacecraft trajectories, an area I had grown fond of while studying at Iowa State. I ended up with Mr. Brown and his band of eccentric engineers.

According to Brown, they were very impressed with my summer's worth of work. A government hiring window had opened and they wanted to bring me back to NASA, this time for good. He cautioned that he couldn't guarantee how long the offer would be available; the window could close just as quickly as it opened.

But I turned them down. Too close to finishing my master's degree at Iowa State, I took a sizable risk that an offer would still be available upon graduation.

Yet, unlike my father's wagers on the horses at Fonner Park in Grand Island, my gamble paid off. Just prior to my graduation from Iowa State University in May 1983, my friends in MPAD called again, the hiring window apparently still open. This time, with a master's degree in aerospace engineering firmly in hand, I said yes and packed up my bags for another long (and maybe final) drive to Houston.

My foot was in the door. Now, if I could just get the damn thing open without breaking my leg!

In the summer of 1983 I was scared shitless. I was heading off to Houston, Texas, again, not for fun and frivolity. This time, I was to be officially employed by the National Aeronautics and Space Administration. Holy crap!

As I had learned from previous experience, timing one's arrival in Houston during June of any year is pretty stupid, but I had no choice. With a humidity level that hovers around 95 percent, and temperatures that reach the midnineties and then graciously drop to a balmy seventy-two (if you're lucky) at night, the weather is less than desirable. Throw in a city that at the time was one of the fastest growing in the nation, complete with the accompanying traffic problems, and this naive young Nebraskan was once again in over his head.

But things were calmer this time. I was returning to the familiar Mission Planning and Analysis Division with two solid JSC summers under my belt, and all things NASA were becoming clearer to me.

Small stuff remains stuck in my memory about those early days as a brand-new full-time NASA employee, like my lack of a business wardrobe, and my mom heading out to the Omaha stores to get me clothes. One weekend before my departure for Houston, she presented me with three pairs of polyester slacks, each with matching polyester polo shirts, and a pair of tan leather Hush Puppies. Wow! I was a young engineer and dressing like one.

During the first few months of my budding career, I lived in the small town of Arcadia, Texas, with Mickey Donahoo and his wife, Doris, who were dear friends since the summer of my second internship in 1982. They had graciously opened their home to me rent-free as I searched for an apartment nearer the NASA facilities. Mickey was now officially my "lead" engineer and mentor. We worked well together, but recalling the first time we met, I never would have guessed it would work out that way.

I was standing nervously in a large corner office on the third floor of Building 30 at NASA JSC, fidgeting and rocking back and forth, trying to look confident and professional while feeling neither. Having reported for my first day of work during my second summer tour at JSC, I was waiting for my new supervisor, Robert

W. Becker, and his lead engineer, Michael E. Donahoo. They were destined to enter the office and escort me, a second-year graduate student in aerospace engineering, back to my temporary work area. Having no idea what to expect, I imagined that these two NASA engineers would be highly intelligent, somewhat nerdy, and possibly a bit on the introverted side. The division secretary, a commanding female presence named Faye Broussard, informed me that they were on their way down the hall.

Eager to see my new bosses, I slipped out into the hallway to catch a glimpse of the key NASA employees who would shape and mold me for the next two-and-a-half months.

My vision of a NASA engineer was shattered immediately as two men, almost identically dressed, strode confidently down the hall, their leather-soled boots making loud thumps almost in unison on the solid tile floor. Their bright plaid flannel shirts were partially tucked into well-worn faded blue jeans held up by leather belts with ornate belt buckles the size of a small platter riding just below their protruding bellies. I thought, "What have I gotten myself into?" Sporting full beards on their taut and weathered faces from what must have been years spent outdoors, Becker and Mickey, as I would come to call them, were not your typical engineers.

Neither was Richard "Deke" Kincade. Deke, also normally clad in cowboy boots, jeans, and a flannel shirt, was a space shuttle rendezvous trajectory designer who hailed from the backwoods of Louisiana. The story of Deke, Laurie Norton Hansen, and her Oreo cookies was destined to become a classic.

A co-op student from the University of Michigan, Laurie would one day rise to the rank of director of engineering at the Johnson Space Center. Always a giver, early in her first MPAD co-op tour, she brought in a package of Oreo cookies one morning and offered them to her office colleagues. Deke graciously accepted her overture of kindness and downed a couple of the chocolate morsels in single bites. Laurie, appalled at his unbecoming behavior, chastised Deke with the remark, "Don't you know how to eat an Oreo? You have to grab both sides, spread them apart gently, and then lick the insides."

Deke, a true redneck, chauvinist, and thirty years her senior, listened to her words carefully, then began to leer at this young coed from the north. His evil grin grew slowly into a toothy smile. Laurie, so matter-of-fact just seconds ago, came unglued. Her face turned a blazing shade of red as she realized Deke had interpreted her words much differently than she had intended. Standing abruptly, she yelled, "No, Deke!" and stormed out of the room.

The next time Laurie reported to NASA for a co-op stint, we made sure her desk was adorned with a brand-new package of Oreo chocolate sandwich cookies, complete with a red ribbon and bow.

Life in the offices on the third floor of Building 30 was crazy to say the least. We "newbies" were working with some of the finest minds in the history of the U.S. space program. The Mission Planning and Analysis Division was home to some of our country's true "rocket scientists," guys who invented concepts like stable orbit rendezvous and Apollo entry guidance algorithms, and had done the work that helped to place men on the Moon. They had already accomplished so many great things, yet it seemed to me their motivation for the then-fledgling space shuttle program was at a bit of a low. They were often more interested in having fun than meeting deadlines. Their responsibility to the overall shuttle program was minuscule compared to what had been required of them for Apollo, and their waning enthusiasm was reflected in their day-to-day behavior.

For example, my supervisor, Bob Becker, had somehow created a NASA urban legend around his briefcase. He had two—one he carried with him at all times and the other he allegedly left sitting open on his desk—so that when people came looking for him, his officemates could all honestly respond, "We don't know where he is but his briefcase is here, so he must be around."

You just can't make this stuff up!

The time was ripe for a changing of the guard, so to speak. Given a rather substantial hiring window by the government, NASA and MPAD took advantage, and several of my compadres reported for duty at roughly the same time that I did.

Blair, Jerry, Rick, Kim, Eric, Dave, Tim, Steve, Rex, Kevin, Laurie, and I gave MPAD (and other JSC organizations) a bit of a youth movement, and what would turn out to be a pretty good mix of young talent with veteran leadership. But on a daily basis, things remained pretty crazy.

We all took to our differing assignments, beginning with the requirement to read a horde of NASA manuals. Many of us were fortunate in that our mentors took us under their wings, actually giving us important work to do. In my case, Mickey, along with Becker and his rendezvous experts—Ken Young (Becker's boss) and Al DuPont (Mickey's colleague, now a godparent to my kids)—were more than willing to provide me with opportunities that allowed me to learn and grow while at the same time building a reputation that would serve me well in the future. Others were not quite as fortunate. Their workloads were low-level and sometimes assigned without regard to their specific areas of expertise. Deadlines were out there, but the work we were doing was often theoretical, and in those days computers were not ubiquitous. We sometimes had to wait hours and even days for access to a data terminal. At times it was a struggle for us to find meaningful things to do. So we improvised.

One of our favorite improvisations was "Larry Bird," a cheap plastic ornithopter purchased from a nearby toy store. Larry's plastic body was shaped like that of a bird, with appropriate aerodynamic surfaces of wings and a tail, and made from a very thin and lightweight plastic material. Propulsion was provided by a rubber band running from a hook mounted inside his head just behind his beak to a small plastic crank near his tail. By giving the crank about fifteen to twenty revolutions, we wound him up like a balsa wood flying airplane kit available at the local five and dime.

Larry made his office debut in austere fashion. The rubber band fully twisted for maximum flight time, his triangular tail was tilted at just the right angle for straight, level flight, easing into a slight left bank. Rick Deppisch and I served as his air traffic control team. We departed our office space on the third floor of Building 30 and approached the open door of the administrative area that housed our capable support staff of Faye, Jeanette, and Sandy diligently typing, filing, and answering phones. Carefully leveling

Larry for takeoff, my right hand firmly grasped his body on the underside of his chest cavity. Raising my right arm to eye level and pointing Larry along the chosen flight path, my left maintained its steady grip on the crank to counteract the force of the tightly twisted rubber band.

With all systems go, Larry was prepared for his maiden voyage. A gentle push, timed with a simultaneous release of the tail crank, freed Larry. His wings began their rhythmic up-and-down motion generating the thrust needed to drive him noisily into the wide-open spaces.

Screams erupted from within the administrative vista. Larry performed perfectly, the slight bend of his tail enabling him to fly in tight, level circles through the limited airspace. Audible thumps of his wings added to the confusion as this alien being took center stage on an otherwise normal and uneventful day.

It's entirely possible that the secretarial staff never forgave us for this interruption, but I'm guessing hard feelings subsided quickly as the resulting rush of adrenaline dispelled any inclination to take an afternoon nap.

Larry Bird bonded our group of young engineers. The "young guns" were thinking outside the box. We weren't going to conform; we were establishing new NASA traditions.

As we continued to grow as engineers, we greedily soaked up whatever our senior engineer counterparts were willing to share. Gene "Geno" Ricks, Dave Scheffman, Richard "Deke" Kincade, Jim Kirkpatrick, Rocky "Mule Head" Duncan, Rocky Avento, Bill Springer, Jerry "J.B." Bell, Arnie "Good Buddy" Loyd, Daryl "Loss" Lostak, Al DuPont, Sam "I may be wrong, but I don't think so" Wilson, John "Wheels" Wheeler, Ed Lineberry, Hal "Beckface" Beck, Charlie Gott, Dave Homan, Cynthia Wells, Marty Jenness, Larry Davis, Brody "Al" McCafferty, Claude Graves, Al "King Olaf" Lunde, Lee "Razor Tongue" Norbraten, Mike Collins, Ernie Smith, Jon Harpold, E. "Mac" Henderson, Marty "Lucky" Linde, Mike Tobin, J'Ann "J-Bird" Siders, Charlie Buchanan, Ken "Yippee" Young, Cathy "Oh So Good" Osgood, and Alex Benny were all willing to share their knowledge and experiences, technical or otherwise.

That willingness to share information led us rookies to discover a large notebook binder stashed within the cabinets of the Division Office, which included copies of all our senior colleagues' NASA security badge photographs taken during the history-making period of the Apollo program.

The photos were typical and, to our young minds, hilarious. The men were almost universally clad in white long-sleeved collared shirts with dark skinny neckties, many with pocket protectors loaded with government-issue retractable black ink pins. The women, some engineers and some administrative support personnel (back then they were always referred to as secretaries), were visions of loveliness in their dark horned-rim glasses and bouffant hairdos.

The pictures unleashed a flurry of laughter and a bit of nostalgia, but more importantly, they gave us the idea to honor our mentors and leaders with a dress-up day we christened "NASA Nerd Day."

We began gathering wardrobes that would make us look like they did back in the sixties. We added some appropriate "freestyle" touches: black horn-rimmed glasses with white tape, slide rules hooked to our belt loops, and calculators appropriate for the era when NASA took the lead from the Soviet Union in the race to put men on the moon. The date for our inaugural NASA Nerd Day was set. We planned a grand lunch at the local Fuddruckers's across the street from the space center.

NASA Nerd Day built a great sense of camaraderie between the senior members and us juniors. Most had wonderful senses of humor. Their smiles at our willingness to behave in an unorthodox manner made our efforts worthwhile. The culmination of this inaugural version included a happy hour at the local hot spot, J. Larkin's. We carried all our gear (including authentic college textbooks) into the bar exactly at opening time in order to get prime seating and a clear view of the doorway through which patrons (many of them beautiful women) would enter.

As the end of the workday approached, more and more folks came into the bar, and our gaggle of nerds, buoyed by the strength of adult beverages, began to assert itself in perfectly nerdy ways. If a beautiful co-ed strolled in, a loud chorus chirped, "Hiiiiiii, girls," followed by the classic snorting laughter, made famous in the 1984 movie *Revenge of the Nerds*. In much the same way that actors Robert Caradien and Anthony Edwards portrayed the life of a nerd in the now-classic movie, we universally rebuked any one of us who dared approach a potential partner for the dance floor.

We had arrived!

The older of the two Johnson Space Center cafeterias, the one known as Building 11, held considerable significance in my NASA career. As a young engineer, I quickly learned from my elders that the daily luncheon special awaited huge appetites promptly at eleven o'clock. Same time, same table, each and every day; the only difference was the menu item selection.

Costing a mere $2.75 back in the early eighties, the daily special featured favorites like "chicken fried snake (steak)" and "donkey dick (BBQ sausage link)." It could only be bested by occasional forays to the "all you can eat buffet" featured at Ron's Krispy Fried Chicken on Bay Area Boulevard.

Early in the summer of 1990, the Building 11 cafeteria would change my life. Standing at the counter of the small gift shop positioned at the cafeteria's far end, I was writing a personal check for the purchase of a small NASA knickknack for one of my friends. Glancing toward the nearest entrance, waiting for the cashier to ring up my purchase, I saw an incredibly attractive woman, smoothly manipulating the double doors of access.

She was extraordinarily beautiful. Tall and blonde, dressed in a dark green dress, she sauntered into the cafeteria, making her way to the salad bar line. Back then I never ate salad, but that day I made an exception. Grabbing my checkbook, I bolted for the salad bar and reached for a tray, capturing the spot directly behind this gorgeous woman.

More than likely as obvious as a train wreck, I moved casually, trying to catch a glimpse of the name adorning her NASA civil servant badge. "Don't I know you?" was the pickup line that gushed forth from my inexperienced self.

"I don't think so," the young woman replied, her smile captivating me even more than her luscious figure and stately legs. I mumbled and stumbled, seeking a new approach that would garner her attention as much as she garnered mine.

We reached the cashier and it was over—except for the fact that I did get a look at her nametag—the nametag of NASA's Susan Harreld.

I returned to my office, but I remained relentless in my pursuit of this woman who would one day become my wife. With no email or Internet resources to call on, I turned to the weathered pages of my Johnson Space Center telephone book, heading directly to the H section, my heart rate increasing with the turn of each page.

I discovered that she worked in the Human Resources Office in Building 45. I reached for my phone and nervously dialed the five-digit extension of the employee I so longed to meet. The call was answered by her secretary, a young man who told me she was not in her office at the moment. I thanked him and asked if he would please ask her to call Clayton Anderson, and left him my own five-digit number.

Incredibly, days ran into weeks and I never got a return phone call. Taking that as the snub I was expecting, I turned my attention to the other important aspects of my mundane single life: recreational sports and basketball officiating.

Sitting alone in my house, maybe a month or two following my attempt to contact Susan, new city phone books were delivered to residences throughout the NASA area. Not having anything to do that night (as with many of my evenings), I grabbed the smaller than normal phonebook and began to leaf through its thin gray pages, looking for the names of women I knew. Yeah, I know, pretty pathetic.

I came across a name that rang a bell. Cindy Jicha, who had dated a colleague of mine for many years, was my first target. With no reason other than the fact that I knew her already and she was very attractive, the lonely NASA engineer from Nebraska took a chance. I dialed her number.

Having no idea what I was doing or what my expectations were, Cindy's mother picked up the phone. Not expecting to get her mother, I stuttered and I stammered, eventually getting around to identifying myself and asking her if Cindy was available. She was gracious and kind, letting me know she remembered me, but forthright in gently informing me that Cindy had a new boyfriend. Shot down like a Kewpie doll at a carnival pistol range, I quietly thanked her and asked her to tell Cindy I said hello. Embarrassed, deflated, and further depressed with my inability to meet women, I wallowed in self-pity for at least two situation comedies.

During commercials, I lectured myself. Clay, you are a thirty-two-year-old man, a NASA engineer with a fun personality. Get up off that couch, pick up that phone, and call another one!

I did exactly that, dialing the number of the second name that caught my eye. It was my salad bar acquaintance, Susan Harreld. Nervously I dialed my pushbutton telephone, waiting as the pre-set number of rings gave way to her recorded voice. Listening carefully to the message from her answering machine, I froze. In another terrible moment of embarrassment and panic, I slammed my phone down in its cradle as if I were sixteen years old again, leaving no trace as to who triggered her tape recording. Alone in my home, I was pitiful.

I decided to try one more time. This time I vowed I would be a man and at least leave a message. No more wimping out from me.

The second dial was performed with renewed confidence. After all, what was the worst that could happen? She could tell me she wasn't interested. Not like that hadn't happened before.

Standing casually in my kitchen, pinching the phone's handset between my ear and right shoulder, the rings were interrupted by a click at the other end. But this time it was her! No recording; it was Susan who answered the phone.

Panic set in again quickly as I searched for some suave and debonair words that would capture her interest and keep her on the phone just long enough for me to ask her on a date. Sweating profusely, I introduced myself, reminding her of our introductions in the cafeteria salad bar. She acknowledged our meeting and that she knew who I was. I engaged her in classic small talk, learning she had just returned from a rec league co-ed softball game at NASA. Excellent, I thought, she's athletic too; something in common to build on.

Not wanting to press my luck, our five-minute conversation

ended with me taking a shot. I invited her to lunch and she agreed! I was overwhelmed.

Anticipating our lunch date, I headed to Men's Warehouse. I would need new clothes. I certainly didn't want to approach this seeming like an engineering geek. The day of our lunch date, my secretary, Debbie White, was the first to notice my new attire and inquire of its purchase. She knew right away I was meeting a lady friend and her teasing comments did little to put me at ease.

I picked up Susan in her office on the first floor of the Human Resources Office in Building 45. When I arrived she was on the phone, standing near her desk wearing an above-the-knee pale pink suede leather skirt, high heels, and a white blouse. She looked incredible! My panic returned.

The lunch date was wonderful, and as I walked her to the entrance of her building, my brain raced as I searched for more words that might lead to a second date. I had done my homework, though, having asked my sister-in-law, Gina, a former model, how to proceed. "If the date goes well," Gina said, "don't wait. Ask her out again before you drop her off." I took her sage advice and secured a second date with this incredibly sexy, highly intelligent professional woman from Elkhart, Indiana.

Thus began a friendship and romance now lasting more than twenty-three years and boasting two wonderful children. Susan has been a tremendous partner on this incredible journey, and I couldn't have done it without her.

Who says nerds can't get the girl?

4

Hey, There's an App for That!

The fact that I applied to become an astronaut fifteen times has not been lost on my friends, followers, or fans. Jokes and snide remarks have hinged upon the ugly truth that on fourteen of those fifteen attempts I was a complete and abysmal failure. As a matter of fact, there's a NASA public service announcement highlighting how it took me fifteen tries. I like to cling to the reality that I can always say "better late than never," but at this point it's all academic.

The process of applying to become a United States astronaut is actually quite simple. All a person has to do is head to the computer, call up an Internet search engine of choice, and type in the website www.usajobs.gov or http://astronauts.nasa.gov.

Now, be forewarned. These websites are not for the faint of heart. After all, they come from a government entity. Yet with a little luck, entering the keywords "astronaut" and "Houston TX"—provided the federal government is actually looking for new astronauts—your search will lead you through the official process to put your name in the hat for (potential) astronaut selection.

In the mideighties the application request cycle for astronaut hopefuls, comically shortened to "As-Hos," occurred annually. Partly because of the successful launch and landing of the space shuttle *Columbia* and her crew of Commander John Young and pilot Bob Crippen, things were really picking up steam in April 1981.

Three subsequent shuttle test flights (STS 2–4, again all highly successful) had the shuttle program managers salivating over the "operational potential" of a fleet of four space "U-hauls," that is, orbiters, sleek and beautiful in simple white-and-black, ferrying humans and cargo satellites to and from low-earth-orbit (LEO). The need for new astronauts to serve as crews was keen, and the selection office was not lacking for dedicated young Americans waiting to step up and begin the greatest job in the universe.

Having decided that I met all the initial qualifications, in late 1983 I decided to submit my very first application. As I'm sure most applicants do, I thought I would only need one (insert laughs here). Now I just had to figure out how to navigate the application process.

First I had to acquire the physical application forms and relevant process information. While not as simple as logging on to your computer, in 1983 a properly addressed, stamped envelope with a personal request would do the trick.

My inquiry produced a fourfold brochure adorned with the NASA "worm" logo (used predominantly in the eighties until the return of the NASA "meatball"). Entitled *Announcement for Mission Specialist and Pilot Astronaut Candidates*, it covered everything required to educate a potential applicant on the astronaut candidate program.

Verbatim, the *minimum* requirements for mission specialist, to be met *prior* to submitting an application, were:

1. Bachelor's degree from an accredited institution in engineering, biological science, physical science, or mathematics. Degree must be followed by at least three years of related, progressively responsible, professional experience. An advanced degree is desirable and may be substituted for part or all of the experience requirement (master's degree = 1 year, doctoral degree = 3 years). Quality of academic preparation is important.

2. Ability to pass a NASA Class II space physical, which is similar to a military or civilian Class II flight physical and includes the following specific standards:

    a. Distant visual acuity:
        i. 20/100 or better uncorrected, correctable to 20/20, each eye.

b. Blood pressure:
   i. 140/90 measured in a sitting position.
c. Height between 60 and 76 inches.

(Today, according to NASA's website, mission specialist candidates must have 20/200 or better visual acuity, and height limits are 62 to 75 inches for astronaut pilots and 58.5 to 76 inches for mission specialists.)

Pilot requirements were nearly the same. Visual acuity needed to be 20/50 or better (correctable to 20/20), with passing a Class I flight physical and being at least sixty-four inches tall the key differences. The added expectation of "at least 1,000 hours pilot-in-command time in jet aircraft" and that flight test experience was "highly desirable" made it clear they were looking for the best of the best.

The brochure cited the need for United States citizenship. Degrees that were *not* considered qualifying were those in technology and psychology (except for clinical, physiological, or experimental psychology, all of which *were* qualifying), nursing, social sciences, and aviation or aviation management.

Following a detailed description of the space shuttle program, it laid out the expected duties of an astronaut mission specialist who, working with the commander and pilot, would have overall responsibility for the coordination of shuttle operations in the areas of crew activity planning, consumables usage, and experiment and payload operations. He or she would be required to have a detailed knowledge of shuttle systems, as well as detailed knowledge of the operational characteristics, mission requirements and objectives, and supporting systems and equipment for each of the experiments to be conducted on their assigned missions. Mission specialists would perform extravehicular activities (go on spacewalks) and payload handling using the remote manipulator system (fly the robotic arm), as well as perform or assist in specific experiment operations. (There was no mention of a space station during those times; it wouldn't enter the game for several more years.)

Pay and benefits were outlined as well, but I could not have cared less what it paid or what the benefits were. I wanted to be an astronaut!

My official request for the appropriate application package needed to go to

NASA, Johnson Space Center
Astronaut Selection Office
ATTN: AHX
Houston TX 77058

and would end up on the desk of Duane Ross, a quiet and somewhat shy man with an ample supply of snow-white hair and good humor. He was short and slightly built, a dedicated long-distance runner and a career government employee.

Ross, as head of the Astronaut Selection Committee, worked at the Johnson Space Center in Houston, the home of the astronauts. Duane (as he would eventually become known to all "multiple" applicants—as if we all had a close personal relationship with the man) was assisted by his longtime associate and the true administrator behind the scenes, Teresa Gomez. Between the two of them, I think they knew every single thing there ever was to know about selecting U.S. astronauts.

Your application materials (or "app" as it was lovingly referred to by veterans who applied many times) would be delivered some seven to ten days later, packaged officially in a 9 by 12–inch manila envelope bearing the NASA logo in the upper lefthand corner.

Complete with a cover letter thanking you for your interest in applying for the astronaut candidate program, it provided all the governmental forms and issuances designed to strike fear into the hearts of U.S. citizens who dare to misuse her system. Not to be missed was the crystal clear guidance as to how one must proceed or else face the risk that "your application may not be considered."

The necessary forms were standard—an SF-171 (Personal Qualifications Statement), an SF 93 (Report of Medical History), the JSC Form 465 (Supplemental Medical History), and the JSC Form 490 (Supplemental Information). For my application to be considered complete, I would also need to provide full college transcripts (legible copy acceptable).

It was now that the real work would begin.

While the application process seemed to be an art form in and of itself, my personal SF-171 would be far from a work of art.

In *my* day (what may now be defined as both historical and fruitless applications from years one through fourteen), the process of actually filling out the forms was quite different from today. An applicant

(a) did *not* require a computer (weren't many around back then, and you needed a warehouse to store it in),

(b) *did* require ample amounts of paper and a black or blue ballpoint pen or typewriter, and

(c) if the rumors were true, serious applicants required a sufficient supply of Liquid Paper or maybe a spiffy Corona electric cartridge typewriter with the correction-tape cartridge to fix all the mistakes.

The 1983 version of United States Government Standard Form SF-171 consisted of four pages (unless the SF-171A Continuation Sheet was required). The astronaut rumor mill said that your application would not be judged on content alone but would need to be free of errors or mistakes. For those of us who know how difficult it is to erase black or blue ink, the ability to paint a smooth, thin layer of a white sticky substance over the boo-boo, blow on it with coffee breath until it was TOTALLY dry (another key technique of my generation), and finally rewrite or retype whatever we goofed up was essential to the success of your submittal.

Another area of concern was learning to play the "astronaut application game." As an early entrant into the application process, I assumed (rather naively) that I should follow each and every instruction on the SF-171 form to the letter. When it called for the addresses of my residences over the past twenty years, I provided them. When the form requested I state my full name and birthdate, "Clayton Conrad Anderson" and "02/23/1959" were squeezed into the tiny box. When further instructed to provide "three references that are familiar with your work and character," that's what they got. Three.

Follow the instructions, stay within the lines, no typos, and don't give them anything not specifically asked for. It was not until my twelfth application that I learned my competitors were submitting packages that contained not only the names and addresses of their references but also piles of letters with accolades so glowing that surely astronaut corps selection was only days away.

Being a standard government form, the application form featured a significant number of irrelevant fields. For example, section 14 asked your willingness to work in Washington DC, anywhere in the United States, or outside the fifty United States. Everyone already knows that the astronauts (at least the American ones) live in Houston, Texas, near the program's home at the Johnson Space Center.

It really got interesting when you reached the sections calling for work experience and education. Using a typewriter on the standard form's tiny data fields did not leave room for details. It wasn't until much later in my "application career" that I learned what a "supplemental" application really was.

My work experience was limited at that point (less than a year on the job), almost two if I counted my summer internships. I could only hope that my degrees in physics (BS from Hastings College) and aerospace engineering (MS, Iowa State University) would hold up reasonably well against the expected deluge of PhDs from my competition.

From the various designations of special skills, accomplishments, and awards, all the way to references, my app was a crap shoot. I had no idea whether anything I had accomplished thus far in my career could or would stand up to anyone else's. Honestly, I knew I had no chance in hell of being selected on my first submittal. I didn't kid myself; I knew it would be a long, long time before I even got a sniff from the committee.

Now an application expert, personally certified after fifteen years of trying, I always found it interesting to see just how few *disqualifying* standards were provided in the application package.

As mentioned above, besides the visual and blood pressure guidelines, a mission specialist need only be five feet tall and not taller than six feet four inches. Jim Wetherbee and Scott "Scooter"

Altman at six feet four were two of the astronauts I was aware of who pushed the upper end of this envelope (and they were pilots). Numerous female astronauts were near the lower limit, with Nancy Currie (five feet), Barbara Morgan (five feet four), and Wendy Lawrence (five feet three) immediately coming to mind.

Auditory acuity (hearing ability for us laymen) was also dictated, but only for a set of three frequencies across the aural spectrum. So from my limited perspective, I figured someday my chances would be as good as anyone else's.

I am often asked if the process of applying to become an astronaut is hard. My answer is easy: Nope. I would simply label it as time consuming. The basic requirements asked only for submittal of the standard government employment form, properly filled out, with three references. There's some medical stuff to get through, but basically that's it. Sign your John Hancock, date it, pop it in the mailbox, and off it goes to the Johnson Space Center mailroom by way of the U.S. Postal Service, perhaps to languish in someone's in-box for eternity. Then, with your fingers and toes tightly crossed, wait, wait, and wait some more!

Positive receipt of your hard work comes in the form of a confirmation note, returned with a loving and personal message: "You will be notified as soon as possible of any determination concerning your application." Ugh, more waiting.

When the time finally comes and your submittal is received, reviewed, *and* deemed "viable" by the review committee, things get more interesting. The review committee is not really about selection, it is about reviewing thousands of qualified potentials and paring that number down to something manageable.

A hand-chosen group of veteran astronauts determine if a PhD is better than no PhD, military jet pilots are better than nonmilitary jet pilots, and whether a specific institution of higher learning really matters.

So how did I get selected? Beats the hell outta me!

For most of us wannabes, multiple submittals are required. But the hardest part is putting together all the information required for your *first* application. Digging up details of previous residences, finding and securing copies of all relevant high school and college transcripts, figuring out who to use as your references—those are the things that take the most time. Once you have completed all that, the rest is simple.

The Astronaut Selection Office asks that you update your information annually. So for most folks, once your basic info is complete, you just add the things you deem relevant since your previous application.

As recently as 2013, Duane Ross shared some key information during a briefing to astronaut hopefuls about the current state of the astronaut selection process, and how, based on his thirty-seven years of experience, it has changed. With the space shuttle program complete and commercial space companies emerging, the search for U.S. astronauts now focuses on long-duration space travel.

Historically, not including the statistics from the 2013 selection, some 50,758 people have applied for the position of astronaut, beginning with the very first class of 1959. Three hundred and thirty-eight NASA (U.S.) astronauts have been selected throughout the years, and an applicant has a 0.6 percent chance of being selected. Statistics for nonpilots selected from civilian life showed 39 percent completed a master's degree and 38 percent achieved their PhD.

In the "selected as pilots" category, 53 percent had a master's degree and 43 percent had only a bachelor's degree.

In total, nearly half the astronauts selected had a master's degree (46 percent), challenging the long-existing notion that a PhD is required in order to stand a good chance of being selected. A nontechnical bachelor's degree is essentially useless, suggesting that a candidate pursue a higher-level degree in a field qualifying for "desired astronaut selection."

Today's selection process can be divided into five steps:

1. Review of basic candidate qualifications.

2. Candidates are given an initial rating of "qualified" or "highly qualified" and sorted into similar groups based on background and skill set. This helps prevent "apples to oranges" comparisons, for example, fighter pilots being compared to teachers. These discipline groupings are physical science, biological sci-

ence, engineering/operations, flight test engineering, education, and pilot.

3. Candidates are rated and ranked within their grouping.

4. Interviews and medical checks are begun. (This lasts five weeks.)

5. Final selection is made.

Once selected, candidates have several months to relocate to Houston.

Becoming flight-certified takes an additional two years of basic training, at which point you *may* qualify for up to three years of mission-specific training.

In the most recent group of potential candidates, whose selection process began in 2012, the expectation was for missions to the International Space Station (ISS) only, and it could take up to eight years, maybe longer, before they would experience their first flight.

The formal (selection committee) interviews attempt to answer the interviewer's basic question, "Would I want to go to space with this person?" The committee is not looking for hyperfocused individuals, but people who can do a little bit of everything.

They hope to obtain answers to these questions:

1. Why do you want to be an astronaut? Is it a passion or do you just think it would be fun?

2. Do you have operational capability, i.e., can you fix things like a car or a computer?

3. What is your applicability of experience?

4. How well do you communicate?

5. How well do you cope with others, and how to do you respond and adapt to change?

6. Would this candidate be a good representative of NASA?

7. Does this candidate have a personality that is too intense?

8. Are you a team player? A self-starter?

9. Who are you as a person? Are you a hard worker? What is your humility and ego balance?

10. Do you have good situational awareness and sound judgment?

Qualifications must be met before your application is reviewed. For example, if you *anticipate* getting a pilot's license, a new degree, or a few years of work experience, that won't cut it. Everything must be finished by the application due date.

The personal interviews are conducted by a panel made up of current astronauts and key Johnson Space Center leaders. The recommendations for new astronauts set forth by the panel must then be approved by the JSC director and passed along to the NASA administrator for final approval.

According to Ross, while the basic requirements for consideration may appear to have been loosened a bit, medical requirements have not. They are nearly as stringent as they were for the Mercury, Gemini, and Apollo programs; planning for long-duration flights requires astronauts in top physical and mental condition. The examinations are thorough, including eye and dental, MRIS, heart and cardiovascular checkups, and a volumetric oxygen (lungs) maximum stress test.

There is no documented age limit; passing the medical exam is all that is required, but your chances of meeting all the medical requirements definitely decrease with age. Astronauts have been selected with ages ranging from twenty-three to forty-six. Younger is considered an advantage because NASA can utilize your skills over a longer period of time.

Some medical conditions disqualify you immediately, like kidney stones, even if you've only had one. Vision requirements remain one of the key considerations for astronaut candidates. If you have 20/400 vision, correctable to 20/20, or if your vision is no worse than 20/800 and LASIK surgery could restore your vision to the 20/400 and correctable to 20/20 category, you may qualify as long as two years have passed since any type of eye surgery has been performed.

Recent ISS data have revealed that a number of astronauts serving on long-duration missions have experienced degraded vision.

Numerous studies are ongoing to try and determine why this is happening and the potential for appropriate countermeasures.

Today it is imperative all aspirants understand clearly that even if you are selected as an astronaut candidate, you are not guaranteed a space mission assignment. If at any time during your astronaut candidacy period you cannot achieve success in key areas of Russian language, robotics, or spacewalking, you may be disqualified.

Over the thirteen-plus years I was updating my application, I figured things were going to have to change for me to be considered. With the selection office providing almost no feedback, it was difficult to know how to change my "relevance" in the eyes of the committee.

Some things were easy (albeit costly). For example, many applicants go off and get their private pilot's license. Others learn to SCUBA dive. Still others go so far as to learn how to jump out of airplanes or climb the world's highest peaks. All noble endeavors, they serve the same purpose—they show the Astronaut Selection Office that

(a) You are trying to better yourself,

(b) You are not adverse to learning new skills,

(c) You are aware of many of the skills required of a new (or old) astronaut, and

(d) You are not afraid to try anything.

With encouragement from Susan, I followed that path. We got our SCUBA certifications together—on the same weekend we also became pregnant with our son, Cole (okay, the significance of the two events occurring on the same weekend is minimal, but it does show that we both have incredible stamina).

I worked hard to complete the requirements for obtaining my visual flight rating (VFR), the ticket for flying single-engine aircraft. Eventually, I even decided to take a new job at JSC, becoming the manager of the Emergency Operations Center.

Because most of the applicants were doing these same types

of things, or had already done them, I doubted they would set me apart from the rest of the field. I needed something unique.

By year thirteen, Susan and I had pretty much given up. With nary a hint that they were taking my application seriously, we journeyed to Seattle, Washington, to visit friends and look for job opportunities. Upon our return, unsure of our next move, I was surprised to receive a phone call from Duane Ross. He needed to know my availability for participating as a member of the fifth group of astronaut candidates for the class of 1996.

My flame burned anew. Sorry, Seattle!

As I went through the interview process, I wanted to stand out. I needed something I could relate to the committee that was truly unique, something most astronaut applicants would know very little about and almost certainly wouldn't do. With a little bit of digging, I discovered I may have had something I could consider my "ace in the hole." There *was* one thing about me that truly was different. I was a high school and college basketball official—a referee. I was a zebra!

Performing as a basketball official is an excellent analogy to astronaut. Both professions require you become a student of the "game." A basketball referee has a tremendous number of rules to know and understand, and if you officiate contests for men's and women's college and high school contests, you have many subtle differences between them to keep track of, and these rules must be applied correctly in any given situation.

For an astronaut, the rules are known as systems knowledge, situational awareness, and "boldface" (i.e., execute from memory) procedures. As a space-centered "referee," you must know exactly what to do, quickly and sometimes from memory, when encountering specific situations.

When you are officiating a sporting contest, the consequences are typically not critical. As an astronaut, your incorrect application of a rule, or correct application at the wrong time, could possibly put your life or your crew's lives in jeopardy.

Like basketball officials, astronauts are also *expected* to be in excellent physical condition. While there is absolutely no requirement for an astronaut to exercise, you are responsible for passing an annual physical fitness assessment: a one-and-a-half-mile run or stationary bike ride to check your oxygen intake and exchange levels, performing as many sit-ups, push-ups, and pull-ups (a minimum of two) as possible in one minute, a hand grip test (to determine hand strength for spacewalking), and a flexibility measurement (to see if you can touch your toes). It is not necessarily a difficult set of tasks for most astronauts to perform but rather a broad, general measurement of overall fitness capability.

The bottom line is that if you can squeeze your fat ass (or chest) into a spacesuit, you're good to go. (But you *will* be talked about around the water cooler by the folks that had to stuff you in!)

The ultimate analogy, perhaps most important for comparison purposes, is the ability to perform under duress. I recall many instances in my high school and college basketball officiating career where the only people in the gymnasium who were on my side were my two officiating partners, and sometimes that was debatable.

The pressure could be enormous. Playoff games, the outcomes of which were to be decided by the players, were exciting, stressful, and often downright scary. Some venues in East Texas might have you running from coaches at the end of the game or looking for security to protect you from overzealous fans or coaches' wives not impressed with your performance.

When longtime Angelina Junior College coach Guy Davis stares you down from the confines of his bench, arms crossed tightly across his chest and egged on by his vocal son affixed in his usual gameday seat by the scorer's table, a great deal of self-confidence was needed to make a call against the home team in the closing seconds of a tightly contested game.

Analyzing situations in an instant and deciding whether or not to bite down and blow on the rubber-tipped end of your black Fox 40 referee whistle was, in truth, astronaut training. Even if your call was correct, you still had to control the action. With all eyes on you, correct execution will let everyone understand the situation is under control. Whether in a striped shirt or spacesuit, it is very much the same.

The final, critical component of the two skill sets is ego. A basketball official for over twenty-five years, I observed ego levels as varied as a week's worth of orbital sunsets. A healthy ego, a major feature of most astronauts, requires care in how it manifests in behavior.

A strong high school and college official must exude confidence, not cockiness and arrogance, for which confidence is often mistaken. The fine line that separates the two can be crossed too often if you are not careful. Your ego, and the corresponding attitude with which you carry yourself, provide an "open book" on you and your personality. The same is true for an astronaut.

From my first year as an astronaut candidate it was evident that if you wanted it, you could be treated differently than anyone else. Simply by donning the blue flight suit, people looked at you with an awe they might share with a rock star or professional athlete—and that can be intoxicating.

Small things were proffered, like the time one of our colleagues was given "free pizza coupons for life" or when we were told that during launch preparations the Kennedy support staff could "keep our wives apart from our girlfriends." Withstanding these temptations went a long way toward establishing your reputation, but inappropriate responses did not necessarily place you in a bad light.

My astronaut-referee analogy at the interview was good, but not good enough. I didn't feel too depressed after getting yet another rejection note from NASA. I was pretty much used to it. But this time I didn't just get a postcard, I got a real letter.

Received on May 7, 1996, Duane Ross thanked me for trying and told me that twenty-five mission specialists and ten pilots had been selected from over twenty-four hundred applicants. He said the competition was keen and the limited number of slots precluded highly qualified candidates like me from being chosen. I was highly qualified. I had a chance!

The letter gave me a feeling of hope. I had made it to the interview round and at least had a chance to present myself to the selection board. This time, however, I figured that since most applicants receive postcards, a letter sent on stationary meant something. I had more work to do.

I waited two more years to receive another interview. This time I had more experience on my side, and even better, I had a plan.

Feedback solicited from my first interview let me know the selection committee had concerns with my technical knowledge and skills. Finding myself seated once again at their conference table in 1998, I focused first on sharing my technical accomplishments from a fifteen-year career as an engineer. But what I think pushed them over to my side was the gist of my closing statement.

I referred to the annual automobile issue of *Consumer Reports* and its rating of cars for the model year. To aid their readers in the quest to purchase new vehicles, the experts used three descriptors: highly recommended, not recommended, and insufficient data. These descriptors were key to my plan.

I proposed to the committee that each of them walk the grounds of JSC at random, stopping every person they encountered. Then, I suggested, they should ask that person if they knew or had worked with Clayton Anderson. More than 50 percent, I speculated, would respond in the affirmative. (I had been there a long time.)

At that point, I argued, actual data would be available to the committee, just like in the magazine. The individuals could be asked how they knew me, what kind of person they thought I was, did I work hard—anything. They could ask if they thought I would make a good astronaut. Would they recommend me, not recommend me, or did they not have enough data to decide?

I concluded my remarks by telling the committee I had the one thing no one else could give them—I was from Nebraska. When asked by Greg Hayes of Human Resources why they should pick someone from Nebraska, I calmly explained that being the first from the state would provide a wealth of new outreach possibilities, not to mention the fact that it would give Nebraska's representatives in Congress a very specific reason to support the space program. Finally, pointing directly at committee member and veteran astronaut Steve Hawley, I flashed a quick smile and said, "Well, you picked a guy from Kansas, didn't you?"

Sign me up, baby! I'm ready.

5

Answer the Phone, Will Ya?

It is known as "the call." I imagine most astronauts remember their call—the day, the time, the place—everything associated with one of the most important events in their life. It's the call that takes ordinary U.S. citizens and gives them the opportunity to become extraordinary, to become a United States astronaut.

Susan and I were in Florida, at the Kennedy Space Center to be exact. She had been awarded an all-expense-paid trip to the famed Rocket Center as part of a NASA promotion called "space flight awareness." This prestigious award is given to NASA and contract employees who have made significant contributions to their organizations in the name of the space shuttle program. Susan was being cited for her excellent work in the Shuttle-Mir Phase 1 program, the precursor to the International Space Station program in which we would one day be so intimately involved.

We were at Cape Canaveral to witness a shuttle launch firsthand. STS-91, the final Shuttle-Mir docking mission, was poised on launchpad 39A, ready to lift off and secure its place in NASA history as the final visit to the Russian Mir space station. Commanded by veteran astronaut Charlie Precourt, the space shuttle *Discovery* would carry a crew of six uphill, and seven, including Mir resident and native Australian Andy Thomas, back down. Pilot Dom Gorie, along with mission specialists Wendy Lawrence, Janet Kavandi, Franklin Chang-Diaz, and Russian cosmonaut Valery Ryumin, rounded out the shuttle crew.

The space flight awareness activities, most often scheduled two days before launch (L minus 2), were numerous and varied. Included was a luncheon featuring a briefing from brand-new astronaut candidate Lisa Nowak (a member of the sixteenth group of astronauts, she was to become infamous as the diaper-clad, pepper-spray-packin' woman spurned by astronaut William A. "Billy O" Oefelein.). Bright and eager in her royal blue flight suit and yellow turtleneck, Nowak flashed smiles, shook hands, and signed autographs. It was a wonderful luncheon, and Susan and I got to be photographed together in front of the space shuttle *Discovery* launch background.

The biggest and most interesting party during the trip was the reception at the nearby Cape Canaveral port and cruise ship terminal. Attended by astronauts, NASA managers, contractors, and the awardees, the place was packed with folks enjoying fancy hors d'oeuvres and adult beverages. As we mingled with the crowd, we ran across several people with whom we were very well acquainted. Some of these VIPs made what we felt were strange comments. Brock "Randy" Stone, a former flight director and the head of Mission Operations at Johnson Space Center (and at the time my boss), told me it was "okay to relax." The remark didn't really sink in, although I did make a mental note of how odd it seemed for him to say something like that. While Susan and I were exchanging a subtle glance (complete with raised eyebrows), Jeff Bantle, then the head of the Flight Director Office and also a former flight director, sauntered over to where we stood with Randy. After he entered the casual chitchat, he suggested, "Don't get too far from the phone." I began to put two and two together. Jeff was a member of the Astronaut Selection Committee. I had recently stood before him and a plethora of other bigwigs to tell them all things Clayton Anderson in the hopes of solidifying my position as a viable astronaut candidate.

It wasn't until Dave Leestma, another veteran astronaut and at that time the leader of Flight Crew Operations, happened by and said, "Hey, Clay, when are you going back to Houston?" that I dared begin to daydream. Quickly regaining consciousness, I doubt my answer was timely or succinct, but Dave's response of "We'll talk to you then" was intriguing. Having only spoken to him during the astronaut interview process, it seemed doubtful

I would ever talk to him again—unless of course . . . maybe . . . you never know.

No, I told myself. Absolutely not. I simply couldn't let myself think about selection. I was worried that if I let hope intercede, only to have it pulled away, the disappointment would be too great. Susan and I refused to discuss it any further, except for acknowledging the strangeness of the various interchanges. Though bolstered by their positive nature, we were still apprehensive about their intent. Oh well, we thought. Let's drink more wine.

The next party, a huge celebration on the day before launch (L minus 1), was held at the Royal Mansions, a well-traveled Cocoa Beach condominium resort and regular hangout for Houstonian NASA folks. We were attending because Susan, as a member of the Shuttle-Mir Program Office, was invited. This bash commemorated the fast-approaching final mission and linkup between a space shuttle and the Mir space station.

We found ourselves on the patio, enjoying seasonally cool weather and the excitement surrounding the anticipation of another successful liftoff. Susan, looking gorgeous as ever, was in huge demand. Not only was she an effective employee but she was damned good-looking and thus the target of many of the inebriated males in attendance—any one of whom could make or break her career. It was not easy for me to stand by and watch these guys hug my wife and try to get "final mission kisses." Susan was up to the challenge, though, politely fending them off with a smile and a quick hip bump. Always a pro, she was gracious and calm. I admired her moxie.

Many key players attended this gathering: Frank Culbertson, the Phase 1 program office manager and Susan's boss; George Abbey, the Johnson Space Center director; Yury Glazkov, the decorated cosmonaut and hero of the Soviet Union; and former astronaut Mike Baker, the director of operations in Russia. Abbey and Glazkov were seated together at one of the patio tables, enjoying the revelry . . . perhaps a bit too much. Eyes struggling to stay open, Mr. Abbey was well known for snoozing right in the middle of critical conversations, then waking immediately, seemingly not having missed a single second of the transfer of information. He is a truly amazing and brilliant man.

The staff arrived at their table to deposit a watermelon fruit bowl. Cut from the rind of the melon, with jagged edges gracing the top of its circumference, the natural container was filled to the brim with various fruits, beautifully done and perfect for an outdoor party on the Florida coast.

I stood quietly on the patio, a good distance away, hoping to appear a typical nonchalant partygoer. Having attended the space-flight awareness gathering the night before, and hearing the innuendo that was prevalent regarding the astronaut selection process, I figured my best bet was simply to hang out and not do anything stupid. Keep my distance, observe silently, be polite. Minimal chatter would be my ally in the quest to avoid messing this one up in the final hours.

Yet here I was, only feet from a former cosmonaut and the most senior official of the Johnson Space Center, both well past their normal levels of sobriety.

Mr. Abbey made the first move. Awaking from one of his brief power naps, he spied the newly provided sustenance in the table's center. Without missing a beat, and with the vigor and command presence of a bear chasing salmon, he stuck his large hand directly into the watermelon bowl, securing a solid handful of melon balls, strawberries, grapes, and whatever else lay within. His hand moved quickly to his mouth and deposited the entire fistful into a cavernous waiting gullet. Yury wasted no time following Mr. Abbey's lead. His motions were identical, although his hand was considerably smaller. This was amazing—and disgusting. Anyone watching would undoubtedly lose their appetite for whatever remained in the bowl.

What happened next became a vision forever etched into my memory banks. An attractive woman, probably in her early fifties, with short blond hair and quite well put together, approached the table with enthusiasm and a wonderful smile. As she neared, Mr. Abbey leaped to his feet—or at least he tried his best to, given his current state of "relaxation." Obvious acquaintances, they exchanged a few pleasantries, and then, with a swoop of his hand reminiscent of his attack on the fruit bowl, Mr. Abbey grabbed the back of her head and pulled her in for a French kiss that would have made James Bond envious.

Tom Cremens, a JSC budget expert and one of Mr. Abbey's righthand men, was also observing the male-female bonding exercise. With more courage than I could ever muster, he yelled, "Jesus Christ, George! My wife won't even let me do that to her!"

I am not sure whether Mr. Abbey even heard the remark or cared, but a roar of laughter erupted from the small crowd witnessing the sensuous exchange. I sank deeper into my incognito persona, observing everything. This was pretty humorous and revealing at the same time. I wondered how these guys would ever be ready for the launch.

On the morning of June 3, 1998, parties and celebrations had finished. Possibly suffering hangovers but most certainly carrying the memories of a lifetime, thousands of people were heading home from their visit to Spaceport USA. The space shuttle *Discovery* had done her part, delivering a spectacularly beautiful and safe launch into orbit. She was now less than two days from her rendezvous with the Russian-built dragonfly-like collection of anodized aluminum modules known as Mir as it orbited some two hundred miles above the Earth.

Totally exhausted but enthused about the United States and her space program, Susan and I had several hours to kill before our flight home to Texas. Traveling without our two-year-old son, Cole, our adventurous side prevailed and we left Cocoa Beach for Highway A1A, bound for the U.S. Army Corps of Engineers' Canaveral Lock station. Florida's Beeline Expressway, and ultimately Orlando's bustling international airport, would just have to wait.

Other launch guests had told us the Canaveral Lock was a great place to view and possibly interact with those huge masses of gray homeliness known as manatees. As we strolled leisurely around the area in search of some of these Wilford Brimley lookalikes, my pager began to vibrate at approximately 1006 (it's funny how I remember that; today I can't even remember what I had for breakfast). As head of JSC Emergency Operations, I was leashed to my job with this now ancient technology known as a pager. I looked at the telephone number on its tiny pale-green screen. The pager continued its buzzing, suggesting I push the button signifying receipt. I was racking my brain trying to identify the number. Usually I was able to at least identify the city or state by checking the area code: 402 was Nebraska, 515 Iowa, and 713 signifies Houston. The numbers 321 predominantly displayed in the pager's LED window did not ring a bell.

"It has to be for you," I told Susan. "I don't recognize the number at all." Handing the pager to my well-connected wife brought an initial look that was equally questioning but followed by her swift response, "I think I know this area code. It's Florida."

Still not certain of the originator of the pager's digitally cryptic message, I was feeling a desperate need to return the call. While my gut was telling me it was likely intended for Susan, the fact that the number meant nothing to her either presented another, more serious possibility—an emergency situation could have arisen at JSC. In my position as its emergency manager, it was imperative that we find a phone. Any hope I harbored for becoming an astronaut would be dashed against the rocks if I failed to respond to the needs dictated by my current job responsibilities. Keep in mind this was happening back in the dark ages of the late nineties, when we didn't carry cell phones.

Finding a telephone at the U.S. Army Corps of Engineers' Canaveral Lock presented a problem. It's not your standard Florida tourist attraction. Aside from the two of us, nary a soul could be found anywhere in the vicinity. The only structure within view was a small shack set back from a concrete walkway twenty or thirty yards from the lock.

We approached it cautiously, searching for signs of life, feeling much like the cops on a *Special Victims Unit* episode on TV. A single metal-casing door with a square glass pane stood as a silent sentry, ready to serve as a staunch deterrent in our quest for the telephone holy grail. We continued our stealth approach, as if command leaders in the mountains of Afghanistan, until we were within inches of the window. We discovered a Windex shortage existed at this government facility. Peering through the dirty glass like a spy in a B-roll movie, I gingerly cracked the door open. Susan's soft hand squeezed the trapezius muscle on my right shoulder. Using the door as my shield, I craned my neck to maximize my view of the interior. The place was void of humankind.

I took a deep breath. "Hello? Anybody here?" I called without much confidence. The words seemed to bounce around like unreturned serves in a racquetball court.

My eyes scanned the space for any signs of life. A black rotary dial telephone (parents, please explain this one to your children) sat in the middle of the room's single desk. The five clear plastic pushbuttons on the bottom of this ancient communication device were dark, signifying that at least for now, no one was using the line.

Clutching my pager in my left hand, I grabbed the receiver with my right. Not knowing how to get a line out, I randomly pushed in the clear plastic button at the far left. It lit up and I heard the necessary dial tone. Feeling like a sophomore making his first call to ask a girl for a date, I fumbled through three misdials. My nerves were heading toward fever pitch. My breathing must have been twice its normal rate. Finally a connection was made. A calm, soothing female voice came on the line: "Astronaut Crew Quarters."

Area code 321—I finally figured it out! A neophyte in the Kennedy Space Center area, I hadn't known that 3-2-1 was chosen in honor of the many launches from the Space Port.

I politely identified myself and explained how I had received a page and was simply returning the call. The patient voice asked if I had dialed the correct number. Had I? I wasn't sure. I said, "I think so, but Susan Anderson is my wife and it's possible they are trying to reach her."

The voice said, "Please hold. Someone will be with you in a minute."

The fog began to slowly lift in my brain. I was putting it all together.

With a rush of adrenaline and anticipation I hadn't felt since the birth of our first child, my body and mind began to tingle. "Susan—I think I know what this is!" I whispered to my beautiful bride.

Susan knew, too. She began to cry. The first of many dominoes had fallen, starting a sequence that was destined to change our lives forever.

David Leestma came on the phone. After some agonizing small talk with this highest-ranking astronaut, he asked me the question I had been waiting to hear since I was five years old. "Are you still interested in being a long-duration mission specialist?"

Trying to sound as astronaut-like as possible, I stammered, "Yes, sir. Absolutely, sir!"

No longer interested in manatees, we headed to Orlando International Airport. We were so excited we couldn't contain our enthusiasm, yet we only had each other to share it with, like when you have a big secret and are dying to tell someone but you can't. Once inside the airport and safely checked in for the flight back to Houston, we initiated an attack on the nearest set of pay telephones. The first call went to my mother—who wasn't home. The second call went to my sister—who wasn't available either. The third call? You guessed it—my brother, but he wasn't in his office either. We did hit the jackpot when we dialed up the in-laws in Anderson, Missouri.

My father-in-law, Jack Harreld, answered the phone and was the first to actually hear the news. Not much of a telephone conversationalist, he said nothing but burst into tears on the other end of the receiver. I was truly touched. Since my father had passed away in 1984, Jack had served as the father figure I now lacked, and he did it unconditionally with pride, honor, and understanding. I was excited that he was the first to hear the news. We randomly continued our attempts to contact all our other family members until we had to board the plane. The rest would have to wait a bit longer to get the wonderful news.

The week after NASA had issued the official press release announcing the astronaut class of 1998, I found myself playing right field at JSC's Gilruth Recreation Center softball field complex. Roaming the green grass of field number 3, feeling like I was still twenty-five years old, I was enjoying one of my favorite pastimes of my early middle age.

Hearing a ping from the aluminum bat and seeing the red-stitched, white leather softball soaring rapidly my way, I instinctively put into action the training techniques that had been drilled into me from years spent on the baseball diamond. Hearing my father's baritone voice saying, "Son, it's easier to run forward than to run backward," I rotated to my right and, continuing to accelerate, ran ever deeper into the far corner of right field. Sensing that this one was well hit and might recoil off of the top of the eight-foot-high chain-link fence surrounding the outfield, I slammed on the brakes to give myself room to play the carom.

While my mind was willing, my body was not. I felt a sharp pop in my left knee. The intense pain was short-lived but not the instability that came with it. As I tried to slow down to establish a good fielding position it felt like my knee was going to break sideways.

All I could think was "This isn't good" as I gingerly braced myself to throw the now-retrieved ball to the infielder screaming at me from second base.

Recusing myself from the remainder of the inning, I managed to jog off the field to the dugout, telling myself that nothing had really happened to my leg and I would be able to finish the game after a short break to let my knee return to normal. As the minutes wore on and I took my turn in the batter's box, it became painfully obvious something serious had occurred and I wouldn't be playing any more softball for a while.

The next week I had an appointment with world-renowned orthopedic surgeon Daniel B. O'Neill, son of mission operations director John O'Neill. It took him only one tug on my lower leg to confirm the diagnosis I had been dreading. I had torn my left anterior cruciate ligament (ACL). I zigged when I should have zagged. The damage was severe enough that I would now need the good doctor's services and a boatload of rehabilitation.

Since Dr. O'Neill knew I had just been selected as a new astronaut candidate, I was scheduled for what turned out to be very successful surgery on June 26, 1998, just forty-eight hours after the injury and less than two weeks since receiving my life-changing phone call from Dave Leestma. Feeling sheepish and fearful that my time as an astronaut had lasted all of two weeks, I put in a nervous call to Duane Ross, the dean of astronaut selection. In a roundabout way I mustered the courage to ask him if I was going to be kicked out of the corps because of my softball ineptitude.

He laughed his quiet unassuming laugh. After a slight pause for effect, he said, "No—short of being arrested, once you're in, you're pretty much in."

Relieved at having survived my first obstacle, I threw myself into a daily, three-hour-plus rehabilitation regimen, fully expecting to report for astronaut duty in August no worse for the wear. I did make sure that I wore long and loose triple pleated slacks to my office in the Emergency Operations Center every day to cover up the fact that a full-length knee brace was part of my wardrobe.

The "cool factor" of astronaut selection set in very quickly. Well wishes were continuing to come in by email and telephone, including a call from Texas Democratic congressman Nick Lampson of Beaumont. Then representative for NASA's home district, he provided kind words of congratulations. Being a native Nebraskan, I had speculated that this type of call might come from the representatives of my home state; it hadn't dawned on me yet that I had been a Texan longer than I had been a Nebraskan and I now lived in Mr. Lampson's district.

Being a novice astronaut, the phone call that ultimately blew me away was the one I received from the PE (Personal Equipment) Shop at nearby Ellington Field. I was told I would be receiving a "holey joe" (NASA lingo for interoffice mail envelope) containing a couple of forms for me to fill out. Once that task was completed, I would then be able to head out to Ellington Field for a meeting, the content of which was not clear.

For me to be journeying to Ellington Field was a major deal. This was a special, almost revered place where United States astronauts challenged the skies in high performance T-38 jets. So recently bestowed with the title of astronaut, I still considered myself an outsider. I was in awe as I headed for Hangar 276.

A huge white hangar with massive thirty-foot sliding doors at both ends served as the parking garage for NASA's fleet of sleek T-38 jets. Having never before been to the PE Shop, I parked my car and headed for the interior of Hangar 276. It was midmorning and the hangar was only partially full of its cadre of aircraft. Many were on the flight line, prepared for pilots and astronauts to take them out on a sortie or two.

I took in a huge gulp of air as I entered the hangar, perhaps more from reverence than anything else. I was spellbound, my eyes fixed on these graceful supersonic air force hybrids. I was snapped from my trance when one of the flight line mechanics noticed me and asked if he could help.

"I'm supposed to go to the PE Shop," I blabbered. He pointed me to a royal blue door on the hangar's southwest side, where a sign, also royal blue, read "PE Shop." I opened the door and climbed rubber-lined steps to the home of astronauts' personal equipment.

There was not a lot of activity in the large open rooms. To the left was a room full of sewing machines. Royal blue jackets and flight suits cluttered the tabletops in this cockpit for highly skilled aviation haberdashers.

Faded photographs in cheap black frames adorned the walls, featuring famous astronauts and mission montages signed by crewmembers. To the right was a long, narrow room with two tables pushed end to end. On top, a myriad of components of the aviators' parachutes were strewn. There were the beige chutes themselves, and the army green backpacks that would eventually carry the carefully folded cloth. Bulbous water floatation devices for the chute's shoulder harnesses sat ready in the sequential and highly critical order required in packing the chutes.

I stood in the chute packing room mesmerized by its sights, smells, and secrets. A gentleman in navy blue pants, athletic shoes, and a gray cotton t-shirt stepped into the room and said, "Hello, Clayton!" While I was still trying to figure out how he knew my name, he introduced himself as "Sarge." He was there to provide me with my equipment—my astronaut equipment.

Sarge, born Ervin Knehaus, led me to the end of the chute room and into a much smaller area that contained, surprisingly enough, a wooden picnic table. It was a break room of sorts, but on one wall was a full-length mirror. Along the other walls stood drab government-issue storage and filing cabinets. Sarge disappeared into an even smaller room, more like a closet, and emerged with a huge army-green duffel bag which he plopped down on the picnic table. He unzipped the bag and began quickly handing the items to me with only the briefest of explanations.

Like a barker at a carnival, old Sarge announced: "Here's your flight boots, here's your kneeboard, here's your flashlight, here's your wristwatch, here's your flight jacket, here's your sunglasses, here's your pub bag, here's your flight gloves, here's your garment bag and your duffel bag, and here's your two blue flight suits. Try them flight suits on." A bit embarrassed but feeling like a kid in a candy store, I dropped trou and threw off my shirt in a hurried effort to begin donning my royal blue flight suit for the very first time. A size 42 long, just as I had indicated on the paperwork, it felt scratchy and stiff, carrying the smell of a garment fresh out of the package. I stood silently in front of the mirror, gazing at the reflection that most certainly was me but not believing my eyes.

"How's it fit?" Sarge asked.

"I guess it fits great," was my uneducated reply. "How does it look to you?" I wanted confirmation from someone who was not as ignorant as I.

"Looks good to me," Sarge replied. "Now try on the jacket."

Sarge had obviously done this before. Under his watchful eye and patient guidance, the sizing process proceeded smoothly, ensuring a proper fit for the jacket, flight suit, and standard-issue boots and gloves. Sarge was unrelenting in his quest to make sure everything met my satisfaction. I was in awe.

"Now you need some custom-made flight boots," Sarge nonchalantly stated.

"I do?" I can only imagine the silly look on my face that greeted this salty old veteran. After all, he'd just given me a fine pair of boots.

"Yep, we need to measure your feet. Take a seat and pull your socks off."

With an ancient, well-worn tailor's tape, he carefully measured every inch of my feet, mumbling and making notations on a form that would serve as the blueprint for my custom footwear.

"What kinda boots ya want?" Sarge asked expectantly.

"Uh, what kinda boots ya got?" I queried, not certain of the meaning of his question.

"Well, we got yer lace-ups, we got yer zippers, and we got yer buckles," he stated matter-of-factly.

"Uh . . . what kind do most people get?"

"Most astronauts, they like the buckles."

"Well, that's what I want!" I blurted enthusiastically.

"What color boots ya want?" He asked.

Fighting the urge to let him know that I thought this was getting ridiculous, my response was a hesitant. "Uh, what color boots ya got?"

"Well, we got yer Italian brown leather or your cordovan or your basic black," he offered.

"Uh . . . what kind do most people get?" I repeated.

"Most astronauts, they're kinda partial to the Italian brown leather."

"Well, that's what I want!" I confidently responded. I was starting to get the hang of this.

"What kinda heels ya want?" he asked.

"What kind of heels do I want . . . really?" I was beginning to feel like part of an Abbott and Costello comedy routine. "Uh, what kind of heels do you have?"

"Well, we got yer rubber heels and we got yer leather heels."

"What kind do most people get?"

This time his reply to my constant question caught me totally off guard. "You don't wanna slip and fall on your ass, do ya?"

"Uh, no, sir."

"Then ya wants the rubber heels."

"Okay, that's what I want, the rubber heels."

Wrapping up his tape measure and gathering his tools, Sarge signaled that I had satisfied his near-insatiable need for boot specifications.

Our next endeavor was getting a flight helmet. He led me back down the steep staircase and across the hangar floor to another door, once again matching the royal blue motif but this time bearing a sign: "Helmet/Chute Room."

Inside this crowded room were rows and rows of shelves subdivided into individual bins. Each bin contained a military-green soft-sided bag. At the base of each bin were blue placards with the last name of the bin's owner. The names of several astronauts, including Culbertson, Camarda, and Coleman, commanded my attention as we moved down the center row toward the back of the room.

Along each wall were evenly spaced thick wooden pegs, each one supporting the weight of a hanging parachute. All the chutes were facing the same direction, as if in military formation.

From there I was escorted into an even smaller room behind the rows of shelves and the stash of dangling parachutes.

"You're going to need a flight helmet," said the new personal equipment "helmet guy," Chris Sandoval.

"Okay!" Another brilliant reply from the rookie astronaut.

"What color of helmet would you like to have?" he asked.

Oh no, I thought, a bit exasperated, we're going to do it all over again. This time, though, I allowed my brain to do a small amount of processing before reentering the world of comedy routines.

Preemptively striking against my friendly foe, I asked, "Can I please look at some of the other astronauts' helmets?"

"Sure, let's go take a look," was his accommodating reply.

We began to grab random helmet bags from the shelf of bins just outside his office door. The first one revealed a baby blue (that's right—totally baby blue) helmet that belonged to the eccentric but brilliant astronaut Story Musgrave. Not my style. The PE Shop expert grabbed the next bag and unzipped it to reveal a bright yellow helmet with black lightning bolts painted on each side. This was the helmet of Frank Culbertson. Again, a helmet color scheme that was not going to float my boat. The third and fourth bags contained identical helmets, painted darker blue, with a metallic finish one might see on a sports car or a Texas Tech Red Raiders football helmet. It looked good to me—simple yet elegant and "astronaut-like." But when the PE Shop guy told me that many of the astronauts of the 1996 class had chosen this type of helmet, I no longer wanted one. I wanted to stand out among my peers.

I searched other bags, trying to hone in on something that would work for me. Not having much luck, we returned to the office for a chance to look through a huge three-ring binder containing all the various colors and styles that were available. It was then that I had my helmet epiphany.

"How about maybe a solid red helmet with a white visor?" I asked. My thought was that the red and white could stand for my beloved Nebraska "Big Red." It also occurred to me that as an equal opportunity school advertisement, it also represented the colors of my alma mater, Hastings College, and one of the colors of the Iowa State Cyclones. Not really a concern, the happenstances were an added bonus.

I learned that I could also get a customized logo painted on the helmet's visor. As I looked through the mammoth binder, the NASA meatball and the symbol some call the "NASA swoosh" caught my eye. The swoosh logo is basically a representation of the innards of the NASA meatball—letters on a field of stars with the red chevron across the letters. In its purest form, this logo has the NASA letters in white, the chevron red and the stars are blue. The meatball logo, the more recognized of the two, is represented by a basic circle, predominantly blue, and is smaller than the swoosh. The size of the meatball would be quite small on my helmet visor, so I suggested that we go with the swoosh. With that major decision documented on the requisite forms, we moved to the next phase of my equipment orientation and adornment.

"You can get something on the back of your helmet, too," my trusted aide revealed. I asked what he meant by that.

"Well," he said. "You can get your name, or your wife's name, or your girlfriend's name or," after pausing briefly, "your wife *and* your girlfriend's names," he stated matter-of-factly.

Shocked by his candor—and the deadpan delivery—I was speechless for a moment before stuttering, "H-h-how about Clayton C. Anderson?" I asked.

"Sure, that would be fine. What kind of font do you want it in?"

"What do most people get?" Here we go again, I thought.

"Usually they like to use the scripted font, like this one." He pulled down one of the helmets and pointed out a name beautifully painted on the back, a military flier's call sign that I didn't recognize. Accepting his recommendation with a perceptible nod, I had apparently answered all his design questions.

Chris now told me we needed to figure out the type of oxygen mask best suited to the shape of my face. We tried several different styles (who knew there would be multiple styles?), hooking them up to a generic gray flight helmet, two bayonet fittings sliding into the two silver slots affixed to the outside of the helmet's ear cavities.

I put it on and was struggling to breathe through a mask supplying no oxygen when he grabbed the end of the hose now sprouting from in front of my nose and attached it to a black military-type oxygen supplier. He flipped the dial to the "on" position and my breathing became easier. Satisfied that this might be a good fit, Chris moved the knob to the "test" position.

The shock to my system was intense. A serious push of oxygen came through the mask at a constant flow level. Air began to shoot out from under the mask just under my eye sockets. It became difficult to blink as the flow battered my untrained eyes. Chris noticed and turned the system off. He took the mask off and I watched as he delicately maneuvered the straps attached to the metal triangles serving as stabilizers on the sides of the rubber container.

"Try it now," he instructed. I went through the newly learned ritual of clipping in the bayonet fittings. We did the test again. This time the mask felt awfully tight from the bridge of my nose to near the bottom of my chin.

The rotary switch in the "normal" position, he asked again, "How's that feel?"

"I don't know. How's it supposed to feel?" I asked, my voice muffled by the thick military-green rubber mask.

Not at all affected by my attempt at levity, Chris asked, "Does it feel uncomfortable on your face? Is it too tight?"

I released the right bayonet from its locked in position. "Yes!"

Having apparently exercised all his options for sizing on this mask, we went to a second larger, and more rounded, style. The process was repeated, but this one was way too large. We ultimately returned to the first mask and resized the straps, finally being able to secure a fit that while a bit snug did everything necessary to keep the oxygen flowing within the confines of the mask and not leaking out anywhere on my face.

Chris asked the inevitable question, "How does that feel?"

I held to the exact same reply I had used earlier, and in an effort to be a team player, I suggested I would "try this for a while and see how it works."

This would be the very mask I would wear while amassing over 650 hours of flight time in the T-38.

I walked away from Ellington Field that day with a bit of a hop in my step. Knowing little to nothing about the unbelievable adventure I was about to undertake, I felt for the first time like a real live astronaut.

The rest, as they say, is history.

6

Baby Astronauts

My son, Cole, is a pretty darned good football player. According to his coaches, teammates, and a plethora of NCAA Division 1 football institutions, he is capable of playing "at the next level." While attending Junior Day at the University of Houston in the spring of 2013, we were greeted by numerous coaches in Nike dry-fit slacks and polo shirts. They were all intent on relating to Cole what a great place it was and how he could greatly contribute to their red-and-white clad Cougar football squad.

The most telling aspect for me that day wasn't the level of kow-towing to my son. It was a speech by one of the university's football team staffers, a gentleman named Mikado Hinson. Hinson served in the position of campus director for the Fellowship of Christian Athletes at the University of Houston.

As he stood in front of the small group of "invitation only" athletes and their parents, he began to relate the various aspects of his job. His excitement was evident as he told of working with young athletes on the Houston campus and throughout the nation. Wrapping up his time with us, he summarized the team philosophy and struck me with one of his final comments. He said, "If you wear a [Cougar] jersey, you have influence."

So it was with the completion of a press conference in August 1998, when thirty-one Penguins—Group 17 in NASA terminology—were ready to don their "jerseys."

We had influence.

When astronauts are selected to the corps, they are designated only as astronaut candidates. For the first two years of basic training, astronauts are constantly being evaluated. It is a time to tread softly, to "keep your head down and color."

At any point within that time period, through an error in judgment or a physical ailment, it is possible to lose the coveted status of astronaut. Although rare in the history of the program, it has happened, more so in recent years than ever before.

We are like newborns—baby astronauts, if you will. In much the same way we raise our children, astronauts are "raised" as well.

Whether referring to technical data, NASA history, or simple social interaction, baby astronauts are molded and shaped to ultimately assume the role of spacefarer and all its associated duties.

From the process of selecting our class nickname, Penguins (other flightless, ugly, and intelligence-challenged choices included Dodos, Dumbos, and Emus) to the choice of our class leaders, everything had significance for us as we "grew" into our positions.

Shortly after our August reporting date, our class leader, Gregory C. "Ray J" Johnson, a retired captain in the United States Navy and a NASA veteran since 1990, told the Penguins, "If you want to fly in space, don't screw up in a T-38 or a simulator."

All thirty of us took Ray J's words to be sound advice, although I often wondered why mistakes can't be made in the simulator. Isn't that where you are supposed to make mistakes and then learn from them?

I would come to find out that while some mistakes are tolerated, others are not.

We ASCANS traveled the country as a group, visiting every NASA Center, including NASA Headquarters in Washington DC. We were paraded around and put on display for all to see. From the desert landing strips of Edwards Air Force Base in California to the Goddard Space Flight Center in Green Belt, Maryland, we visited each center and learned of their storied contributions to the U.S. space program.

In anticipation of one day serving as NASA spokespersons, we were trained (somewhat) in the art of public speaking and interviews. We were primped and we were photographed—because we were big news.

We had influence.

But as a class, our judgment was not always sound. Just as back in elementary school, there were troublemakers—individuals who challenged the status quo by sticking their necks out in the name of having a good time while ignoring the consequences.

We had some Penguins like that.

We had our version of the "What happens in Vegas, stays in Vegas" mantra. The "two-TACAN rule" (referring to the two-hundred-mile spacing of the tactical air navigation system that aircraft use for bearing and distance) is astronaut-speak for "If it happens more than two TACANS away, ignore it."

We had classmates who jumped, probably inebriated, from the balcony of a condominium near Washington DC to the swimming pool below. We had Penguins who went skinny-dipping in a small river during a survival training exercise. There was the time we returned from a soiree in Thermal, California, extremely late at night and found ourselves punch-drunk the next day from too little sleep. Acting like silly children, we embarrassed ourselves and our hosts while listening to a PhD professor at the Jet Propulsion Lab in Pasadena.

But perhaps, just perhaps, we shouldn't have gone to Mardi Gras.

We found ourselves in New Orleans, perched high in the bleachers rising above the southeast side of Saint Charles Avenue, watching a Mardi Gras parade. Fortuitous timing had placed our ASCAN familiarization trip to NASA's Stennis Space Center and the nearby Michoud Assembly Facility right in the middle of the greatest party in the South. Stennis was home to NASA facilities for engine testing, and Michoud manufactured the orange foam–covered external tanks.

Guests of the City of New Orleans and thoroughly enjoying the marvelous weather, we watched the parade pass by. Everything adorned in gold, green, and purple, it was a marvelous pageantry.

It didn't take long for the males in our group to locate the section of beautiful young women seated across the street. Numbering in the thirties, these Mardi Gras princesses sat in special reserved seating.

Suddenly a fellow Penguin stood and shouted, "Look, across the street! There's Foreman and Fergie sitting with the princesses!"

Looking in that direction, I saw them. Two astronauts sitting tall and proud directly in the midst of the young royalty, acting as if they belonged.

They waved back at us, grinning like Cheshire cats. They had influence.

Leaving the parade early so we'd have time for exploring, I made a baby astronaut mistake of agreeing to accompany a group of my classmates to Bourbon Street in the famous French Quarter.

Covering the distance on foot in a little under thirty minutes, our group of five was greeted by a mass of humanity. The street could have used "standing room only" signs, and the pulsating Zydeco music was intense. It reeked of stale beer and urine, as amid the thousands of partygoers were those who whipped out their business to "mark their territory" in the public streets.

Packed in like sardines, movement was difficult, and I clung to the leather belt of one of my fellow classmates. Having no idea where we were headed, I followed blindly, maintaining a solid grip on the thin piece of leather.

Crossing the street would be a formidable task. The wall-to-wall people barely moved as if little straws tightly packed in an unopened box.

A police officer riding on a majestic roan cut through the masses like an icebreaker pushing slowly to the North Pole. As the horse passed by, the human ocean parted and then closed again quickly.

We jumped into the wake and reached the door to an adult-themed establishment on the street's opposite side. We were met by a young man serving in the capacity of bouncer or maître d'—I wasn't sure which.

"Twenty-five bucks each," he said as he carefully looked us over.

Twenty-five dollars—he's got to be kidding, I thought. That's five trips to Burger King. Nothing could possibly be worth that much.

One of my compadres, loaded to the gills with NASA memorabilia, chided, "I have NASA mission patches. How about we give you John Glenn patches? He just flew in space." He was referring to the recent highly publicized launch of the aging senator and former Mercury astronaut from Ohio.

"No patches, twenty-five bucks a head," he repeated forcefully, now seeming to be more of a bouncer.

"Aw, c'mon, man," the rookie astronaut repeated. "Give us a break. I've got these authentic NASA mission patches."

"No deal," the doorman reiterated.

As I turned from the entrance certain that our offer was insufficient, the bouncer made a counteroffer.

"She shows us her tits, and you all get in," he nodded in the direction of our only female companion and fellow baby astronaut.

Without further negotiations, our female's shirt and brassiere shot up as a single unit, exposing her B-cup-sized breasts.

Nodding graciously in approval and displaying a sly grin, the victorious doorman moved from his post, allowing all of us to pass.

Cover charge waived. She had influence.

This was not your normal bar. Packed to the gills just like the street outside, every fifteen feet or so were color televisions mounted on ceiling brackets, playing inaudible full-color pornographic movies.

Uncomfortable and preoccupied with the pornographic TV, I nearly ran into a young lady leaning against a stool at the bar dressed in a Halloween cat costume.

Upon further review I realized she wasn't wearing a costume. In fact, she wasn't wearing anything at all—unless you count a coat of body paint. Chalk up another new astronaut experience for the rookie from Nebraska.

Following my crewmates up the stairs to the second floor of the raunchy establishment, I was wondering how long I could stand to stay in this place. We found an open table near the center of the room.

Ordering beers all around, we relaxed for a bit (as much as possible in a place like this), discussing our travels and the things we had seen in this crazy and unique venue of New Orleans.

While chatting, I noticed our NASA paraphernalia–laden ASCAN had moved to a window that faced the street. It had been opened wide to let in the beautiful weather and no doubt the sounds. I joined him on the iron-grated balcony. Watching the multitude below and taking it all in, my compatriot was still interested primarily in the upper portion of the female anatomy. Drinking his beverage and yelling at the top of his lungs, he chanted like a carnival barker, "Show us your tits! I have patches! I have John Glenn NASA patches! Show us your tits!"

Apparently John Glenn NASA patches are not in vogue in New Orleans during Mardi Gras. The fully clad women below responded nearly in unison, "We don't want any patches. We want beads!"

Having only a stash of embroidered patches that were apparently worthless—at least if you want to see women's breasts—my friend continued his futile efforts.

To our left were two Asian gentlemen talking vigorously in a language that sounded like Japanese. They constantly pointed to their wristwatches and then gazed and pointed across the street to another balcony. I watched them and their actions keenly, trying to decipher the meaning.

Noting that their excitement built with every glance at their watches, I surmised the appearance of their objective was imminent.

As their timepieces struck the apparent witching hour, a beautiful young blond woman seated on the opposite balcony leaped to her feet, turned in our direction, peeled up her shirt and exposed two beautifully round peach-colored breasts.

My Asian friends squealed with approval, clapping their hands as if at a burlesque show.

As her top came down, the Asians began to reset their timers. I watched, curious to see if it would happen again. It was only a matter of time until their efforts were once again rewarded—several times. What a great city!

But the novelty of the bar was wearing thin and my patience was growing short. I pleaded with one of my rookie cohorts to head back with me to the hotel. Not yet ready to depart, he placated me with "One more beer, then we'll go."

I patiently waited for that one more beer, but it grew obvious to me I would be heading back alone. Fearful of the journey, given what I had witnessed so far, I let the group know I'd had enough and I would see them in the morning.

On my way to the safety of the hotel lobby, I met two more of my classmates heading to the French Quarter as the clock struck two in the morning. "We're heading to Café Du Monde for some beignets and coffee. Wanna come?" they offered.

Tempted only slightly, I politely declined.

Entering our room, I noticed that my roommate, Marcos Pontes of the Brazilian Space Agency, was not yet in, as his bed was fully made. I gave it nary a thought, as I longingly climbed into mine—totally expecting his highly audible return would be just at the moment I was falling asleep.

Waking the next morning, it took a few moments to shake the cobwebs from my head. Then I noticed Marcos's still-untouched bed. Oh my God, I thought, where could he be? What should I do?

I quickly showered and dressed, ready to tackle the mystery.

Pacing the room, hoping to stumble upon a solution, I stumbled on Marcos. I found him sleeping—totally naked—in the fetal position on the floor on the far side of his bed.

He was sleeping like a baby. A baby astronaut!

7

Hail *Columbia!*

Thrust immediately into training activities and initial job assignments that would one day see us as fully functioning, authentic astronauts, the Penguins were bonding well. We mucked through the two-year-long process together and got to know each other, at least from a job performance perspective.

With each passing week we became more comfortable with the people who comprised our office. We began to more fully comprehend day-to-day operations and the responsibilities of our job. We participated in both shuttle and space station simulations. We flew in the T-38 training jets with veteran astronaut and instructor pilots and got to know our potential crewmates better, including those who might be selected to command us.

I cannot speak for my Penguin classmates, but as I went through my first few years as a fledgling astronaut, I constantly compiled mental notes and lists, storing them in the recesses (I loved recess as a kid) of my brain. Two of the most important lists could be loosely titled:

1. "Those who I would rather NOT fly in space with," and

2. "Those who I would prefer NOT to have as my commander."

While I had other mental ledgers comprising a myriad of subject lines, the creation of my lists, especially these two, provided me with a personal, albeit unofficial, validation of the astronaut selection process. Both lists were surprisingly short.

Tragically, seven prominent names would be permanently

absented from all my lists. Though I would never have the opportunity to fly in space with any of these seven, my life became uniquely entwined with theirs through the horrific accident known simply as *Columbia*.

I had not been familiar with the *Columbia* crew until a relationship began to take shape on the rugged slopes of the Wind River Mountains in north-central Wyoming as part of a training expedition. My time in the mountains with them—Commander Rick Husband, pilot Willie McCool, and mission specialists Mike Anderson, Laurel Clark, K.C. Chawla, Dave Brown, and Ilan Ramon (covered in more detail in chapter 10)—came simply by chance, providing a lifetime of memories fueled by their incredible mixture of talents and personalities.

A few months before their scheduled launch on January 16, 2003, I got a call from STS-107 commander Rick Husband. Smiling as I thought of our meaningful days in the wilderness, I had no idea my relationship to his crew was about to change.

The conversation was cordial, and he began in his typical warm, caring fashion: "Hello, how are you doing?" Sitting at my desk, I wondered why he was calling me, an unflown rookie.

After a few seconds of catching up, he got down to business. Would I be willing to be a family escort for their mission?

I had no idea how to be a family escort, and I certainly had no idea how one was selected. I didn't have the faintest idea of what a family escort was supposed to do, but it didn't matter to me. I was thrilled and honored he would even consider me (and I did not ask him how many other folks he had asked who had turned him down).

In keeping with my astronaut persona, I gave him an "excitement-concealed" response of affirmative, thanking him profusely for asking. I stammered and stumbled enough with my delivery that he may have been reconsidering his request.

Officially a family escort for the very first time, I would now need to figure out what escorts were supposed to do.

Fortunately, most of my worries were unfounded, as the escort team was comprised of two veteran space fliers, Steve Lindsey and Scott Parazynski, me, and fellow unflown astronaut (astronaut class of 2000), Terry Virts.

The only thing that seemed to present a possible wild card with this flight was the Israeli air force colonel, astronaut Ilan Ramon. The first space flier from Israel, his presence on the crew created a highly dynamic environment given the post-9/11 timeframe. Concern for security was an extremely high priority.

Our escort job started a few days prior to launch. We arrived in Florida, landing our T-38s at the Kennedy Space Center's Shuttle Landing Facility, and were immediately required to attend a mandatory kickoff meeting. The meeting would address all levels of security and include the FBI. Each astronaut escort would have an FBI agent assigned to them, sharing responsibilities for the families.

Reflecting a substantial federal budget, each agent had their own vehicle, as did the astronaut escorts. The astronauts would have primary responsibility for driving the crew's families, and with everyone using large sport-utility vehicles, we presented a presidential-like motorcade any time we needed to "move out."

On a near-perfect day for launch, the Columbia crew was beginning their strap-in process on the pad while we were loading our respective crew families into SUVs for the trip to the Launch Control Center (LCC). In a private area of the building we would bide our substantial free time during the countdown until watching the liftoff together from the LCC's rooftop.

On launch morning I was the chauffeur for Lani McCool (wife of Willie), Doug Brown (brother of Dave), and J. P. Harrison (husband of Kalpana "K.C." Chawla).

The origin of our morning jaunt was the parking lot of a beachfront condominium in Cocoa Beach east of Highway A1A. The main drag, A1A runs north and south through Cocoa Beach, paralleling the coastline and providing a reference for all surrounding destinations.

With our departure point a good forty minutes from our launch viewing location, schedules dictated we leave the condo about the time the crew would be boarding their spaceship. Due to security protocols, we had to follow a specific predesignated route to limit traffic and allow for the quickest transit time.

To accomplish this objective, we would drive onto KSC territory by passing through the adjacent government property known as Cape Canaveral Air Force Station, itself a secure facility. I was fascinated as we neared the guard shack standing sentry over Canaveral's southern entrance: more than fifty police and state trooper motorcyclists were on hand to escort our SUV motorcade onto the KSC grounds.

Air force security, per their military protocols, directed us to stop just outside the entrance. In awe, we listened and watched as the motorcade "bikes" fired up their engines, turned on their flashing lights, and leaped single-file into a parade line that would both lead and follow our dignitaries down the highway to launch. We would encounter no traffic this time.

As a rookie in the family escort department, accompanying a crew's brood to liftoff would prove to be an educational experience. I absorbed as much as possible during the hectic time, filing it away for later when I could share it with my family.

Crew family escorts serve in many roles during their brief (and stressful) two-week tenure. I was a space flier consort, part-time babysitter, driver, waiter, ex-officio advisor, playtoy, and entertainer, and I soaked it all in with a smile on my face!

Launch morning was no different. Having arrived at our prelaunch destination, the crew's children, running the gamut in ages, eagerly grabbed dry-erase markers and began their turn at an old shuttle tradition. Their task that morning was to draw on a massive whiteboard their personal mission tribute to the crew.

In a display of teamwork worthy of an actual shuttle crew, each family member staked out a place at the special surface hung just for them. The resulting artwork would be framed, serving to document each family's venture, and would forever adorn those walls.

While the neophyte artists composed their masterpieces, plenty of food was available, and well-wishers gathered within the suite of offices overlooking the launchpad. Excitement was prevalent, as were calm, reassuring words and glances and compassionate hands on shoulders.

Yet people's sensitive nerve endings accompanied increased levels of anxiety, keeping most from consuming anything more than an occasional strawberry or bite of cantaloupe.

After polling his launch team, the launch director keyed his microphone, and the call to resume countdown from its nine-minute hold, rattled the room's speakers.

We made our way up the small flight of stairs to the LCC rooftop. It was a tense time. This close to liftoff, the families are separated from their closest friends and loved ones who are bused to a private viewing area known as "Banana Creek." (NASA policy now allows a mission crew's immediate family to choose where they will watch the launch. Besides the LCC rooftop, a private balcony in the Saturn 5 Building, close to Banana Creek, allows families to mingle briefly with their loved ones prior to returning to the private balcony just before launch.)

A mere three miles from the pad, the families were alone on the rooftop. Struggling with their innermost fears, they had only the other crewmates' families and astronaut escorts to help. Our job was to provide comfort and compassion. Memories of the *Challenger* accident undoubtedly tugged at the heartstrings of each person who watched the tiny shuttle on the distant launchpad.

There was no escort training for this.

As the countdown clock moved within ten seconds of launch, continuing its silent, steady movement toward the hallowed 00:00, tears welled up in the eyes on the rooftop. Silent prayers pleaded to an all-seeing, compassionate God.

Six seconds prior to liftoff, the shuttle's main engines roared to life. A fiery torrent of rocket exhaust mixed with thousands of gallons of water spewed forth from the sound suppression system, forming a cloud worthy of Mount Vesuvius. Thus began the thunderous climb of humankind's most complex machine.

All eyes fixed on the now-blazing horizon. Eerily, no sound accompanied this controlled explosion. It had not reached us yet from our vantage point three miles away.

It took only seconds for the "oohs" and "aahs" uttered from the mouths of transfixed viewers to change to laughter, cheers, and applause.

Then, in a display of power like no other, an invisible wave rushing from the pad at the speed of sound pummeled us, shaking our very being.

Hearts pounding and tears flowing, we stood our ground on the rooftop watching *Columbia* soar higher and higher, her trajectory tracing a golden arc across the bright blue sky above the aqua-green waters of the Atlantic Ocean.

With *Columbia* passing fifty thousand feet in altitude, tension was high. We collectively held our breath, hearing CAPCOM's call of "*Columbia*, Houston. Go at throttle up." We knew full well the history associated with those words and the crew of the space shuttle *Challenger*. Then the calm reply of Commander Rick Husband crisply echoed back: "Roger, Houston. Go at throttle up."

The first significant milestone behind them, at two minutes and five seconds since ignition, the solid rocket boosters were violently but safely liberated from the stack. Pyrotechnic charges had detonated to break the motors free, enabling them to drop safely into the cold, blue Atlantic where they would be collected and towed back to Port Canaveral for reuse.

There would be no repeat of the *Challenger* incident today. The *Columbia* crew was safely on their way to orbit and a perigee (closest point) some eighty miles above Earth.

After the eight-and-a-half minute ride to orbit, the CAPCOM call of MECO (main engine cutoff) was confirmed. Stress melted away from the families (and us escorts). Smiling again, their loved ones were now experiencing the joys of zero gravity.

I thought we were home free.

Days passed quietly, NASA Television providing snippets of highlights from the crew's daily efforts. My escort job continued in a nominal fashion, mostly dull and uneventful, until I received a cell phone call from Evelyn Husband, wife of the STS-107 commander. She asked if I would be available to lead a tour of NASA's Johnson Space Center for their dear friend, gospel singer and recording artist Steve Green. In Houston for a mid-mission concert at Gloria Dei Lutheran Church in Nassau Bay, Texas, Steve wanted to take advantage of his proximity to the space center. Accompanying him would be his right-hand man and sound engineer, Carry Summers, and his guitarist, Charles Garrett.

We spent the afternoon touring Mission Control and climbing through the life-sized mockups of shuttle and space station, all housed in the space vehicle mockup facility. Afterward we took a short detour to the Husband home where Evelyn played a special videotape for Steve. The tape showcased a NASA-provided video describing Rick's rise from a grinning young man from Amarillo to decorated aviator and, ultimately, NASA astronaut. Prominent was its soundtrack, featuring music from Steve's recording of "God of Wonders," one of Rick and Evelyn's choices for wake-up music during the mission.

As landing day approached, we found ourselves back in Florida at the Kennedy Space Center, preparing for return of the crew. Things seemed to be proceeding normally, as evidenced by a chance meeting with Jon Clark, a medical doctor, NASA flight surgeon, and husband of crewmember Laurel Clark, at the local Dunkin' Donuts near the condo.

Our conversation was short but pleasant. We chatted about normal things, making small talk the way folks do when they're a little nervous. My overall sense remained positive, but my thoughts continued to turn to a conversation I had overheard between some NASA engineers during dinner on the day of the launch. Videotape had shown a small chunk of foam dislodged from the external tank, and it may have struck the port wing of *Columbia*.

No one seemed to be giving it much credence, and most judged nothing potentially dangerous with the situation. I dismissed it as easily as the next guy and did not discuss it with Jon. We focused on the overwhelming success of their nearly completed mission.

The weather was looking reasonable for a space shuttle landing in Florida as we loaded the crew families into our respective SUVs. As on launch day I would be driving Lani McCool, Doug Brown, and J. P. Harrison to the family viewing site adjacent to Runway 15/33.

We returned to the site with much less fanfare than had met us during launch. Because our destination was the Shuttle Landing Facility rather than the Launch Control Center, we had about twenty minutes to kill during our ride.

Conversation was light, and the air inside the suv seemed tense. Lani was preoccupied with the weather. Married to a navy fighter pilot and familiar with aviation weather concerns, she quickly alerted us to the potential for the morning's low-level clouds and fog to hamper landing operations.

Sensing her growing anxiety and using my most official nasa astronaut voice, I tried to allay her concerns by explaining that the weather she was seeing was typical of ksc in the months of January and February.

I continued my attempt to reassure her, stating that even though fog often blanketed the ground during the first part of the morning, landing time was over an hour away. The rising sun and Atlantic sea breeze would team up to burn off and blow away the fog.

She continued to exhibit ever-increasing signs of worry, and I sensed something else was at work in her brain. My thoughts turned again to the foam conversation, but I had not received any updates or heard of any real concerns during the two-week mission. To me, it didn't seem to be important.

It was obvious she needed more information, so I made further attempts to put her at ease by explaining the process followed by the control center team on launch morning. I told her that prior to our leaving for landing that morning, the folks in the control center must have been very confident in the predicted weather forecast for landing time, since the "go" had already been given to the crew for an on-time deorbit burn.

By directing the astronauts into the preparation steps for the burn that would drop the shuttle from orbit, the control team was giving their blessing for the onboard programming of the shuttle's five general purpose computers to ready *Columbia* for her largest maneuver since launch day.

With everything set into motion, once the burn took place, landing would be less than an hour away. That the process could not be reversed implied things must be looking very good from the perspective of the ground team, and they believed the weather was going to be fine.

Lani still wasn't convinced.

The drive continued, and I was thinking that my words may have helped Lani. She did seem more calm—at least until we passed a famous KSC landmark.

Standing tall and straight above the low brush is a Norfolk pine that is home to a bald eagle's nest. Easily spotted by its massive size and conical shape, the nest is consistently a highlight of daily KSC tour buses. Viewers are encouraged to be on the lookout for the "mama" eagle, and much excitement ensues when she is spotted perched on her fortress. (KSC is a National Bird Sanctuary and home to a tremendous number of wildlife, none more majestic than our national symbol.)

Lani, knowing the story as well as anyone, was the first to note that the nest was empty. She also knew the tradition—to see the mama eagle seated proudly atop her nest on launch or landing day is a very good omen. With the eagle not there, more uncertainty flooded into Lani's consciousness, further adding to her already high stress level.

Still, our arrival at the Shuttle Landing Facility felt festive. The weather was turning out to be perfect (much to Lani's satisfaction), and the viewing area for the families provided ample room for everyone to spread out.

Similar to the setup at Banana Creek for viewing the launch, the landing site area was open grassland. The grandstands stood near the midpoint of the fifteen-thousand-foot concrete runway.

Kids were playing in the grassy area, running happily, tossing a Frisbee, and burning energy pent up from being confined in vehicles and conference rooms with stuffy adults.

A wooden snow fence separated the private family area from the stands that held the large number of VIPs. Protected from unwanted attention by a KSC security officer and the fence, the families were able to relax. An enormous digital countdown clock and a color television sat directly in front of the bleachers.

Their private section of the bleachers would offer a great view of the landing strip when the shuttle and its T-38 jet escorts came screaming down the runway right in front of our eyes. I stood near the bleachers, chatting with Laurel Clark's sister and Steve Lindsey, the lead family escort, who was never far away from Evelyn Husband. We discussed the excitement of the day and our anticipation of being able to see everyone reunited again and to celebrate a job well done.

The clock's red numerals, preceded by a minus sign, showed the time to landing growing ever smaller. But the countdown clock falsely reflected a state of normalcy. While everyone else seemed content, as if at a family picnic, my awareness turned to the television audio.

Most of the morning it was simply white noise—Mission Control verbiage, monotonously and stoically delivered by the professionals of the ground team and crew.

Then Steve and I, trained to recognize exchanges between ground and crew, heard something that didn't fit the standard communication protocols. With the countdown clock showing 0859 EST and touchdown expected at 0917, we heard Mission Control CAPCOM Charlie "Scorch" Hobaugh radio the crew from Houston.

CHARLIE: "And *Columbia*, Houston. We see your tire pressure messages. And we did not copy your last."

RICK: "Roger, uh, but—"

Charlie tried again to contact the shuttle.

CHARLIE: "*Columbia*, Houston. Comm check."

There was no reply . . . just silence. He tried again.

CHARLIE: "*Columbia*, Houston. UHF comm check." (Ultra-high frequency, an alternate radio frequency for communication between ground and crew, is used only in situations where the prime system has failed.)

Steve and I looked at each other, wondering why Houston would be calling for a UHF comm check. "Perhaps they're experiencing ratty comm," Steve speculated. "Ratty comm" happens when the orbiter antennas are blocked from reaching communication satellites because the shuttle nose and tail surfaces create obstruction regions with the signal and the ground. It usually dissipates quickly.

Scorch's words now commanded our total attention. Charlie would repeat his last call two more times. I glanced to my left and noticed the KSC security officer who had been previously standing there businesslike in her white shirt and blue blazer. She slowly lowered the radio to her side, having just received a transmission. Her face underwent a transformation I shall never forget. In an instant, she turned ashen and a look of sorrow hollowed out the sockets of her eyes. It was at that moment Steve Lindsey grabbed my arm and said quietly, "Get ready."

I knew exactly what he meant. I had no time to think; I simply reacted. As the family members continued to watch the clock and ask when the sonic booms would occur (the shuttle creates two sonic booms as she nears the landing strip, one from her nose and the second from her tail), I began to gently urge my riders to "Come along, please. We need to go to our cars."

I saw people beginning to acknowledge the uncertainty of the situation as they looked around and then back to the clock. Still reflecting its continuous countdown, it was long past 00:00 and now counting back up. People clustered together, searching for their family members with unsettled, questioning looks.

Some rose in the stands to better see the clock below. A hush settled over the clearing. It no longer felt festive. It was as if a black cloud of fear and doubt had descended from nowhere on this cloudless pristine Florida day.

It was a somber and unscripted parade back to our SUVs. No one knew anything. Few words were spoken as the families tried to come to grips with what was happening. Pushing their worst nightmares to the far recesses of their brains, they climbed into the SUVs.

As I slid into the driver's seat, without thinking my first reaction was to reach for the radio and make sure it was turned off. But it made perfect sense; with no official information as to what was going on, I didn't want my passengers to hear anything that might not be true.

My mind was racing. Knowing the standard entry timeline, I racked my brain trying to figure out what may have happened. With their trajectory bringing them in over southern California, maybe they had bailed out over the Gulf of Mexico, I speculated. A bailout would mean something had gone seriously wrong, but it would at least give them a fighting chance at survival.

The silence within the vehicle was deafening. No words were spoken until I engaged the gearshift lever, getting ready to take our place in the line of vehicles leaving the parking lot. Then Doug Brown, Dave's older brother, began to speak in a matter-of-fact tone.

He said that he and Dave had talked about this. They had discussed how something disastrous could happen at any moment during a spaceflight. How the crew was trained and prepared for anything that could happen, but the limitations of the system could ultimately cause their demise.

His words were not welcomed by his captive audience.

I encouraged him to think positive. "We simply don't know what is happening," I told him. "We need to focus on what we know, not on what we don't know." I asked him to keep his thoughts to himself during the short drive back to KSC crew quarters. My mind was also fighting to drive anything negative away, as I sent silent prayers at a rapid-fire rate asking God to make this all turn out right.

Arrival at astronaut crew quarters was chaotic at best. As with any emergency planning process, what's written down on paper may look appropriate and correct, covering every detail, but actual implementation when the emergency truly arrives is another thing entirely.

The crew quarters staff were all there, hoping to help, but the stoic looks on their faces belied what I knew they were feeling in their hearts. We had no concrete data from anyone to help us move forward; we were in the dark and had no time to confer with those who knew what was truly going on. We were acting totally on gut instinct and adrenaline, doing what we thought was right and necessary in the moment. Our only consolation was that we were keeping busy. The more we did, the less time we had to think about the situation.

Entering the building, the families headed to the crew's private rooms. They were obviously in shock. Some went into the rooms together as families. We crew escorts acted like ushers in a movie theater, trying to provide assistance wherever we could. We hustled some of the younger kids into the TV room in order to keep their minds occupied and give the adults some time alone.

Unfortunately, the only thing we could offer the kids was a television set and outdated video games, a flaw in the contingency plan that would one day require correction.

With kids ranging in age from young adults (the McCools) all the way down to Matthew Husband and Ian Clark (about Cole's age of six at that time), we were finding it difficult to deal with all that was going on.

The adults were eventually directed to return to the main conference room of the facility. Here, only fifteen days before, their loved ones sat at the table preparing for their journey into space, getting weather briefings, making last minute checks of procedures and equipment, and signing STS-107 memorabilia. Now, hoping against hope, their families prayed to see them here again.

I was in a quandary. I felt in my gut something terrible had happened. But my training, coupled with the shuttle program history of more than one hundred successful shuttle landings, had conditioned me to expect landing day to be a joyous occasion.

Today was not a good day.

NASA prides itself on exactness: exact launch times, exact orbital maneuvers, exact docking and undocking times. Everything on board, from the most ambitious activity down to when we eat our breakfast, is planned out to the minute. But now, we were so far from the normal timeline that it couldn't be good. I searched for reassurance in the faces of my fellow escorts, Steve Lindsey and Terry Virts, and the lead flight surgeon for the crew, Smith Johnston, but saw nothing. Their faces were blank. It was frantic and frustrating all at the same time. I needed and wanted to help, but I didn't have a clue what to do.

I walked briskly down the hall to the office of the manager of the KSC group called the vehicle integration and test team (VITT). Run by veteran astronaut Jerry Ross, VITT is an integral (some would say critical) part of the astronaut training and living experience at the Cape. They provide personnel to aid the crew in all aspects from learning hardware to be flown on the shuttle and space station to taking care of the crew while they are living in crew quarters.

Ross was standing in his office quietly discussing the situation with Colonel Bob Cabana, another space shuttle veteran and former shuttle commander, currently the boss of all things astronaut serving in his role as the chief of the Flight Crew Operations Directorate back at JSC. As I listened to their words, I had to bite my lip to fight back a wave of emotion threatening to break forth.

"This is what we know," Colonel Cabana began. "The vehicle came apart over Texas at about two hundred thousand feet. We have to go tell the families." I pushed down the urge to vomit when he continued: "And we can't give them any false hope that the crew survived. There is no hope. We don't know exactly what happened, but there is no hope. We must tell them."

Colonel Cabana would know. His position in the organization put him directly in the critical path; whatever was known at the time would be provided to him. They headed to the conference room, ordering me to ensure that all the family members were there.

The families sat together, forming a half circle around the far end of the enormous conference table cluttered with t-shirts, photos, plaques, and other mementos waiting to be signed by the crew.

They appeared stunned as Colonel Cabana entered the room. Assuming his marine-bred military stance—legs together, back straight, and hands calmly at this side—his facial expression gave every indication of hopelessness. His ability to maintain this commanding presence appeared to require every bit of internal fortitude he could muster.

As he gathered his thoughts and began to share his story of no hope, the families bowed their heads and began to sob.

They were now living their worst nightmare.

I stood as strong as I possibly could, taking it all in. But when Mike Anderson's two young daughters began to scream, it was all I could do to keep from breaking down myself. I stepped into the hallway, knelt down in a corner adjacent to the door and prayed like I have never prayed before.

Wiping tears from my tired eyes, I pulled my cell phone from the pocket of my flight suit and dialed Susan's number. As she answered, I could tell she knew about the tragedy. Through a voice quivering with fear and sadness, I told her I was okay but the crew had perished. As the words came forth, I burst into tears. Forcing myself to control my emotions, I told her I would be home that night and asked that she call our family. Knowing full well I didn't have to ask, I requested that she please take care of the kids. On the verge of another breakdown, I choked out the words, "I love you."

I then called my mother. It was even shorter than the call to Susan. I reassured her that I was okay and would call her soon. Quietly, she said she was praying for everyone involved.

I rose with new resolve. Now was the time for me to be stronger than I had ever been in my life. My courage and strength were needed; I found myself thrust into the role of family escort far more than I ever believed would be necessary.

The families began to disperse as they dealt with the horrific news. Parents held their children tightly, whispering lovingly into their ears. The sobbing continued, broken only by random screams that seemed to reverberate throughout the room. Laura Husband, held closely by her mother, Evelyn, asked quietly, "Mommy, who will walk me down the aisle at my wedding?"

Matthew, her younger brother, simply tugged at his mother's side, repeatedly asking, "When can we go back to the hotel and swim? I want to go swimming."

My heart felt like it was being torn to shreds as I listened to these forlorn pleas. I continued praying silently with every bit of my being, asking God to ease the pain these people were feeling.

Across from the conference room entrance is a short hallway with a few chairs and cabinets lining the walls. The focal point of the hallway is a collection of autographed crew photos above the cabinets. It had been the custom for years that crewmembers provided these photos along with their words of thanks to the people who helped make their service possible.

In this hallway I found Ian Clark. He was standing near one of the small cabinets, leaning on its top, staring up at the photo of his mother in the row of pictures on the wall above his tousled blond head. I stopped and knelt beside him as it became apparent he needed someone to listen.

"Mommy, why did you go?" he asked. "I told you not to go, Mommy. I didn't want you to go."

As I knelt there silently, listening to his questions that would forever go unanswered, I felt as helpless as I had ever felt in my life. I searched frantically within my heart, soul, and mind to find words that would comfort this youngster who had just lost his mother.

Carefully, I put my left hand on his tiny shoulder and told him that sometimes things happen that we don't—or can't—understand. These things can be very good or very bad. I turned to my early lack of understanding with Santa Claus and his ability to slide down chimneys at everyone's house on Christmas Eve.

"Ian," I said. "I always wondered how he did that. How did he get down the chimney?"

Ian did not respond to my words. He just kept looking up at the wall, talking quietly to the picture of his mother, having his own private conversation with the person who brought him into this world.

I watched intently while fighting back tears, knowing I must keep them hidden from this stricken young boy. I told him that someday he would begin to understand what happened, and as he grew older, he might find answers to many of the questions life had already presented to him.

While I may never know whether my words had any impact on Ian, I did realize that the things I was saying to him were things I needed to hear myself.

President George W. Bush spoke to the nation that day, but not before he called and talked privately with the families by telephone. His remarks in both instances spoke of resolve. He reminded us of the importance of what we do: "Our journey into space will go on. In the skies today we saw destruction and tragedy. Yet farther than we can see, there's comfort and hope."

In the late afternoon we landed at Ellington Field with the families. As we slowly filed down the steps of the NASA business jet, a huge crowd of people awaited us, mostly NASA managers and law enforcement officers. The weight of the tragedy clearly showed on their solemn, tired faces. As I moved toward the crowd, still clad in my flight suit, I saw Randy Stone.

Now JSC's deputy director, he was my longtime friend, mentor, and former boss. Our eyes met but no words were spoken. I held out my hand and he took it in his. I fought to hold back my tears but was again unsuccessful. His tired, sad eyes acknowledged my grief and we hugged tightly.

I had additional duties to perform, returning to the plane's cargo hold to retrieve luggage and load it into waiting vehicles. For the families that day, the ride home would be short in distance but long and lonely in grief.

The Astronaut Office had called an immediate "all hands" meeting. We were to report to the space center, then assemble in Building 4 South in conference room 6600.

The atmosphere was tense and silent. I anticipated a status report from management on the current situation and perhaps preliminary directions for a "plan of attack" to deal with the aftermath of the *Columbia* disaster.

Visions of flight assignments and one day reaching orbit had been slammed to the deep recesses of my mind. There would be no telling how this tragedy would affect the flow of astronauts to space, but I was sure it would be a long time before Americans would reach space again.

The meeting was short—for once. We were told of what transpired. Having been an eyewitness at the scene in Cape Canaveral, I gleaned little new information. The technical details were unknown to all except for *Columbia*'s now deceased crew.

We were ordered to not speak to the press; that responsibility was reserved for a select few in management. We were cautioned about what to share within the NASA family, to not speculate or put forth anything that wasn't supported by data. Rumors were already running rampant, including the unlikely theory that terrorists had brought down *Columbia*.

In instructing us what not to say, astronaut management and NASA public affairs had reverted to standard operating procedure. Their fear of unverified information being captured by the press superseded their confidence in our ability to do the right thing. Yet the story would be splashed on the front page of every newspaper in the world by morning and aired on television before I would make it home for the night.

The day's events, which started out as ordinary, would soon be transformed into another exposé of NASA. It would be Apollo 1 and 13, the tragedies of *Challenger* and *Columbia*, all rolled into one.

Being placed under a "gag order" made me angry. Perhaps it was frustration from the helplessness I felt, and the fact that my friends had been ripped away, but I knew that for me and likely for others, coming to grips with what had happened would take time. And it would take discussions.

In my grief I wanted to deal directly with the situation. I needed to speak to someone, to share my personal relationship to the crew and my feelings of helplessness. I needed to be a part of the team that would piece together the scenario that brought down *Columbia*. I needed my wife, my children, my pastor, my friends, and maybe even someone in the press corps.

My first encounter with someone uninvolved in the day's tragic events came as I was driving through Clear Lake Shores, just east of my home in League City. A police officer stopped me for speeding. I can only imagine how haggard I looked after a day of too much emotion and too little food and sleep.

He asked for my driver's license and studied my face against the photograph. He asked why I was going so fast, and I tried to explain that I was an astronaut and on my way home having spent the entire day dealing with the *Columbia* disaster. Apparently familiar with what had transpired, he asked if I had anything to prove I was an astronaut.

Emotions on edge, I was tempted to say something I might regret. Holding back, I explained slowly that the only other ID I had was my NASA badge, but it said nothing about me being an astronaut. He graciously acknowledged my offer and said he was truly sorry. He asked me if I would please just slow down a bit. Managing a faint smile, I pulled away, with the next stop being home and my family.

As I pulled into our driveway and waited forever for the garage door to rise, I tried to anticipate what I might face within. Dragging my small carry-on and backpack, I went inside. Clearly, Susan and Cole had already been struggling with the *Columbia* tragedy. I grabbed Susan and hugged her for all I was worth, with Cole—just six years old—grasping us both around as high as he could reach.

I buried my face into Susan's shoulder and cried. I knew she was experiencing her own pain, but she dutifully and graciously held me tight, knowing that I needed her love and support.

Cole, not possessing a true understanding of what was going on, looked up at me with sad eyes, conveying that he loved me and wanted to make his Daddy's sadness go away. I tousled his hair and smiled at him, telling him how much I loved him. His reply was that of a six year old who had questions that needed answers.

"Daddy, did they die?" he asked.

"Yes, son, they died." I answered.

With a maturity belying his years, he continued: "Did they have children, Daddy?"

"Yes, son, they had children."

"Did I know them?" was his final, heartfelt question.

Squatting down to be at his level, I told him, "Yes, Cole, you did know some of them."

With that, he looked up into my eyes, then turned quietly and walked away.

Our lives proceeded from that point in near-normal fashion. We didn't really discuss the *Columbia* accident, not when I was assigned the task of working with the aerodynamic reconstruction team rebuilding her trajectory from the scant data available, nor even when I was finally assigned to fly in space.

Cole never mentioned anything about the events of that day, not to me or to Susan, until I returned home from space in 2007, just shortly after my five month stint on board the ISS.

We were in my daughter Sutton's bedroom—Cole, Sutton, and me—playing at one of our favorite activities (at least it's one of Sutton's favorites), wrestling. I usually never passed up an opportunity to get down on the floor with my kids. We were rolling around on the carpet, laughing and giggling and having a grand time. I had only been back on Earth for a few days, and her frequent pleas for a wrestling engagement had been met continually with the deferral "not until Daddy can get a bit more of his strength back."

While taking a rest period (called by Daddy, of course), I attempted to initiate conversation with the two of them, trying to discern their thoughts and feelings about the launch, landing, and my five months away from home they had so bravely accepted.

Now aged ten and six, respectively, Cole and Sutton had not yet shared any of their feelings with me since I touched back down on Earth. With the mind of a six year old, Sutton provided the expected colorful responses: how famous she felt, how much fun it was to ride on an airplane, and how she got to swim in the Atlantic Ocean. Nothing of true substance but everything expressive of the innocence and energy of a child.

Cole was a different story. As a youngster, he was never one to engage in any kind of discussion that didn't center around Yu-Gi-Oh! cards, Little League baseball, or elephant jokes. Yet now I sensed he was holding something inside.

Like a mountain climber letting out more rope to a fellow climber, I asked him strategic questions. I hoped that if I could draw him out, helping him share his inner feelings, we could tackle any fears or inhibitions he may have had, and I could give him a clear understanding of the events that had transpired.

It took twenty minutes before he opened up and shared his experience. He quietly related, head often down, how things played out on the rooftop of the Launch Control Center at Kennedy on June 8, 2007, the day his father launched into space.

Cole spoke of the other crew's families, how he didn't really know the adults and their kids "because Dad had been added to their crew at the last minute." He spoke of the other astronauts who were hanging out on the roof, and how he didn't know them either.

The tears began to flow when he related what happened when the solid rocket motors finally jumped to life. As they lit, right after the roar of the main engines, the other kids began to yell, "Don't explode! . . . Don't blow up! . . . Don't kill them!" Cole sobbed as he told his story.

Those words had been too much for him. He told how he had cried as he stood anxiously with his sister, both cradled in their mother's loving arms, not knowing if he would ever see his father again.

Susan later related her version of the story: "There were people jumping up and down on the roof, and then there were others that were just scared. I heard sniffles, and Sutton turned to me saying, 'Mommy, you don't have to cry.' And then when she looked up at me and realized it wasn't me who was crying, it was Cole—it was a tough time."

Fighting back her own tears, Susan told Sutton, "Your dad is so excited right now—he's so happy! He's doing things he's dreamed about since he was nine years old. And we need to be happy for him."

Those were the same thoughts I had when as a rookie family escort, I stood with the families of *Columbia*.

The courage shown by astronauts and their families is as powerful as the rockets themselves. On that rooftop in 2007, Cole, a proud, strong youngster with a heart of gold, was fighting his own space demons, demons born February 1, 2003, the day the *Columbia* crew perished.

Shortly after the *Columbia* tragedy, Hastings College, my alma mater, asked if I would be willing to share my thoughts on the disaster and how I was dealing with it. On February 7, 2003, I put pen to paper and wrote the following, an excerpt:

> On February 1, 2003, I experienced one of the most difficult days of my life. On that day at 0916 Eastern Standard Time, the Space Shuttle *Columbia* was scheduled to touchdown on Runway 33 at the Kennedy Space Center in Florida. She didn't make it.
>
> I was there at the landing site that day as an astronaut family escort. In that capacity, along with two other astronauts, I was responsible for providing support to the family members of *Columbia*'s crew. "Support" is a broad and general term. . . . We were to give them whatever they needed: transportation, food, smiles, and assurances. We all (or at least I) thought it would be easy. Just get them to their designated

spot near the runway on time for the joyous return of their spouses, then shuttle them off to the place where they would greet their favorite heroes with hugs, kisses, and cheers. How shortsighted I was.

With a somber yet urgent look from a KSC security officer our roles became instantly transformed and I had to call on my faith in God in ways that I had never before imagined. Our astronaut and family escort job had now become "real" . . . with consequences that I have always understood but maybe never really fully comprehended. I can comprehend them now.

I want everyone reading this to understand just how brave the STS-107 crew and their families truly are. Clearly knowing the risks, these seven pioneers moved forward with focused determination and joyful hearts, anticipating the wonders and discoveries they were going to experience in a place that so few ever come to know. With the courageous support of their loved ones, they ventured into their lifetime dream of flying into space.

My personal dreams and aspirations have not changed. I still long for the opportunity to explore the heavens, and I hold firmly to the belief that what we (NASA) do benefits all those back on Earth. Our Space Program will continue. We will persevere. It will be better than before; it has to be, or my friends will have died in vain.

I ask that you continue to pray for the families and friends of *Columbia*'s crew and for the entire NASA family. Please know that Rick Husband, Willie McCool, Kalpana Chawla, Dave Brown, Michael Anderson, Laurel Clark, and Ilan Ramon were my friends, my colleagues, and my heroes.

Clayton C. Anderson

U.S. Astronaut

We would revisit the *Columbia* tragedy again on the grounds of JSC.

President George W. Bush spoke at the service held in Houston. In my role as family escort, I would be able to watch, along with Susan, from a short distance as the president and first lady met privately with the families before the ceremony.

Susan recalls, "As the president looked into our eyes, we could see the pain in his."

His well-chosen words were compassionate, comforting, and sincere:

Their mission was almost complete—and we lost them, so close to home. The men and women of the *Columbia* had journeyed more than six million miles, and were minutes away from arrival and reunion. The loss was sudden and terrible, and for their families, the grief is heavy.

This cause of exploration and discovery is not an option we chose. It is a desire written in the human heart. We are that part of creation which seeks to understand all creation. We find the best among us, send them forth into unmapped darkness, and pray they will return. They go in peace for all mankind, and all mankind is in their debt.

He was right, they *were* the best among us.
Hail *Columbia*!

8

Age of Aquarius

As a kid, I really looked forward to Saturdays. For me and other kids my age, when the school week was over, it was time to play and goof off. One of my favorite parts about the weekend was waking up on Saturday mornings, eating my bowl of bland, sugarless cereal (Mom refused to let us eat anything with sugar on it) and turning on the TV to watch cartoons with my younger brother. In those days the cartoon lineup was always the same, and to the best I can recall, most of the good cartoons were all on the same channel (but everyone had only three channels). The morning started off with Bugs Bunny and the Road Runner around eight o'clock; then our personal *TV Guide* lineup featured a thirty-minute classic known as *Jonny Quest* and ultimately finished with one of my personal favorites, *The Superman/Aquaman Hour of Adventure* (I don't recall the exact name, but this is what *Wikipedia* says it was).

A superhero nut, I loved them all: Superman, Batman and Robin, Flash. And what preteen boy didn't go for Wonder Woman? Aquaman was another favorite, fascinating to me for his unique ability to live underwater and talk to the sea creatures. He was an underwater version of Superman, flying through the oceans rather than the skies.

Aquaman discovered as a boy that he possessed superhuman abilities, which, coupled with his tremendous swimming prowess, he eventually put to use as the defender of the Earth's oceans.

Thanks to NASA, I too would one day possess some of the powers of both Superman and Aquaman, but not at the same time.

As an astronaut I have had some incredible opportunities, including the chance to poop in four different spacecraft! My "out of this world" career also enabled me to sleep more than 225 miles above the Earth and almost sixty-five feet below the surface of the ocean, where for fourteen days I became Aquaman in a place called Aquarius.

Training an astronaut is a science. The skill set required is unique and varied, comparable to nothing else in the world. That not-so-simple fact can present a huge problem. How do we find activities that actually *do* compare to the skills required to be successful in an environment without gravity?

At NASA, we look for analogs through simulations and extreme environments. With the help of the great folks from the National Oceanic and Atmospheric Administration (NOAA) and the University of North Carolina Wilmington, someone finally found Nemo.

Ours was not the famous clownfish Nemo of Disney movie fame but the NASA Extreme Environment Mission Operations (NEEMO), the brainchild of a group led by NASA engineer Bill Todd. An avid SCUBA diver and former member of the Mission Operations Directorate training team, Bill and his cohorts came up with a fantastic opportunity for station crewmembers to "get their feet wet." We would learn about living and working on the space station in an analog below the ocean's surface, a barnacle-and-coral-encrusted habitat anchored near the deep coral reefs of Key Largo, Florida.

We were known as NEEMO 5, the fifth crew in this brand-new experience. Everyone—the crews, the mission support team, the NOAA divers leading our training, and the scientists—was essentially learning on the fly. The idea was simple and elegant: put potential station crew members together underwater in an environment hostile to humans, then have them execute a mission as similar as possible to an actual one on board the space station.

We would have mission tasks to execute, a timeline, and extra-vehicular excursions outside the safe confines of "home" to perform maintenance and repairs, all while gathering scientific data and testing new concepts and equipment applicable to the undersea environs. We would be working in tandem with a mission control team, in near constant communication during our time under the sea. Some of us would even be forced to deal with the concept of family separation, a key component in the life of a crew member experiencing long-duration spaceflight.

Our experiences in South Florida commenced with a week of dive training to help us understand our equipment as well as the danger posed by our home beneath the sea. Under the tutelage of seasoned diver Mark Hulsbeck, appropriately nicknamed "Otter," we worked on enhancing our SCUBA skills, got briefings on the science we were to use and execute, and made sure our personal items were in order for the trip to the ocean floor.

Life was good in the Aquarius habitat, positioned "20,000 millimeters under the sea" and located about four-and-a-half kilometers off the shores of Key Largo, in Florida's National Marine Sanctuary.

In this near-perfect space flight analogy, I loved to relax on my bunk bed and listen to Enya's beautiful "Caribbean Blue." From my perch on the habitat's port (left) side, I could gaze out the aft window and watch spotted eagle rays, Caribbean manta sting rays, and nurse sharks silently and smoothly cruise the ocean floor.

I really enjoy the clarity and pureness of Enya's voice. Her Celtic-laced New Age music, so smooth and mysterious, was the perfect background for the undersea tapestry of NEEMO. That summer of 2003, spending time underwater as a not-yet-space-flown astronaut, I looked forward to the day her songs would gently stimulate my senses against the background of our beautiful blue-green planet Earth.

The Aquarius habitat was our home for two weeks, about as long as a shuttle flight (usually eleven to fourteen days). Six of us—three astronauts, one scientist, and two habitat technicians ("hab techs")—comprised the crew for our NEEMO mission. The size of our crew, as well as many of our activities inside Aquarius, paralleled those planned for the space station. We dined on actual ISS cuisine. We tested equipment destined for the station, some of which I would eventually get to use in space.

The work kept us extremely busy, especially the first few days. I felt constantly rushed, like I didn't have enough time to do everything I needed to do. As it turned out, I felt the same on my long-duration space flight. Typically it takes the crew a couple of days to establish their individual, and then collective, routines.

Mostly rookies, our crew was led by veteran astronaut and native Iowan Peggy Whitson. Peggy was formerly the chief science officer and flight engineer on the fifth excursion to the ISS, and was well suited to teach and mentor us so we could one day quickly adapt to the zero-gravity environment of an eventual space station assignment.

As true mission beginners, astronaut and fellow 1998 Group 17 classmate Garrett Reisman and I would be joined by Dr. Emma Hwang (a NASA human physiology scientist) and our two hab techs, James Talacek and Ryan Snow. While Peggy was obviously a capable mission commander, her cool demeanor and even temperament were her biggest assets when it came to tolerating Garrett's and my weird sense of humor.

Early in our mission, Peggy and Garrett were seated at the habitat's tiny dining table discussing key aspects and benefits of our portable ultrasound experiment in a teleconference with an Iowa newspaper. Garrett, a PhD from California's Institute of Technology and a mechanical engineer from Parsippany, New Jersey, itched to contribute to the conversation, finding it difficult to restrain himself as our commander dominated the technical conversation.

Nearing the end of the session, as Peg summarized for the audience what we had learned so far, Garrett's hand slowly inched toward the microphone. Finishing her comments on the ultrasound, Peggy's finger pressed the mute button. Garrett's lightning reflexes moved the button back to "talk," whereupon he loudly declared, "And we found out Clay is pregnant!"

Not to be outdone by my fellow Penguin, I quickly added, "With twins!"

Peggy dropped her head in disbelief.

I would one day fly in space with Peggy. From our experience on the undersea mission, I truly felt flying in space with her would definitely be enjoyable. It's funny how it didn't necessarily turn out that way.

Dr. Emma Hwang, a biomedical engineer from the Johnson

Space Center, was our NEEMO mission science officer and "steady Eddie" with regard to setting up and troubleshooting our computer equipment. She had the amazing ability to coordinate all our experiments while continually gathering life-science data and fixing equipment problems—for example, our laptops continually required her attention due to the habitat's air pressure being two-and-a-half times greater than on the land.

Our hab techs, James and Ryan, had a simple but important job—to keep us astronauts alive. As James always liked to say, "Sounds easy, doesn't it?" They were the kings of this underwater habitat, knowing her critical systems in much the same way I would come to know those on the station in a few short years. James and Ryan were two of the most easygoing and competent individuals I have ever met. Knowing our lives were in their hands made me extremely happy.

Aquarius was an eighty-two-ton double-locked pressure vessel only forty-six feet long and thirteen feet in diameter. With five other human beings, supplies, science experiments, and a myriad of undersea life forms, our temporary home was a tight fit. While never having suffered from claustrophobia in my life, these living conditions gave me pause to reflect on sage advice from my mom.

Before I headed off for my freshman year of college, Mom and I were discussing how my relationship with my as-yet-unknown dorm roommate might play out. With her thoughtful parental look, Mom said, "You can live with anyone for six months." In the college semester schedule, that was just about the amount of time until final exams.

How prophetic her words would turn out to be, on land, under the sea, *and* in outer space.

So, pretending to be astronauts in space while cohabitating on the Atlantic seafloor, six of us were supposed to be able to live "comfortably" together. We had a single shower and limited hot water. We took "navy showers": turn the water on and get wet; turn the water off. Soap yourself up; turn the water back on and rinse. Turn the water off and squeegee yourself dry. We slept in bunk beds separated by a mere twenty-four inches. In the event of a need for a bowel movement, toilet operations consisted of donning a swimsuit and SCUBA mask, holding your breath and entering the ocean through the habitat's "wet porch." There you grabbed a prepositioned thick strand of rope and pulled yourself (or swam) to an underwater gazebo less than ten feet away.

Once established in the "outhouse" (envision a cup turned upside down in a bathtub full of water)—the upper half of your body in the air pocket, your lower torso wet with the fishes—you dropped your pants around your ankles, shimmied your buttocks beneath the gazebo's lower edge and "fired," all the while using both hands to furiously fan the water surrounding your "hiney." This was a required move to keep the aggressive, hungry—and apparently not-too-picky—angelfish from chomping you on the ass as they consumed the tender morsels emanating from your intestinal tract. A quick swim back inside, another navy shower, and you had successfully executed "gazebo ops."

Now throw in the fact that your living quarters included the kitchen, family room, breakfast nook, office, and workshop all in the exact same place, and you have life in an extreme environment. Sounds a bit cramped, doesn't it?

The analogy between the Aquarius habitat and the space shuttle and space station was almost dead-on. Being an unflown astronaut at the time of my NEEMO endeavor, I had no real-time data about life aboard our nation's spacefaring vehicles. So I drank in the sage words of wisdom from our NEEMO commander, trying to quickly assimilate an enormous amount of information and a better understanding of the demands that my crewmates and I would be under (and that we would make) in circumstances as alien as these. As happens with most astronaut crews living in this extreme environment, we learned to work together as teammates, a very powerful confluence of ability and dependence on one another. The potential was there for meaningful bonding that would undoubtedly last a lifetime.

My mother was right. I *could* live with anyone for six months. Much to my delight, I found that people could live with *me* for six months! How about two years and a trip to Mars? I still hope one day to actually find out.

As NEEMO aquanauts we executed daily "spacewalks" (SCUBA dives) designed to help oceanographers and scientists critically evaluate the coral on the reefs near Aquarius. At the discretion of our landlubber science team, we searched for what they referred to as "representative coral" in order to measure it, videotape it, and then estimate the percentage that was dead or in the process of dying. It sounds simple enough, but do you know how much coral there is in the Florida Keys? Lots more than there is in Nebraska.

The ocean's currents shift on a daily basis, and their strength is as variable as the wind blowing on land. If sufficiently powerful, the currents made a four-hour dive into a hard workout. Successfully completing a dive led to a sense of personal satisfaction accompanied by a ravenous appetite and a desire to relax. (It would have been nice to have a glass of red wine, too.)

Unfortunately, there was more to do once inside our iron cocoon. Battling serious fatigue, we had to stay focused through many more experiments like combating the bends (utilizing Doppler effects and acoustic measurements), performing any necessary medical investigations, and doing exercises for our mental and physical well-being.

The learning process never ends in the world of an astronaut. Sometimes it has very unusual aspects that we—or at least I—could not have anticipated. During the NEEMO experience, I got one of these oddball lessons by observing the traditional ways the crew got their "call signs," or nicknames.

In the astronaut corps, as well as the military, call signs are a must. Typically an individual earns his or her call sign by doing something that stands out (not always in a good way). That person is then permanently stuck with his or her call sign. There are hard and fast rules involved:

1. You can't give yourself a call sign.

2. If you hate your call sign, and people know you hate it, it will ALWAYS be your call sign.

3. Call signs may change as a function of your peer status or subsequent performance. And finally,

4. Call signs of more than two syllables are severely frowned upon and usually don't stick.

In order to illustrate the proper application of these rules, consider the following examples.

"Accidently-Pinched-by-Caribbean-Spiny-Lobster" is an example of a very poor call sign (see Rule 4), but "Pinch" or "Spiny" would be considered fine. Or, after a bit of refinement available from a veteran call sign selector, we may arrive at "Pin" or "Spine." Both serve as excellent examples of easy-to-use call signs that comply with Rule 4.

So, for example, if you were to accidentally injure yourself, say, by cutting your thumb during one of your assigned tasks (more about this later), possible call signs that leap to mind might be "Thumb" or maybe "Slice."

Our NEEMO crew was not exempt from this decades-old tradition of nicknaming. Peggy Whitson, our commander, was given the simple, straightforward call sign of "Boss."

Dr. Emma Hwang, our science officer, provided an excellent example of Rule 3 by being anointed with two different call signs. When she was tasked to serve as our crew's phlebotomist, responsible for drawing our blood for use in a nutritional study experiment, she immediately became "Vampire." However, this call sign, while clever and fitting, did not travel well, which is the requirement of a really good call sign. Thus, during our preflight training, she earned the new moniker of "Fleece." This resulted from her volunteering to procure our mission jackets, made of fleece, of course. To this day Dr. Hwang is known to me as "Fleece."

Dr. Garrett Reisman was dubbed "Chia." If you are thinking this refers to the 1980s TV ad for Chia Pets, you are correct. A classic call sign in the sense that he absolutely hated it (and protested frequently, thereby assuring its use throughout the mission), Chia became Garrett's call sign during a pre-mission training session.

While being briefed on the use of equipment to be operated as part of an experiment investigating the Doppler effect, we learned the experiment's protocol required us to each attach sets of probes to our chest with adhesive backing. The adhesive performed so poorly that additional tape was required to get them to stick to our damp, clammy skin. The adhesive on this supplemental tape was pretty stout, bordering on that of an electromagnet or Poly-grip denture adhesive. The effect of this tape when removed from Garrett's hairy chest was a visual and audibly painful christening. The call sign "Chia" stuck to Garrett as hard as the tape did!

And what was my NEEMO call sign? Since I had a major hand in the creation of the three previously mentioned nicknames, turnabout was to be fair play. Peggy and Emma had plans to nail me to the wall in the very same Doppler training session. With the experiment calling for measurements of blood flow and pulse from your pulmonary artery, the device had to be properly attached to near the center line between pectoral muscles. Due to my steady diet of gym workouts and weightlifting, I developed massive (my word, not theirs) pectoral muscles, and consistently had trouble getting a viable pulmonary artery signal. Possibly something other than my "buffness" was causing the problem, but whatever it was, it was stopping the signal. Not sure at first whether I should be flattered when the conversation turned to the cartoon character "George of the Jungle," I took the high road and assumed they were referring to our similarly chiseled physiques and not to any shared state of constant bewilderment or severely limited vocabulary! My time had come. My NEEMO call sign became "George."

We were not done yet. We needed call signs for our hab techs. This came easily as we had gotten to know our Aquarius "baby-sitters" quite well during the week of training that preceded our mission. James "Base" Talacek got his call sign from one of his favorite leisure pastimes—base jumping off of big structures like bridges. Ryan "Candyman" Snow—in a slight violation of Rule 4—earned his tag by always being the first crewman to reach for the candy stowage bag.

So there you have it: Boss, Fleece, Chia, Candyman, Base, and George. Six crew members and friends, all living and working together for fourteen days in an underwater habitat, designated as NASA's NEEMO 5. I think I liked that call sign best of all.

Prior to my selection to the astronaut corps, I was manager of JSC's Emergency Operations Center, helping—and hoping—to protect JSC from emergencies, whether they were hurricanes, fires, terrorist threats, toxic spills, or medical crises. It exposed me to aspects of life in the U.S. Space Program I didn't realize existed—aspects that could be critical to protecting the people and assets of the Mission Control Center and an onboard crew.

That emergency management experience proved its value during our excursion to the Aquarius habitat.

We had arisen at six in the morning, a typical start for our day. After completing our breakfast and cleanup, we prepared for our daily planning conference with the folks in our "mission control" stationed back in a condo on a canal in Key Largo. This daily planning conference was executed in the same fashion as those on the ISS.

We were evaluating our timeline and tasks for the day. Boss and Chia were headed outside for the first "spacewalk" of the day, continuing an evaluation of new scuba masks for NEEMO ops that allowed the diver to verbally communicate with both the habitat and mission control. While they prepped for their trek outside, Fleece and I remained behind busying ourselves with other daily activities.

After lunch, Emma and I took our turn at going "EVA" to continue our underwater construction project, nicknamed Waterlab. Waterlab, a lattice-type structure made out of PVC pipe, simulated tool use and body position and control during simple construction tasks similar to those we might actually do on the structure of the ISS during a real spacewalk.

Our construction effort was straightforward. During a previous scuba dive, we had carried several bags, prepacked on the surface, outside the habitat. The bags contained various lengths of PVC pipe, joints, and the bolts, nuts, and washers needed to assemble the pieces of PVC into our Waterlab structure. Holes for the bolts had been predrilled so that all we had to do was sort the pieces and connect them properly to build the simplistic space structure.

During our initial "spacewalk," I quickly discovered that what I had perceived as a very simple task was instead quite frustrating.

Many of the predrilled holes for the bolts were not of sufficient diameter to let the bolt easily slip through. I had tried turning the bolt as if the hole were threaded, but finally I resorted to hitting the bolts using a pair of (Nebraska-invented) Vise-Grips like a hammer. These attempts were difficult to manage and ineffective.

Being a forward thinker and engineer, I was excited when I learned the surface team was sending down a PVC pipe–cutting tool to aid in our construction. It had been anticipated that this new tool would only be needed if we had to cut additional lengths of PVC pipe. However, I decided to adapt its use to solve our current problem. Placing the tip of the tool's cutting edge into the predrilled holes, I twisted the body of the tool in order to shave off excess PVC material, enlarging the holes. Implementing my plan on the ocean floor, I felt like a genius! It was working beautifully; I was sailing through the task.

My euphoria was short-lived. Exuding overconfidence, I was thrusting the cutting tool with such vigor it missed the hole in the PVC pipe and flew across the thumb of my right hand. An incredibly sharp utensil, it sliced through both my diving glove and, disappointingly, my thumb. A mysteriously green fluid erupted volcano-like from the cut.

Realizing this was probably not a good thing (and recalling how sharks love to come rushing when they smell blood), I motioned to Emma with a rapid scissoring motion of the first two fingers of my good hand that we should head back to the habitat.

Having reentered Aquarius, I held up my thumb for evaluation by Base and Candyman. They leapt into action.

As James was dealing with my wound, Ryan was acting as the Aquarius "producer" for a live public video cast. Peggy and Garrett, seated at the habitat's dining table, were about to interact with schoolchildren from across the United States.

Back on land, unbeknownst to us, the Aquarius staff was also in motion. Hearing James's diagnosis that my thumb would need a few stitches (James was a certified emergency medical technician), the topside team communicated to Aquarius that our mission doctor, Jay Sourbeer, was diving near the habitat. Conveniently, diving with him was another medical doctor, hand surgeon and author Dr. Ken Kammler. Kammler was taking advantage of this dive opportunity while visiting the topside facilities in advance of an interview he was to have with us the next day.

In order for me to complete the mission and remain in the "saturation" condition, the thumb doctoring had to occur inside the habitat.

The topside team dispatched their emergency boat the *Manta* (which incidentally had been captured by Florida authorities in a drug raid) with Dr. Kammler's medical kit and the needed supplies for the stitching. A mere seventeen minutes later, the ultimate house call was underway as doctors and supplies moved from the ocean's surface into the habitat.

But just as the activity in the habitat reached a fever pitch, the power failed in Aquarius. Peg and Garrett's live video came to an abrupt halt along with all other habitat systems.

Though the backup power system immediately roared to life, we were operating at reduced capacity. While emergency procedures were being executed for the host of power failures, I was repaired by Dr. Kammler's skilled surgical hands. After a grand total of three nylon stitches and a cup of hot cocoa, the docs were off to the surface and all was right with the world. (Dr. Kammler describes the event—"the best house call he ever made"—in a chapter of his 2004 book *Surviving the Extremes*.) Oh, and yeah, I earned a new call sign: "Slice."

That was a very real day, as opposed to simulated. Astronauts spend much of their training in simulations, where instructors try to create emergency situations like these in which we are expected to perform well under pressure. That day reflected real-time operations at their very best. Just a few miles off of the southern coast of Florida, I witnessed a highly trained topnotch professional team perfectly executing their emergency responses.

Since my thumb was injured and had to be wrapped in a huge gauze bandage to protect the stitches holding the gash together, I was benched, called out of the game for a few days. In athletic terms I was now "riding the pine."

As I had been a serious high school and college athlete, riding the pine was not something I enjoyed. I despised sitting on the bench. I loved to compete. From my early days on the sandlots of Nebraska, I thrived on the competitive aspects of sports, whether it was football, basketball, baseball, softball, golf—you name it.

Like all athletes, I had been drilled over and over on the importance of team play. "There's no 'I' in TEAM," Coach Bob Simpson would say on the athletic fields at Ashland-Greenwood High School.

"Football is all about sacrifice. It teaches you about life!" Hastings College football coach Wendell Maupin would call out as he rallied us for the critical game.

While my crewmates worked sorties in the teal blue depths, I stayed in the habitat and tried to live up to those words. I was jealous and terribly disappointed. My ingenious idea had turned into a total faux pas because of my impatience and frustration, and I was paying dearly for it. Years later, after my long-duration flight to the ISS, I would again pay dearly for those exact same characteristics.

I wanted to be out there with my teammates in the worst way. I wanted to contribute to the mission each and every day. From years of participating in athletics I know well that in life or in sport, you must learn how to deal with adversity. When the going gets tough . . . oh, you know the rest.

Much like a starting pitcher temporarily moved to the bullpen to get him back on track, I had to figure out how to get back in the game. I assumed a slightly different role on the team, looking for things that could be done inside while the rest of the team was outside. I brought them Snickers bars and snacks between their scuba dives. I cleaned the dishes that lay in the sink. I tidied up our sleeping quarters and stowed unneeded equipment to give us more countertop space for experiments.

That way, I was able to get my crewmates' tasks out of the way by the time they returned, giving them a few precious extra minutes of time for themselves. This is what the experts label "good expeditionary behavior." It must have worked, because in the midst of my personal struggle the crew was very supportive. They reassured me with words, glances of acknowledgment, or sympathetic touches on my shoulder. They helped to "keep me in the game" by showing me I was needed and a key part of the team.

The two-week underwater adventure, full of excitement and wonderful experiences, as well as difficulty and adversity, was fast drawing to a close. Our final dive from Aquarius was absolutely grand. We began before dawn, venturing out onto nearby Conch Reef to view the deep and her creatures as the sun rose. Our aquatic neighbors were all in attendance: majestic manta rays flying in formation on an underwater sortie; our constant companions the nurse sharks, whose menacing looks belied their passive behavior; the 650-pound-plus goliath grouper and her friends who loved to hang out beneath the habitat; and finally some Ridley sea turtles, the first I had seen. There we were, living among an incredible menagerie of God's unique creation, all stirring to life with the beginning of a new day.

As our three-hour dive limit neared, my crewmates and I took time to cruise around the outside of the habitat for one last look. Then we hopped up onto the deck grate near the wet porch and performed numerous "Stupid Aquanaut Tricks," including synchronized diving, leap-frogging, and other frivolous escapades. It was a blast, and most of it was captured on video, thanks to our dedicated hab tech Ryan.

This last dive was so wonderful there was even a happy thought about its conclusion: we didn't have to put on our nasty-smelling dive gear anymore!

Mission Day 13, our final day underwater, was also known as "dee-co day," short for decompression day. We had to spend several hours in the habitat undergoing decompression so we could safely return to the surface.

For fourteen days we had been doing "saturation" diving. That means we had as much nitrogen in our bloodstreams as our bodies would allow. As is the case with any deep-sea diver, we had to remove that nitrogen or we would suffer from potentially fatal decompression sickness commonly known as the bends.

On decompression day, initiated at 1600 hours, or 4:00 p.m. Florida time, the Aquarius habitat underwent an environmental transformation. Our hab techs, James and Ryan, converted the habitat into a decompression chamber on the ocean floor. Closing and sealing all the hatches, they began to very slowly lower the internal pressure from within Aquarius, which was two-and-a-half times that of sea level (that's why we couldn't whistle in the habitat), until the habitat's pressure approached that of sea level. Through this simple and continuous pressure adjustment, it was as if the habitat—still anchored to the seafloor—were a scuba diver swimming ever so slowly to the surface.

The process takes sixteen to seventeen hours and begins with the crew breathing pure oxygen for short intervals. This helps to quick-start the nitrogen purge process. During this time our pseudo-ascent is moving at its fastest rate. Then things slow way down.

The next fourteen hours of incrementally lower pressure changes were long and boring. Limited to our tiny bunkroom, we passed the time by packing up our experiments and personal effects for "potting" to the surface (the gear is sealed in airtight pots and hauled up to the surface by divers). We also watched some movies that Garrett selected. None of them were on my list of all-time favorites (although *The Abyss* was quite appropriate). We slept (one of my favorite pastimes) and reflected on our time spent beneath the sea.

One of the most spaceflight-like aspects of our undersea mission was the complement of science experiments we conducted. As I carried out the numerous procedures and protocols, my thoughts often drifted back to seventh and eighth grades in Ashland and the science teacher who first exposed me to the scientific method. Alice Raikes was one of the most dedicated individuals I have ever met. Through her guidance I developed a clear appreciation for what science is and can be.

Living in the Aquarius habitat, I participated for the first time in my career in gathering and securing data that would potentially benefit not only my fellow astronauts but perhaps everyone on the planet. This really put into perspective for me an astronaut's ability to impact society.

One of the experiments I worked on during our NEEMO 5 mission involved techniques using the Doppler effect, which is best explained using a railroad train analogy. Imagine yourself at a railroad crossing as an oncoming train approaches. You hear the wail of the train's horn. As the train approaches, the source of that sound is in motion relative to you and the air around you, so the pitch you hear as the train passes is not the same as it would be if both you and the train were stationary. The horn's sound waves are compressing as the train approaches and expanding as the train passes and moves away. The pitch of the horn noticeably drops as the sound fades into the distance.

Fellow astronaut, physicist, and bioengineer Mike Gernhardt, in the role of a principal investigator, was attempting to use the Doppler effect to help measure and possibly "fend off" decompression sickness and its potentially fatal effects in both scuba divers and spacewalking astronauts.

After each scuba dive we would don an apparatus designed to measure the flow of nitrogen gas bubbles through our bloodstream. Fewer bubbles meant less nitrogen in the blood, thus reducing the chance of getting the bends. The potential for application to spacewalking may ultimately lie in the reduction of the time required for prebreathing pure oxygen, a proven process that also eliminates nitrogen from the bloodstream. Less prebreathing would save valuable on-orbit consumables of time and pure oxygen.

Another interesting experiment—with huge payback potential for Earthlings—involved the use of a portable ultrasound machine. We were evaluating our ability to use the ultrasound device in a remote environment on an ill crew member. In essence, we were performing the job of hospital ultrasound technicians but without their specialized knowledge.

In this experiment, Emma pretended to have symptoms of a kidney stone. A surefire way for an astronaut candidate to get disqualified, kidney stones present serious dilemmas if they occur on-orbit or deep under the sea where options are limited. So, we could all relate to how important an accurate diagnosis could be.

Using a portable ultrasound machine and Aquarius's teleconferencing capability, we tied in with a doctor back in Houston. Garrett and I took turns operating the system's probe while the doctor, over the conference line, viewed the ultrasound screen from the comfort of his office. He guided us through the setup of the machine and then told us how to "drive" the probe to give him the views he required. Once he had seen enough to make a solid diagnosis, the doctor would then direct the crew to take appropriate steps to deal with the situation, whether it be medication or, more drastically, a speedy return to Earth (or the ocean's surface in our case).

Fortunately for us—two rookies at the controls of a high-tech medical device—the doctor's prognosis was that Emma would indeed survive her "kidney stone."

Astronauts are often asked to explain why what we do at NASA is important. After my experience with NEEMO, I could answer this question with the story of the ultrasound experiment. Because of the space program, we—NASA—through this NEEMO experience, could provide valuable evaluation data for ultrasound use in remote areas. In a jungle in South America or a desert in North Africa, an ultrasound could help determine the health of a woman's child or the status of someone's kidney in the absence of a hospital or doctors and nurses. Whether performed on the ocean floor or in outer space, the science is real. It is the stuff that a decade ago we were touting as futuristic, the stuff of Hollywood.

Constantly representing NASA, I always try to point out the benefits the public receives from their tax-dollar investments in the space program.

Back when I was in junior high, Mrs. Raikes used to have us read a science journal for kids. Published every week, it had all sorts of cool technology stories that back then were only dreams, but today many of them are reality. I hope that perhaps one day my grandchildren will read about science I had a hand in.

The NEEMO 5 mission was a fantastic experience. First and foremost it gave me a much clearer appreciation for what I might expect on my first flight into outer space. I had a newfound respect for the need to stay on your timeline and not get behind, a perspective that was hard to sense in early simulations in Houston. Fourteen days underwater and the preceding week of premission training helped me to more keenly understand and appreciate the teamwork involved in executing a mission that achieves *all* of its objectives. I became acutely aware of the cooperation, tolerance, and patience required among crewmates in order to live in a confined space for an extended period of time.

My main take-away from Key Largo was an enhanced appreciation of how humor and laughter go a long way to smooth over stressful or disappointing situations. Most importantly, I had a better vision of who Clay Anderson truly was and how he would perform on a demanding and dangerous space shuttle or space station mission. And truthfully, I liked what I saw.

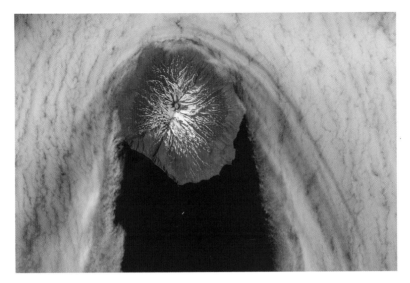

1. An Aleutian volcano diverts Pacific Ocean cloud cover, much like a ship and its wake. (NASA, photo by author)

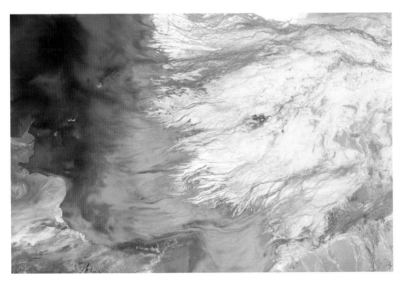

2. The Baluchistan Plateau in Pakistan. (NASA, photo by author)

3. Glaciers in the Tibetan Plateau near Bobogawu mountain peak. (NASA, photo by author)

4. Colorful landscape of the Brazilian state of Minas Geiras. (NASA, photo by author)

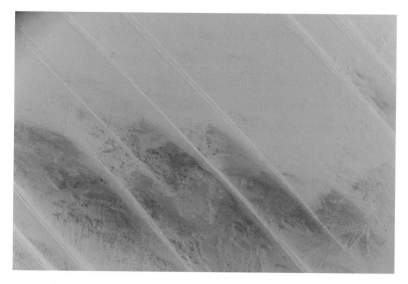

5. Windblown desert landscape illustrates the geometry of parallel lines. (NASA, photo by author)

6. Arms of the Dickson Glacier in Chile. (NASA, photo by author)

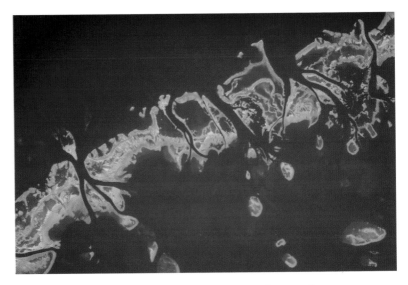

7. The color and beauty of the Great Barrier Reef, Australia. (NASA, photo by author)

8. Forest fires in Idaho captured during the 2007 drought in the northwestern United States. (NASA, photo by author)

9. Author's selfie during his first spacewalk. (NASA)

10. Libyan desert near the border between Chad and Libya.
(NASA, photo by author)

11. Classic view of the North and South Platte Rivers as they merge in the Sand Hills of Nebraska. (NASA, photo by author)

12. The sun's glint gives the eastern third of Nebraska a maplike quality. Omaha, Lincoln, Grand Island, Hastings, and the Platte, Elkhorn, and Loup Rivers are clearly visible. (NASA, photo by author)

13. The Parana River splits Guairá, Brazil, and Salto del Guairá, Paraguay. (NASA, photo by author)

14. Great Pyramids of Egypt and the Sphinx near Giza. (NASA, photo by author)

15. Author's hometown of Ashland, Nebraska, near the Strategic Air and Space Museum and Interstate 80. (NASA, photo by author)

16. "Sea of Red" on October 20, 2007. The University of Nebraska's Memorial Stadium becomes the state's third largest city when filled to capacity. The Huskers lost to Texas A&M University, 36–14. (NASA, photo by author)

17. Hurricane Dean, a Category 5 storm, bears down on the Gulf of Mexico in August 2007. (NASA, photo by author)

18. The Pillar of Hercules. Overhead view of the Strait of Gibraltar. Spain (north) is to the right, Morocco to the (south) left, separated by a mere 7.7 nautical miles. (NASA, photo by author)

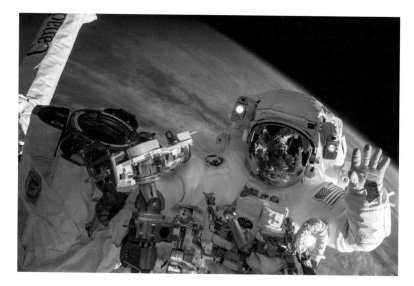

19. Author's first spacewalk: fastening a portable foot restraint to the Canadian robotic arm, preparing to jettison no-longer-needed hardware. (NASA, photo by Fyodor Yurchikin)

20. Author on a spacewalk during the STS-131 mission, waving to the *Discovery* crew while hanging from the European Space Agency's Columbus module. (NASA, photo by Alan Poindexter)

21. Patch of the astronaut class of 1998—the seventeenth group of astronauts selected in the history of the program. (NASA)

22. Official NASA patch of STS-117. The Anderson chevron was added to the patch after the author's reassignment from STS-118 to STS-117, his initial ride to space. (NASA)

STURCKOW
ARCHAMBAULT

FORRESTER
SWANSON
OLIVAS
REILLY
117

ANDERSON

23. Precursor design for the official International Space Station (ISS) Expedition 15 patch. The author first drew it when sending a birthday card to his niece. (NASA)

24. Official NASA patch of ISS Expedition 15. (NASA)

25. The STS-131 official NASA patch.
(NASA)

9

From Russia with Love

International Space Station crewmembers are not immediately assigned to a mission. Instead, they are first placed into the ISS training flow, and international partner approval is sought for each proposed crewmember or flight crew complement. In December 2003 I received word from Kent Rominger, then head of the Astronaut Office, that I was being considered for this training flow. Susan and I agreed that the time was right. I would begin my training in January 2004.

Training would take me to Russia numerous times, to a former cold war top-secret military installation that was decades removed from its feared greatness but still proudly referred to as Звездный городок (*ZVYOZ-dnee gar-a-DOK*) or Star City. Forty-five miles northeast of Moscow, Star City is home to the Gagarin Cosmonaut Training Center, named for the Russian hero Yuri A. Gagarin, the first human to ever venture into space.

I can't remember the exact number of times I journeyed to Russia, but it was a large number. I don't even remember much about my training syllabus in those early days. What I recall vividly is that I went there more times than I cared to. Though I would live in Star City part-time over several years, Houston, my residence for three decades, would continue to serve as home base.

Going to Star City was like the first time your mom takes you to the doctor's office. You find it to be an interesting but scary place and you're not quite sure why you're there. Everything is unfamiliar but you guess you'll be able to figure it out eventually. If your doctor then spoke Russian to you, you'd have the perfect analogy.

My first two trips to Star City were in my capacity as crew support astronaut for the Expedition 4 crew: Russian Yuri Onufrienko and Americans Carl Walz and Dan Bursch. While those initial trips to Star City were a good experience in terms of seeing the place and figuring out where to buy Twix (*tweex*) candy bars and Mountain Dew (*dee-yew*), they were nothing like my later training experiences. I was only there for two weeks at a time and I did not do any training activities. Aside from sitting in on some crew classes and simulations, I was only there to handle various technical issues during their launch preparations (and there weren't many, as those guys were veterans and pretty damn good).

It would be almost seven more years before I would cross the ocean to stay for three to four weeks in a row, sometimes painfully stretching out to five. Our schedules required four to six trips a year over two-and-a-half years to complete what NASA designated as the space station *backup* training flow. All that time traveling and I would not even be declared ready to fly; there would be more training to go.

Once the backup flow was completed, I would enter the prime training flow, which required another full year, for a grand total of three to three-and-a-half years. The best part about it was the frequent-flier miles I could earn with the airlines.

Finally beginning to train as a prime crewmember meant added trips to Star City, but at least in that final year of training I got to wear the official designation as a member of the prime crew. A perk of being prime crew was the Astronaut Office made sure someone else had to carry my parachute out to the T-38!

The training flow was difficult for me and my family, not so much because of the technical knowledge I had to master (although that was significant), but because of a combination of things—fatigue, the language barrier, time away from family, and the stress of having to continually perform at an extremely high level. I had to be "on" all the time.

Classes in Star City were held five days a week, starting at nine in the morning and ending just before six in the evening. Each day contained four periods of about two hours each, with a lunch break from 12:50 to 2:00 p.m.

Most of the training was conducted in a very dismal place within the confines of Star City known as "the territory." Protected by what was once a beautifully sculpted ten-foot-high security wall, the territory was hallowed ground and functioned like the Johnson Space Center in Houston. It was home base for the many monumental successes of the Russian space program and their famed cosmonauts.

The territory was about a ten-minute walk from the dorm-like cottages where we lived. The walk was usually pleasant, even in the worst winter months. As we neared the most often-used entrance to the complex, which came complete with a tiny shack housing the military security guard, we fell into line with the Russian space program employees striding ever so briskly (Russians walk everywhere) to their destinations within the now-crumbling walls.

Reaching the security checkpoint was always an adventure. It was here that some kid usually no more than eighteen to twenty years old in a Russian military uniform would want to see our пропуск (*PRO-poosk*), or badge, for identification. Once they figured out you were a U.S. astronaut, showing your ID become a mere formality. What they really wanted was for one of us to give them a mission patch, and boy, could they be aggressive!

Training classes in the backup flow are broken down by system and are mostly theoretical with a small bit of практика (*PRAK-ti-ka*) or hands-on training in their ISS module mockups. In the theoretical лекция (*LEKT-see-ya*) or lecture, the instructor talks and you listen and take notes—just like in college. Since the "practicals" are more hands-on, they are more fun and entertaining. In those classes you get to see and touch simulation hardware: flipping switches, reading gauges, turning dials, or entering commands into the space station's control computers.

The mockups included replicas of the modules flying in space at that time, which were the Service Module (CM) and the Functional Cargo Block (FGB). (It's a *G* and not a *C* because the Russian word for cargo starts with a *G*. You can start to get the picture on the language thing.)

Eventually, the trainers quizzed us in a sort of midterm exam known as a консультация (*kan-sool-TA-tsiya*) where we were expected to show them from memory where everything is and describe clearly how to operate every system in the vehicle.

My early training as a potential ISS backup also included weeks and weeks of one-on-one Russian language classes, with two four-hour sessions each week, Monday and Wednesday, on every trip. I was hugely thankful I had initiated my own personal study of the Russian language several years before I became an astronaut, when Susan worked for NASA's Shuttle-Mir Phase 1 Program. I think these efforts provided me with a bit of a leg up on the rest of the astronaut candidates. But my goodness, Russian folks talk so fast!

The training was quite possibly one of the hardest things I have ever done. I missed my family tremendously but I was always as honest as possible in my self-assessments, knowing my anxiety (yes, some astronauts do worry about stuff) was mostly due to the newness of the situation. When I was finally able to settle into a basic routine, it helped immensely.

As a family, we focused on the exciting opportunities opening up. The kids seemed to be only looking forward to being interviewed by the newspapers and TV! It was tough for Susan in a number of ways, but I was not overly concerned with her ability to cope. My wife is smart, strong, and sure. With her patient guidance, she and the kids were ready to share in the family's magnificent adventure.

During my first official training weekend in Star City, I was pretty depressed. There were six feet of snow on the ground. In January in Russia, the days are extremely short. I was having trouble coming to grips with whether I had made the right decision to come. Missing my family terribly, I doubted if I was capable of actually performing in a manner that would one day put me on a launchpad.

In a sincere effort to help me acclimate more quickly, my cottage housemate, Jeff Williams (and at that time my commander for Expedition 14), invited me to go with him to Moscow to tour the State Tretyakov (Art) Gallery. I went, as one of my goals in this adventure was to learn more about Moscow and Russian culture.

While wandering through the galleries admiring the paintings, I casually stepped into a room and was instantly captivated by an absolutely stunning painting. It covered an entire ten-foot wall and was held in place by a magnificently detailed golden frame.

Entitled *Христос в пустыне* (*KHREE-stoss vuh poo-STEEN-ye*) or *Christ in the Wilderness*, the painting by Ivan N. Kramskoy (1837–1887) depicted a downtrodden figure of Jesus Christ seated on a bleak rock formation. Alone in a sea of boulders, he cradled his chin in long, thin, gnarled hands. The look on his face was tired, haggard, and forlorn.

I could not take my eyes from Christ's face. Standing there, in the midst of my first battle with the depression that would plague me off and on throughout my three-and-a-half years of training, I could think only of his forty days in the wilderness, the difficulties of his life, and the choices that were tearing at his heart. My personal journey didn't seem quite so hard anymore.

As a newly assigned ISS trainee, I spent a considerable amount of time crisscrossing the Atlantic Ocean, my eyes resting on the blue waters stretching below. During these moments I would find myself contemplating what the heck had I gotten myself into.

The absent generosity of the U.S. government toward her astronauts left me constantly dealing with coach airfare and the accompanying extra-comfy seats ("That would be sarcasm, Sheldon Cooper," for fans of TV's *Big Bang Theory*). More often than not on the trips heading to Moscow, I would end up sitting next to some fat Russian guy who smoked and drank excessively.

The one way I knew I could reduce stress and loneliness was by increasing my mastery of the Russian language. At the time of my initial training in Russia, my children were ages three and eight. One could read and the other was learning the English alphabet. But what of their middle-aged father who must also learn to speak, read, and understand a different language? I wondered if I could apply the same principles and techniques being used on my son at Ferguson Elementary School back in League City, Texas.

From the perspective of a supposed grownup (I do realize that some may see this as a stretch for me), I thought learning the alphabet would be a pretty easy task. It just requires you to memorize some symbols and the sounds they represent. Once that is mastered, you learn what the symbols look like in small and capital letters, both printed and cursive.

Next comes the effort of trying to "glue" those letters together into words. Then you move on to piecing the words together to form sentences until finally you can group sentences into complete thoughts and stories. A couple of weeks of this and we'll be done, right?

Not so fast. It gets more complicated when you realize Russians don't use the same alphabet that we do. The Russians use the Cyrillic alphabet. That means you have to think back to your high school and college days when you had math classes requiring you to know some of the Greek letters: delta (д), phi (ф), gamma (г), and so on.

To further complicate the learning process, for you to fully master the Russian language you have to "unlearn" much of what you learned as a child to help you speak English. For example, you know the English letters *C, K, B, E, H, P,* and *Y* and the various sounds those letters make. *C* can be a "seh" sound as in cessation, or a "kuh" sound as in Clay. In Russian and Cyrillic, those letters don't necessarily match our English. *C* is "ess" and *K* is "kah"; *B* is "veh," *P* is "err," *E* is "yeh," *H* is "en," and *Y* is "oo." It makes my brain feel like *bleecccchhh* (which is not a Russian word, although it does contain the requisite plethora of consonants and limited vowels). Note also that when you write a Russian word in cursive, lowercase letters may also be different than their capitalized versions—so different that an "*m*" represents a "т" and "*g*" represents a "*D*." For me, the concept of unlearning was paramount and I don't think I ever got really good at it.

Russian words that are spelled nearly the same can have very different meanings depending on pronunciation and which syllable of the word is accented. For example, пи-са́ть, spoken with the accent on the second syllable (pronounced *pee-SATS*), means "to write," while пи́-сет, with the accent on the first syllable (pronounced *PEE-sets*), means "to pee." The speaker's accuracy, or lack thereof, can make a huge difference.

My Russian instructor loved to tell the story about how one of our early Mir astronauts, Dr. Bonnie Dunbar, was humiliated during one of her first oral exams. It seems that according to Star City lore, Ms. Dunbar was struggling to answer a question about one of the Russian Mir space station systems.

As she reached into her memory banks for the answer, she repeatedly slapped her hand on the desk while repeating in Russian, "Я пи́сала, я пи́сала," sounding like *ya-PEE-sala, ya-PEE-sala*, with emphasis on the second syllable. The Russians were beside themselves with laughter and Bonnie didn't have a clue. Apparently, the shade of red on her face would have made a former Soviet proud when they broke the news to her that she must have peed a lot while she was studying.

I was not immune to mispronunciation. Imagine my chagrin when, always trying to be the life of the party and the guy with the weird sense of humor, I learned that the American slang word "hooey" (which I was throwing around like a Frisbee) was Russian slang for a male body part that is oftentimes referred to as prick or cock. So much for détente.

Even while I was in the midst of a very successful five-month increment on ISS, it was still crystal clear to me just how formidable the Russian language could be, but at least I knew how to say "Меня зовут Клейтон Андерсон, и я астронавт" (*Meen-YA za-VOOT* Clayton Anderson, *ee ya ASTRO-navt*). My name is Clayton Anderson, and I am an astronaut!

It was my very first visit to a true Russian баня (*BAHN-yah*). I had heard about this classic Russian tradition of a small group of men—usually naked—relaxing, telling stories, and experiencing male bonding in the warmth of a sauna or steam room. It was not part of my formal training syllabus (and I was most certainly *not* naked), but in the end it was definitely a part of my cultural training.

Our crew arrived in midafternoon on a frigid winter day. Somewhere north of Moscow, we (Sasha Lazutkin, Jeff Williams, and I) were greeted by our Russian host, Igor, chief editor of the popular Russian technical journal *Новости Космонавтики* (*NO-vuhs-tee kahs-mah-NAFT-ee-kee*) or *Space News*.

Crossing over a long narrow bridge spanning a snow-covered

waterway, Igor approached us with a huge smile and a digital camera around his neck. With him was our soon-to-be friend, Коля (*coal-ya*), or Tom for short (apparently his last name was Tomarov). Igor directed us across the bridge toward a small wooden building. Inside this rustic cabin were three chambers, each just big enough to hold a quartet of fully grown men, separated by thin wooden doors.

The first chamber had a tiny window, four chairs, and a card table covered with food. We were instructed to go into the middle chamber, where a galvanized water pipe stood in the floor with a spigot and attached rubber hose, and change into our swimsuits. Following a brief welcoming orientation from Igor (given totally in Russian), he directed us into the final chamber, the business end of the establishment, known to all Russians as a "сауна" (*saw-oo-na*), or sauna.

Wearing baggy Bermuda-style swimsuits, Jeff and I were in marked contrast to Sasha. He sported a red, white, and blue Speedo, traditionally skimpy in the European style. Having my lower body covered turned out to be a good thing. As we would later learn via Igor's photo album, many of our Russian colleagues appeared totally naked.

The album did nothing for my self-confidence, but it did provide considerable data for calculating length, width, diameter, and circumference of the anatomically cylindrical shapes adorning my gifted cosmonaut colleagues. Post-calculation, from a personal perspective, the word "inadequate" leaped to mind.

Now I have been in a sauna before, but not like this one. Upon entering the wooden room—complete with a step and wooden bench—we were ordered to don hats reminiscent of an Errol Flynn–era Robin Hood movie (to shield our balding heads from the searing heat reflected from the ceiling). Igor provided us with slippers and seating mats to protect our delicate body parts from excessive temperatures.

The final necessary implement was a wood-handled brush similar to what Nebraskans might use to curry their horses. When instructed, we were to use it to rub our skin everywhere we could reach. As we sat there on the scalding bench, elbow to elbow, wearing silly hats, rubbing our bodies with horse brushes and soaking in the heat, Igor began to pour ladles of water onto the already scorching pile of rocks that served as our heat source. A cheap plastic thermometer on the back wall had been reading near ninety degrees (Celsius). As he poured the water across the rocks, the temperature soared rapidly to over one hundred degrees! Christ, it was hot!

When the heat was absolutely overwhelming, Igor pulled tightly wrapped bundles of tree branches, leaves still clinging to them, from where they were presoaking near the blistering hot stones.

He instructed us to stand up and pull our hats down tightly over our faces. Then, like a jockey flogging his steed to the pole, Igor proceeded to whack our chests and backs, supposedly releasing venomous toxins from deep in our skin cells. Pausing only momentarily to fan the heat source with those damned branches, he returned to flogging us with the vigor of a ten-year-old playing a carnival arcade game. At that point, the heat *was* unbearable, and with my body as red as a North Dakota college student after spring break at the beach, I was seriously considering a call to the nearest fire department!

Suddenly, Igor yelled "три минуты" (*tree min-OO-tee*), or three minutes. I gritted my teeth, hoping to survive that long. At the end of our beating, the door was finally flung open. We quickly donned our slippers to follow Igor down a well-beaten path through a snowbank to a six-by-six-foot hole in the ice (yes, that's right, a hole in the ice).

Considerably overweight and proud of it, Igor stood calmly near the water's edge, his gut and his manhood prominently displayed by the tight confines of his Speedo, waiting for us to build up enough courage to jump into the icy water. Tom had already been in and out of the frigid pool. Igor, camera at the ready, encouraged us to follow his lead.

Fearing the worst but hoping for the best, I jumped in. I couldn't remember ever being so cold. My heart rate shot clear through my head and I quickly scrambled to the hole's icy edge, pushing and pulling to get myself out of there as quickly as possible. There I was, standing out in the snow with the temperature hovering near minus eight degrees Celsius, yet almost miraculously, I felt pretty good. Cold, but good. I felt terribly invigorated.

Throughout the rest of the afternoon and early evening, we alternated periods of sharing conversation over food and beverages, floggings in the sauna, and trips back to the hole in the ice. The only variation was the obligatory jump and roll in a snowbank, performed in lieu of a dip in the pond. I am still not sure which one I preferred. Maybe neither, but the snowbank was much closer to the warmth of the *banya!*

We departed under cover of darkness and a beautiful snowfall, heading back to Star City to, as Igor put it, "sleep like a baby."

It would be a wonderful and Спокойной ночи (*spa-KOY-noy NOCH-ee*), a peaceful good night.

I try hard to carve out time in my days to work out and stay in decent shape. Not so much as a requirement for the job, but given my family history (Dad was not a really healthy guy), for peace of mind. During my time in Houston and Star City we were provided with many ways to maintain physical fitness.

Cottage 4, in the middle of the American-style duplexes where the astronauts lived while training, had a small fitness center in its dirty, dingy basement. The "gym," implemented at the whim of Expedition 1 astronaut and station commander Bill Shepherd, included a limited number of free weights, a few Cybex weight machines, and a treadmill, bicycle, and step machine. It also had a few "astronaut specials" like the arm cycle (imagine pedaling a bike with your arms) and other machines designed to strengthen our shoulders and forearms, which are critical in the performance of spacewalks.

Being an avid weight lifter, I spent a lot of my free time there "pumping iron." Often I would run a few miles on the treadmill or pedal for thirty minutes on the bike while watching a movie on the outdated TV-DVD system. However, during what was to become one of my more memorable trips to Star City, I allowed some astronaut friends to coax me into going for a run in the woods.

Having completed the requisite stretching ritual, our group of five started off slowly, a cluster of pumping arms and striding legs. We had covered about a half-mile inside the territory, heading southeast from our cottages, when we turned onto a trail into the woods that led to a break in the perimeter fence.

After squeezing through the narrow opening, we were off the territory, running among the beautiful birch and Norfolk pine trees. It's a beautiful run, especially when the weather is good. I believe the most beautiful time of year is Russia's version of Indian summer.

It was my turn to lead and set the pace. I liked to keep the pace slow and steady to guarantee that I could actually return to the starting point. I chose a path that would take us southwest toward the edge of Star City and the tracks of Moscow's electric train.

As we took a quick перерыв (*peri-REEF*), or break, our plans for a leisurely six-kilometer run were changed by a complete stranger, now our newest Russian friend. Volodya, or "Jack LaLanne-ski" as we affectionately came to call him, was a fifty-eight-year-old former Soyuz engineer and cosmonaut trainer.

Volodya ran three or four times a week through these woods. He carried an old fishing pole to whack away weeds, tree limbs, and stray dogs trespassing on the jogging trail. He was one of the fittest fifty-eight-year-olds I have ever seen.

"Пошли, пошли" (*posh-LEE*), he yelled. "Let's go!" And off we went. I increased my pace so I wouldn't fall too far behind. This man, some fourteen years my senior, merrily trotted along, chatting as if he were in his easy chair sipping hot tea and watching his favorite television program. We ran and ran and ran while he chatted and checked on us to ensure we were doing okay.

With the kindness of the grandfather that he probably was, Volodya finally dropped us off fifty yards from our cottages. While we gasped for air, Volodya bid us a hearty goodbye. With a wave of his fishing pole and a nod from his head, he ran off into the woods . . . again!

I have never considered myself to be of particularly high intelligence. I'm not stupid by any means, but when I first became an astronaut I was intimidated by my incredibly talented classmates. Drs. Greg Chamitoff, Stan Love, and Nicholas Patrick were particularly gifted, and it seemed to me they were genius caliber, with the uncanny ability to grasp, retain, and fully regurgitate technical information.

Their attention to detail was incredible. As fellow ASCANS we were touring the launchpads at Kennedy Space Center when we stopped to read a plaque at the site of Alan Shepard's initial launch in 1961. It imparted technical information about the speed of ascent during his history-making trajectory. My PhD astronaut candidate companions quickly declared it to be incorrect.

Rushing back to our bus and grabbing their pencils and paper, they began performing back-of-the-envelope calculations. After ten minutes of kibitzing about starting formulas and proper assumptions, they declared that the numbers were indeed correct. A guy like me never doubted that the numbers were correct in the first place—and I wouldn't have known where to begin to try and prove them otherwise.

Given that I am not of genius caliber (as an astronaut, I always wanted to be just slightly above average), spending weeks in Star City focused solely on training was a mental strain for me. Each session included a multitude of theoretical classes designed to provide the crew with a working knowledge of the systems on board the Russian segment of the ISS. We also needed to be well versed in the technical data and operations of the ISS Soyuz vehicle, which served the role of "lifeboat" in the event of an on-orbit emergency. Following the space shuttle *Columbia* accident and the eventual cancellation of the shuttle program, the Soyuz was the *only* way to deliver and return ISS crews.

In any given monthlong training session I was expected to pass a test on three to four different systems. Just a measly three or four systems to study in four weeks, I thought. No problem.

One trip stands out in my mind as being particularly difficult.

We were to learn the Soyuz-ISS docking and attachment system, and the Russian ISS segment's thermal control system, electrical power system, and propulsion systems, with the most challenging by far being the thermal control system. Reality hit when it became evident I would be studying three of those systems simultaneously and would have exams on each of them—all in the first three weeks. It would take three weeks just to cover all the training material!

At night in my cottage, I studied the documentation (i.e., "textbooks") to reinforce the day's discussion. It was very tedious and mentally fatiguing. It reminded me of long nights at Hastings College and Iowa State, but way more intense. In this case, understanding the material and being able to execute the resulting procedures was a life-and-death situation.

Exams were the most stressful part of the training. Typically you were given a review session, another version of the consultation (*kon-sul-TAT-zee-ya*) the day before the exam. There you could ask questions to clarify your understanding of the system and its functionality before facing the Russian "inquisition" the next day.

It was not at all unusual for system designers from Energia (pronounced *En-AIR-gee-ya*) to make the hour-long trip from Moscow to Star City. They claimed they were there to help you to understand their system. Sometimes I felt like they were there to make me look stupid (or make my instructor look stupid, I was never sure which). They seemed to *always* be at *my* exams.

The exams were oral and practical. Garrett Reisman, my NEEMO 5 crewmate and an ISS flier, was fond of bragging about answering his exam questions in Russian. It wasn't that he sought to amaze them with his command of their language. Rather, because he was so bad at it, he took twice as long to answer the questions in Russian, thereby cutting the number of questions they could ask him in half!

The specialists from Energia were given control of the floor. They would ask you any question they could think of and you had to convince them you knew what you were talking about. They pelted you nonstop, forcing you to be on your toes, to show them your knowledge was thorough and committed to memory. It was rumored that during my hour-long personal exam on the thermal system, I was asked, and correctly answered, more questions than any other astronaut ever!

Often you would be asked to perform specific functions in a simulator or on the station's laptop computers. If things began to get too intense, the instructor, perennially annoyed when the specialists tried to make his pupils look bad, would interject a Russian diatribe chastising the specialists for ill treatment of American astronauts.

An hour later, the exam would conclude. Smiles, handshakes, and backslaps would abound while you waited for them to give you your score. The unofficial scale was 1 (fail) to 5 (excellent) or отлично (*ot-LEECH-na*). Between uber-competitive astronauts these scores were points of comparison, sometimes leading to heated debates over the evening meal. I never scored less than a 5, not because I was exceptionally intelligent (although that's what I would have liked to believe), but because, unless you really screwed up, 5 was pretty standard among the astronauts.

Looking back on that thermal system preparation trip, I'm amazed at how much we had to cover. We talked about the active and passive parts of the overall thermal system. We talked about the various aspects of the internal and external subsystems including the air conditioning, ventilation, and control systems. We discussed the Russian version of freon, fans, filters, and fires. We covered it all and still had time to chat with instructor Sasha Larin about the history of the city of Moscow, great Russian works of art, and his personal rock collection.

It was a great feeling to have completed the course successfully, all while maintaining my status of being just slightly above average.

When I was in high school our music teacher, Bette Starnes, asked me to serve as piano accompanist for both the girls' chorus and the mixed chorus in the annual district music contest. Shortly after the mixed chorus's performance (which would receive the contest's highest rating of "1"), our high school band director, Gene Walden, pulled me aside to tell me that he did not know how accomplished a piano player I was and that he was really impressed with my work. I considered that the ultimate compliment, because to anyone who had ever heard Mr. Walden "tickle the ivories" it was clear he knows what he is talking about. On that day I felt I had accomplished, and been recognized for, a great thing.

In my years of training in Star City I would have many of those special days. Days that elevated my morale and allowed me to truly believe I *would* one day fly into space. They were days that made all the travel between Russia and the United States, and all the family separation and hard work, seem worth it.

The day I was fitted for my seat on the Russian Soyuz TMA-10 spacecraft was definitely one of those days.

At nine in the morning, an old, beat-up Russian van pulled up in front of Cottage 4 to take us to the Zvezda ("Star") Space Facility southeast of Moscow, about sixty kilometers from Star City. It was a long ride on a poorly maintained single-lane road full of potholes and traffic.

For decades, spacesuits such as the Orlan (Eagle), the Sokol (Falcon), and the Penguin were manufactured at this rundown Soviet-era factory. (Using bird names for spacesuits was a Russian tradition.) Craftsmen, engineers, and workers at Zvezda created ejection seats for military jets, high-altitude pressure suits, space station airlock components, and the like. They even manufactured a "day" suit for children with cerebral palsy to provide them with sufficient muscle rigidity to enable them to walk.

As soon as we entered the building I was handed a package of clothing that would be critical for the day's activities. Three sets of classic European cotton briefs (in a stylish zebra print—woohoo!), white socks, and knee-length long johns. I was ordered to retire to the bathroom and change. Never having jumped into the realm of European-style underwear, the experience of donning an official "banana hammock" for the first time in my life came off as rather drafty to my untrained loins.

I thought I was looking mighty spiffy until I glanced in the full-length mirror hanging near the changing room door. The long johns were too thin to conceal the zebra-striped "Speedo" that continued to creep up my backside while doing little to effectively conceal my privates. Far from spiffy, I looked like the cover of a trashy tabloid magazine.

Having taken my sweet time in trying to reconfigure my new outfit, I could avoid an exit from the changing room no longer. I was greeted by a team of engineers waiting patiently to measure me in every conceivable way.

The worst part of the process was the gorgeous young Russian woman who, tape measure in hand, was smiling at my zebracrotched, white-clad vulnerable self. Tall, brunette, and built like a "brick chicken house with the corners whacked off," she was stunning. Her legs were her finest feature, starting in a pair of spiked heels and heading upward until they vanished beneath a European-style leather miniskirt. Little was left to the imagination. In her high heels, she faced me—a near-naked rookie cosmonaut—almost at eye level.

She began gathering measurements in places I didn't even know I had. With tape measure firmly in hand, her first target was my inseam. She was not at all bashful in her technique. Her smile increased exponentially as she calmly placed the end of the tape, ever so gently, high against the inside of my right leg. I shivered only a tiny bit as I tried to take my mind off of anything that would make the contents of my "hammock" change in any way.

Ultimately she reached my upper body. I tried to reduce my nervousness with a feeble attempt at small talk in Russian.

She responded to my benign advance with another smile. Her face too close to mine, she briefly responded in Russian.

At that point, my honor was saved.

Dental hygiene in Russia is not a high priority. Her breath reached my nostrils about the same time her mustache came clearly into view. The scent of cigarettes and decaying food snatched away the glamour of her body. The interlude rapidly turned workmanlike and I just wanted it to end.

Next, a team of seat-liner engineers moved us to an adjacent room containing a crudely constructed mockup of a Soyuz seat made of plywood and Plexiglas.

Imagine yourself playing the position of catcher on a baseball team while lying on your back. That's how you sit in your Soyuz seat. With me curled up in the fetal position, more measurements, apparently of a critical nature, were taken.

That done, I was directed to a third room containing a more advanced mockup of a Soyuz seat. This one looked like a really tiny bathtub. I lay down, once again in the "catcher's position," as engineers in white lab coats and rubber gloves ran toward me carrying buckets full of something.

Plaster. They were toting fast-drying plaster. They poured it into my "bathtub" all around me. The goal was to form a mold of my entire backside (quick, bring more plaster!) which they would use to manufacture a seat liner that fit my body contour in my Sokol launch-and-entry spacesuit. A snug fit helps to offset a potentially violent ground landing.

They poured the upper half of my body first. A few moments later when it had almost fully dried, they told me to grab a huge strap affixed to a chain positioned directly over my chest. The chain was attached to the ceiling with a pulley—much like an auto repair shop's engine lift—and by pulling on the chain, the staff manually plucked me from my plaster cocoon. Standing, dripping slow-drying globs of plaster of paris, I watched as they grabbed tools that reminded me of my grandfather's farm implements, and began to carve and smooth the hardened plaster form.

Once they seemed satisfied that the upper body mold was in suitable condition, they sent me back to the changing room to put on new long underwear, after which they then poured the lower half of my body (this process seemed to be much easier). This ritual would happen several times as they refined the final mold's shape. Each time I would have fresh pristine "skivvies" and each time I would be chain-lifted from the grasp of the gooey plaster.

When time came for the ultimate fit check, the one with me clad in my Sokol suit, I would change my underwear one last time—into full-length long johns. The Sokol is the suit you may have seen on television. Sized to better accommodate the on-your-back fetal position, it forces you to stand or walk hunched over. It is one piece, white with blue trim, with an attached helmet and a pair of detachable gloves. This was the real deal! I climbed back into the finished mold and assumed the launch position. The hovering technicians attached my air-cooling hose and closed my launch helmet's visor. I laid back and tried to relax my entire body, imagining myself sitting on the launchpad with just minutes to launch. I was focused, trying to sense if there were any "hot spots" in the suit causing me to feel uncomfortable. I wiggled here and there and shifted my weight. I wouldn't want to be stuck in a launch countdown with the feeling you get with a rock in your shoe. As the minutes passed, it became clear that these folks in this dilapidated and outdated factory really knew their stuff. They were artisans, not technicians.

Just as I had felt years ago at the high school music competition, I sensed this was one of *those* days, too. My dream was inching ever closer to becoming a reality.

The constant travel and high stress began to take their toll. As the months passed it became a near-constant battle to remain positive about my international training.

I might have given up had it not been for some unique experiences that illustrated for me, as a faithful believer in God, that he was constantly letting me know he was still in charge of my life and that I was doing exactly what he intended for me to do.

I am a huge fan of astronaut and navy captain Sunita Williams. Over the years she became my "space sister" since she and I were training partners for most of our mission preparations.

Suni, as she is now universally known, is an adventurer and free spirit who is well known as a result of her forays into space. Raised in Needham, Massachusetts, Suni has always enjoyed having a good time. She is highly intelligent, with a good heart and a deep affection for animals, especially her wire-haired terrier, Gorby (named for Mikhail Gorbachev).

Those who know *me* well know that I am much less a free spirit. While I also like to have a good time, and I believe I, too, have a good heart, I am much more conservative when it comes to the adventure department.

The only difficulty I have with Suni, if you can even call it a difficulty, stems from my assignment to serve as her space station increment backup. Her adventurous spirit—and my willingness to agree to her grand schemes—put me in some situations I would much rather have avoided. But then again, she put me in some pretty cool spots, too.

In an effort to break up the monotony of a Star City training trip, Suni convinced me to travel with her to Saint Petersburg, Russia, for the weekend. Her arguments focused on the facts: we would have a great time, we would learn a lot about Russian culture, and we would have a chance to practice our Russian language skills. Within a few minutes she had me agreeing wholeheartedly to an overnight train trip that took us to one of the most beautiful places I have ever seen.

Yet the most amazing thing about this trip was not the beauty of the city, its architecture, or its tradition of Белые ночи (*BYEL-ee-yeh NOCH-ee*), or "White Nights," in the summer. (Due to Saint Petersburg's far northern location, the sun never truly sets at night.) The amazing thing occurred while Suni and I were purchasing tickets to board a tour boat on the River Нева (*NYEH-va*).

We were standing in line behind what appeared to be a young American couple. They were struggling to communicate with the ticket clerk. Suni and I were able to step in and help by serving as low skill level interpreters. Through our newfound friendships, we discovered the couple hailed from places near and dear to our hearts. The young lady was from Waverly, Iowa, and a graduate of Waverly's Wartburg College in the northeast corner of the Hawkeye State. Wartburg College is also the employer of my Iowa State graduate school roommate, Dr. Todd Reiher, who is a psychology professor there. The young lady's male friend was from near Boston, where Suni spent much of her youth. The world is indeed a small place.

On a different weekend, stuck in Star City and looking for another way to battle boredom, several of us decided to venture to Sergiyev Posad, a beautiful monastery located about an hour north of Moscow. The village of Trinity Lavra from the fifteenth century grew up around the great Russian monastery established by Saint Sergius of Radonezh.

Because it is an extremely popular destination, upon arrival we took our place in line to purchase admission tickets. I happened to notice a tour guide holding a clipboard high above her head. The words "Joslyn Art" stood out, the remainder of the clipboard's contents covered by her hand.

I wondered if that could possibly be a reference to the Joslyn Art Museum in Omaha, Nebraska. As I listened to the idle chatter of the gathering crowd, I felt a tiny shiver at the base of my neck when I heard folks speaking English. Being so far away from home, with only other astronauts to converse with in English, it was exciting to hear other Americans. In my Nebraska-Texas drawl I said, "Where y'all from?"

"Omaha, Nebraska," several answered. I just about fainted.

"Get out!" I said. "I'm from Ashland, Nebraska!"

After excited exchanges of "Why are you here?" and "What do you do?" we went our separate ways to enjoy the monastery, but not before I followed up with a hearty shout of "GO BIG RED!" bringing smiles to many of those welcoming faces.

I was psyched! My attitude about what I was doing and where I was doing it made a huge jump in the positive direction. If I was experiencing a bit of depression, it was gone now. I was on top of the world. So far from family, friends, and familiar places, I had been given signs reaffirming that the world is not such a big place after all. Home is indeed where the heart is.

As an eighth grade football player, I was scheduled to pick up my uniform and equipment after school on a clear fall day in Nebraska. Moving into the eighth grade entitled me to receive the newest from the equipment racks; I would no longer be stuck wearing the hand-me-downs of years past. The uniforms were state-of-the-art and dazzling white. They included the latest and greatest snap-in hip and butt pads that hung over the fancy white belt woven symmetrically through the slits cut in the waistline of the pants. I had slipped my knee and thigh pads into the new, tight pockets that would hold them firmly against those critical parts of my body, protecting me from the onslaught of rival eighth graders who would do their best to bring me to the turf.

Feeling like a young gladiator prepping for battle, I headed for home. I walked the entire way in the sparkling white uniform of an Ashland-Greenwood Junior High School Bluejay football player, slinging my helmet by my side as if it were my executive briefcase. I was a football player and I wanted everyone to know it.

Just like Clay the eighth-grade football player, Clay the astronaut in Russia required a fit check of his gear that took over four hours to complete. The testing session also required one of the most physically demanding exercises I have had to perform in my entire life. Wearing my Сокол (*so-kol*) suit and lying in the seat liner, I would be fully pressurized.

In order to live for an extended period on the International Space Station, astronauts must be trained to travel back to earth on their Russian Soyuz spacecraft, which serves as the "lifeboat" in the event of an emergency situation on the ISS. It is not nearly as simple, however, as throwing on a life jacket and hopping into a lifeboat on a Princess Cruise Dreamliner.

Traveling back to Earth from space is unlike any other form of space travel. Any emergency that forces us to utilize the Soyuz may be the first incident in a very long day, but what if the capsule itself experiences a problem?

When the Soyuz has a leak or depressurization and loses all of its air, the crew must rely on their spacesuits. The Russian Сокол, or Falcon, can be pressurized, providing us with our own individual "spaceship" complete with oxygen, allowing us to survive the two-hour trip home. Then we must be able to exit the capsule and survive whatever awaits us on the ground.

Normally, the landing site is targeted by the computers, but the Russian Federation landmass is huge. Its topography ranges from deserts and swamps to mountains and lakes to prairies and tundra and everything in between. If our trajectory goes awry, we must carry the proper clothing to allow us to deal with a landing anywhere.

The Russian Сокол spacesuit, then, is critical in the world of space flier clothing. This engineering marvel is our first line of protection. Having previously donned our Сокол suits while in the tight confines of the Soyuz living compartment, we are prepared to survive the atmospheric reentry and to land on any spot on Earth. If that spot happens to be of the liquid variety and is coupled with the need to exit quickly, we throw open the Soyuz hatch and leap from the interior with our Сокол water wings in tow.

A landing on frigid tundra requires us to first remove our Сокол while inside the warmth and protection of the safely landed capsule. Then, while remaining inside our Volkswagen Beetle–sized container, the crew dons winter survival gear: long cotton under-wear, an itchy slate-blue wool flight suit (comprised of coveralls, sweater, jacket, and cap), and an insulated snowsuit with match-ing boots, gloves, and hood—a.k.a. the "bunny suit."

If the day is to be totally shot to hell, and we end up landing in freezing cold water, our clothing requirements change once again and a burnt-orange, rubber-lined Форель (*fo-REL*) suit, meaning "trout," becomes the outer covering of choice. It goes over the top of all the other gear. The one-piece rubber Форель, which also includes a set of gloves and an accompanying pullover hood, the-oretically seals our body and keeps the frigid water out, enhanc-ing our chances of survival.

In the event that our landing site exhibits other types of weather and terrain, we can add or remove some of the multiple layers available to us, keeping us warm or cool depending on the con-ditions we experience when we exit the capsule for the first time. Fortunately for us, the Russian search and rescue forces *guaran-tee* a pickup within forty eight hours of landing!

In my Soyuz fit check, following a detailed once-over, the suit engi-neers checked my position within the seat liner to see if I had any pressure points, or hot spots. Then my Сокол suit was fully pres-surized with me tightly curled up in the fetal position. For two solid hours, the time it takes the Soyuz to reenter the atmosphere and land, I would remain in that terribly uncomfortable position.

Measuring six feet tall and two hundred pounds, I was very near the Soyuz size limit standards. An hour and a half into the test, the pain behind my knees where the inflated suit bladder cut into my legs became almost unbearable. Crying "uncle" and stop-ping the test would only lead to doing it again later, and the label "weak" would be added to my Russian résumé. It was gut check time. Fortunately, NASA flight surgeon Dr. Robert Haddon was there, telling the most stupid jokes and anecdotes I had ever heard, helping to keep my mind off the excruciating pain.

Undoubtedly, this was another one of my unofficial Russian survival tests, letting Russian management see what I was made of. Imagine my chagrin when I learned that some of my American astronaut colleagues had taken Valium prior to their sessions to combat the pain!

With that traumatic episode behind me, it was time to try on the rest of my survival gear. Everything was donned in the proper order: first, the sweater of the slate-blue wool flight suit, then the coveralls, jacket, and cap. To that we added the down-filled bunny suit. With the final layer, the burnt-orange rubber Форель suit, I resembled the Michelin Man having been eaten by an oversized tangerine.

Before we returned to Star City, I took one last look at my Сокол suit emblazoned with my name in both Russian and English. Next to the suit, standing like exhibits in a spaceflight museum, were my Сокол gloves. Proof of their customized fit came from my Russian initials, K.A., stitched across the back of the glove in blue thread. Man, how I wished I could have worn them home.

In their acronym-laced language, NASA calls a spacewalk an EVA, for extravehicular activity. The Russian space program is also fond of acronyms, using вкд (*veh-kah-deh*) to represent the phrase "Внекорабельная деятельность" (*VNEEH-kah-rah-BYEL-nah-yah DYEE-eh-teel-nust*), which roughly translated means "activity outside the spacecraft." The Russian phrase for spacewalk is "Выход в открытый космос" (*VY-hot vuh aht-kry-tee KOHS-mus*) or "exit(ing) into open space."

The United States version of an EVA suit is called an EMU, or extravehicular mobility unit. The Russian suit is designated the Orlan-M ("M" represents new modifications). Like all Russian spacesuits, this one is named after a strong bird. Orlan comes from the Russian word Орел (*ah-RYAL*) or "eagle." To perform a spacewalk outside the International Space Station in a Russian Orlan with a Russian cosmonaut would be very круто (*KROO-tah*). (Literally meaning "steep," круто is the Russian slang for "cool").

Once Suni Williams and I completed the theoretical portion of the Russian spacewalking training flow and demonstrated our understanding of the Orlan suit design and function, we needed to learn to actually use the suit while performing work outside the station.

We had already accomplished the American version of this task in Houston with training runs in our Neutral Buoyancy Lab, a 6.2-million-gallon swimming pool. By donning an EMU and working underwater in neutrally buoyant conditions, we can simulate the microgravity environment that will be experienced by a spacewalker. The Russians have their own facility called the Hydro Lab, or Гидролаборатория (GHEE-dro-lab-or-a-TORR-ee-ya), but just like in the United States their training requires crewmembers to develop basic skills before even entering their pool.

Obtaining the basic skills in Russia is enhanced by a unique simulation capability we do not have in the United States. They use a clever suspension system connected to individual spacesuits to offset their weight on Earth, thus providing a rough simulation of zero gravity and allowing crewmembers to enhance their understanding of what it takes to work *within* the suits. In addition, their simulator has a mockup of the Russian segment airlock, along with its requisite panels and a functional hatch. (At this time the airlock was a generic version of their docking compartment module, designated as DC-1 on board the ISS. Today newer modules serve this purpose.) This combination allows astronauts and cosmonauts to practice everything that's needed to prepare to go out the door while wearing the Orlan: basic spacewalking techniques, depressurization (and repressurization) procedures, opening and closing the airlock hatch, use of tethers, and most important, executing the necessary steps in the event of an equipment malfunction.

The Orlan presented me with one huge personal challenge. Because it is a "one size fits all" suit, a person of my size has to deal with a tight fit. However, the Orlan could be adapted somewhat to meet individual needs by using various sizing straps within the spacesuit. The arms and legs could be lengthened or shortened, and we could also raise or lower our (head) position within the suit by changing the crotch height. But alas, there are only two sizes of gloves, which I like to say are small and a bit smaller. Once the suit is pressurized, it becomes more comfortable although still snug. But for a spacewalking suit, snug is a desirable characteristic.

As an American astronaut, I would be one of the last to be certified to perform a spacewalk in the Russian suit. Dwindling budgets and the perceived lack of justification for such certification would lead the United States to stop paying the Russians for this capability. It was a distinct sign of the growing segregation within the once highly integrated programs.

My trips to Russia were nearing their end. I had returned to Star City for what was to be the penultimate segment of my spaceflight journey. It was my final episode of training there, one that would include final exams—simulation performances in both the Soyuz and the Russian segment of the space station—for which we would be graded and (hopefully) pronounced fit for our spaceflight.

The four-week trip was not totally in the classroom. This session would also include training unique to the Russian system. I would be spinning in a centrifuge.

Using a centrifuge for training is not new. During the space shuttle era, astronauts were flown to the nearest centrifuge (I would go to an air force base in San Antonio) to experience force of gravity conditions expected in the shuttle. By varying the speed of the centrifuge, the forces provide a "g-profile" similar to what we would see on launch or landing day. A shuttle only pulls between two and three g's during an ascent or entry, so if nothing else, it was a good t-38 training flight from Houston to San Antonio. The Russian version was the same—almost.

Even though I was comfortable with my ability to speak and understand the hugely complex Russian language, I didn't want anything to go wrong in the centrifuge simulation because I couldn't communicate effectively. So in an effort to be safe rather than sorry, I requested the services of a Russian переводчик (*pee-ree-VOD-cheek*) or translator.

Her name was Anna and she had translated for me before. Tall, with shoulder length blonde hair and beautifully Russian, she was typically referred to by the astronauts as высокая (*vy-SOHK-aya*) Anna, using the Russian word for tall, enabling us to distinguish her from a second translator also named Anna, who was much less statuesque and earned the nickname of маленькая (*mah-LEEN-kaya*) Anna or "little" Anna. We thought we were so clever. But on this day, cleverness would be overcome by a severe lack of concentration, worse than a kid with too many presents on Christmas morning.

We arrived at the facility—my entourage included a flight doc and an American RTI (Russian training integrator)—and entered the foyer of the building that housed the two Russian centrifuge machines. Waiting to greet me with her beautiful smile was Anna, dressed in pale peach–colored high heels and a matching see-through dress!

At that moment I needed a maximum absorbency garment, because my first look almost caused me to crap my pants. Working hard not to stare by keeping my chin thrust upward to maintain my focus on her face, I glanced down just long enough to take note of her version of one of my favorite American patents: a low-cut, lacy underwire bra. In a nod to international support, she was also wearing what appeared to be matching French-cut thong panties. How did I know it was a thong? My eagle eyes, aided by soft contact lenses, reengaged as she gracefully turned and led us into the facility. It was going to be a good day!

Our briefing before the centrifuge session was just that—brief. Perhaps it was due to my translator's outfit and a corresponding concentration lapse from the young male instructor. We'll probably never know, but I'm guessing that my theory was correct based on the wide-eyed look and cheesy smile pasted on his face. With the briefing complete, we were herded into the medical area, greeted this time by two fully clothed elderly females in dingy white lab coats who were prepared to see *me* naked, or at least partially so, as I removed the top portion of my blue NASA flight suit and my t-shirt. They attached the necessary electrode harness (which looked old enough to be the same one used by Yuri Gagarin on his first flight in 1961) that would send heart rate, pulse, and respiratory rate signals to the technical support staff in the centrifuge's control room. With medical prep completed, it was off to the cavernous centrifuge chamber. There, at the end of a massively huge arm, which was attached to the floor on a rotational platform, a tiny movable cockpit opened in anticipation of my arrival.

The interior of the cockpit was adequate—not as small and confined as a Soyuz capsule seat but much less roomy than the seats afforded by the shuttle middeck. A basic control panel was mounted above my head and a quick reach-check with my arms proved to me I could manipulate its buttons, dials, and switches if I needed to (and if someone would tell me what they did). The technical support folks got me all strapped down, just as they had in all of my previous Soyuz fit checks and simulations. I was ready to go for a spin.

Fear was not a real concern, but rather my biggest worry was whether the spinning session was going to drive me to my first Russian execution of the "whirl and hurl." Because I had never before been in this simulator, it was explained to me that we would fly two different profiles. The first would be relatively benign, mimicking a standard, nominal Soyuz entry profile. We would pull only three or so g's in much the same vein as we did on the shuttle. I was only to do the entry portion of a Soyuz profile. Since my launch would occur on the orbiter *Atlantis* there was no need for me to experience a Soyuz ascent. I wholeheartedly agreed.

The second profile was more concerning to me and my intestinal makeup. This one would simulate an off-nominal situation of what the Russians referred to as a ballistic entry. Driven by a critical failure of the Russian Soyuz CA (*ess-ah*) capsule's control system thrusters, a ballistic entry happens when the capsule maintains stability control by spinning along its "long" axis. In much the same way that a spinning top remains steady as long as it is spinning fast enough, the CA capsule can do the same thing as it plummets through the Earth's atmosphere. It has happened only a few times in real life, but typically the only bad outcome is that the vehicle lands much farther away from the estimated landing site. Oh, and did I mention that it's possible you will also pull between eight and ten g's?

The g-forces, while high, are actually not sustained for very long. For only seconds you will weigh almost ten times your current weight. No amount of Weight Watchers or Jenny Craig will help you here; your only recourse is to tighten those stomach muscles and grunt like hell, forcing blood up into your brain as the centripetal force tries to pull it away. Failure to execute your grunting could lead to an essentially harmless but tremendously embarrassing episode of passing out, caught on the ancient video cameras perched above your tiny seat and instantly beamed to the control room. You would be forever "busted"!

The session passed without incident and much faster than I would have anticipated. I exited slowly and deliberately from the tiny compartment that had protected me throughout my spins. I felt good, but I was still a bit unsure how my vestibular system would react. I didn't know it at the time, but the resultant motions that my body insisted I take when my feet reached the floor beneath the centrifuge's huge arm were exactly those that I would experience on November 7, 2007, when I exited from the space shuttle *Discovery* after 152 days in space.

Now where was that see-through dress?

10

Survival of the Fittest

Stress can be a great motivator. It can also push people over the edge. Astronauts-in-training for long-duration space missions (those defined as three to six months or longer), both as individuals and collective groups, present NASA with an interesting set of stress-related problems to solve. The ability of a person to survive and flourish in a tin can (actually anodized aluminum) 225 miles above the earth is dependent on how well they take care of themselves in an inordinate number of complex situations as well as how they get along with their crewmates, who may follow entirely different cultural norms.

NASA has long understood the ramifications of short-duration space missions. Most of the flights executed in NASA's storied fifty-year-plus history were on the order of days to a couple of weeks. The space agency's experience with lengthier forays was less: three crewed Skylab flights, each one increasingly longer, but none lasting more than eighty-four days (Skylab 4).

Once NASA began to partner with the Russian space program in the 1990s (Shuttle-Mir Phase 1 and then the International Space Station), it became apparent that the Astronaut Corps needed to find additional ways to help crews prepare for long-duration missions.

More "outside the box" thinking was required to uncover clever, meaningful, and cost-effective ways to provide astronauts with new development opportunities. They would focus on activities that helped crews to implement concepts of teamwork, self-management, and cooperation while functioning in a stress-laden environment.

The ability to manage your personal stress level while keeping track of your "stuff" is key to success in space. When you have little to no control over a large part of your daily life, you must quickly learn to adapt and turn proverbial lemons into lemonade.

It is difficult to develop simulations on Earth that can provide reasonable analogies for the stress. NASA leaders did their homework, and with help from veteran astronauts, looked for guidance from places like our Russian space colleagues, the Canadian military, the National Outdoor Leadership School (NOLS), and the University of North Carolina Wilmington partnered with the National Oceanic and Atmospheric Administration (NOAA).

The result of these collaborations was a new training syllabus. It was designed to place astronauts in unique and stressful situations to find out who really had the "right stuff" for long-duration spaceflight. This collection of training exercises and experiences became known as expeditionary training.

In the military—and I do not speak from actual experience—survival training is intense. Many of my astronaut colleagues in the armed services spoke as candidly as their service branch allowed about their time spent in SERE (survival, evasion, resistance, and escape) school. This specialized training prepared them to confront the unknown through high-fidelity simulations of extreme mental and physical challenges, even capture and torture scenarios, coupled with caloric and sleep deprivation. Not for the faint of heart.

Fortunately for me and my civilian astronaut candidate friends, NASA starts us out slowly, sending an entire class on a two-and-a-half-day exercise to learn basic wilderness survival skills from the experts, members of the U.S. Army.

With fall foliage near the apex of its annual transformation, the astronaut class of 1998 journeyed to Brunswick, Maine, home of the Brunswick Naval Air Station, hoping to survive.

The journey northeast would be one of the first activities undertaken as a class. We were getting to know each other better and learning to become friends and colleagues first, though the competitive juices were still flowing in most of us. So many type A personalities together made for interesting connections and conflicts as we initiated what we all knew (but would never admit) was one of the greatest competitions of our lives.

The quest to be one of the first among us to be assigned a space-flight was our common "that-which-will-not-be-named" goal, and the bragging rights associated with that coup would indeed be powerful.

For the military astronauts in the class of 1998, a two-and-a-half-day quest on survival training must have seemed like a walk in the park. Each of them had experienced this type of training before, more than likely to a much greater extent. For the rest of us, succeeding at survival training was more akin to being a contestant in a reality TV show.

We arrived in Brunswick full of energy and enthusiasm, ready to show the world we did indeed belong in the United States Astronaut Corps.

In what would become standard operating procedure, our class leaders (elected back in Houston during our first week on the job)—navy fighter pilot Greg "Ray J" Johnson and army helicopter pilot Timothy "T.J." Creamer—had chosen someone to lead this short expedition.

Tagged for leadership duty was marine corps fighter pilot George "Zambo" Zamka. A pilot of the navy's F/A-18 Hornet, he was now our official "den mother," charged with bringing order and cohesion to our rookie astronaut version of the Heisenberg uncertainty principle.

Zambo is an amazing individual, a dedicated and gifted pilot. He exhibits a dry sense of humor (I would fly with him as a member of the STS-120 crew) and strong leadership qualities. In typical marine fashion, he divided our class of thirty-one newbies into small groups of five or six for better accountability. For each of these smaller entities, Zambo designated a squad leader. (Later our class would grow to thirty-two after Canadian Space Agency astronaut and medical doctor Robert Thirsk joined the training flow.)

I was preordained by Zambo to serve as a member of the team comprised of Dr. Stan Love (planetary scientist), Dr. Patty Hilliard Robertson (medical doctor), Neil "Lecter" Woodward (CDR, U.S. Navy, Retired), me, and Dr. Bjarni Tryggvason (Canadian Space Agency astrophysicist). We would come to know each other well during this short excursion into the backwoods of Maine.

If nothing else, Zambo was a marine's marine: haircut "high and tight," punctual and disciplined. He decreed we depart early enough to ensure prompt arrival for our first morning at the military base where we would receive our equipment. We were early enough all right—so early we stood around in a parking lot for over two hours waiting for the military personnel to arrive and give us our gear. It would take a while for our platoon leader to live that one down.

The activities we undertook in Maine were of the basic skills variety. Since we would only be there for a couple of days, our curriculum was briskly paced and packed full of information. We were coached on reading and following maps, constructing personal and group shelters, fending for food using simple traps and remedial fishing lines, and building fires.

The more difficult skills (not included in the syllabus) included sleeping on large rocks, listening to Bjarni snore—he was one of those guys who fell asleep in seconds and provided simulated avalanche noises for hours—and staying awake for twenty-four to forty-eight hours straight.

The equipment provided by the naval air station was reasonable and necessary for the time of year. While the weather wasn't awful, a driving rainstorm on day 2 made trying to build fires and shelters that much more difficult.

European Space Agency astronaut Leo Eyharts, a Frenchman who previously flew on Russia's Mir Space Station and one of our new classmates, had participated in survival training with Russian cosmonauts. His classic quote—delivered with a French accent—as he stood somewhere in the forests of Maine, soaking wet in the rain and trying to keep the fire from going out, was simply "This is bullshit!"

Food was provided in the form of meals ready to eat, or MRES. A staple of our military troops for years, they provided adequate nutrition and we only needed them for two days. Our ration was one MRE per day. It took discipline for me to not devour the entire meal in one sitting.

One lesson was on finding food to survive. The instructors pointed out the abundance of wild strawberries that could be eaten straight from the bush and various greens native to the area that were best served after a severe boiling session. We tried each and I highly preferred the strawberries.

A particularly dynamic demonstration involved a caged rabbit. Serving to illustrate how survival can depend on one's ability to "maximize" a catch, "Peter Rabbit" had been previously secured by our instructor team for the sole purpose of the demonstration.

We learned a lot about some of our colleagues that day when the thump of a huge wooden stick to the back of the rabbit's small head ended the life of a creature many consider a pet. Heads turned away abruptly. Quiet cries of "Oh my" were audible after the prolonged silence that followed the swing of the stick.

The art of skinning and cleaning the carcass was demonstrated, accompanied by a stern lecture highlighting the need to use every part of this bunny rabbit: meat for sustenance, fur as feet coverings, protein from the blood, bones used as implements. When an eyeball, a source of protein and salt, was plucked from its tiny head, and the survival instructor requested that a volunteer consume it, my competitive instincts caused me to volunteer.

Hoping to impress my colleagues with my willingness to down something totally disgusting, I turned the eyeball over and over in the palm of my dirty, mucus-covered hand. Having surveyed it for as long as I possibly could, I sensed impatience in the instructor. I finally popped it in my mouth and chewed like crazy.

It was like gnawing on a rubber pencil eraser. My jaws could make no progress in crushing the pupil for swallowing. The more I clamped down with my teeth, the more the eyeball would shoot across the inside of my mouth like a pinball.

Try as I might, I simply could not penetrate its rubbery shell. Finally, in desperation, I choked it down whole. The need to get the horrible taste out of my mouth and rid myself of nausea took precedence over any display of personal courage.

Fortunately, the two days passed quickly. Poorly constructed shelters and two days of rain did nothing for my survival skill confidence. If I was ever to survive as an astronaut, I was hoping it would be in a warm, dry place not too far from a Holiday Inn Express.

Newly designated long-duration expedition trainees look forward to similar but uniquely different "stressor" and "extreme environment" training opportunities. Typically, NASA starts every event with a one- or two-day classroom session focusing on individual preparation for the rigors of life on board the International Space Station.

Typically indoors, the classes cover potentially unexpected aspects of life in space, like personal care, in addition to the better known (and often overused) classics of teamwork, leadership, and followership. The classroom sessions eventually morph into actual fieldwork and training. One such morphing was the National Outdoor Leadership School, which would take us to the Wind River Mountain Range of the spectacularly beautiful state of Wyoming.

I journeyed to Lander, Wyoming, twice in my astronaut career, once in summer and once in winter. Home to one of the NOLS regional offices, Lander is a quiet mountain town full of folks wearing hiking boots, fleece pullovers, and faded jeans, many of whom have an apparent disdain for haircuts and shaving gear.

My first trip to Lander was in August 2002—living in a rustic, hunting trophy–lined, life-sized Lincoln Log hotel—ready to try survival training once again. Two groups of astronauts were there for the training: the STS-107 *Columbia* crew, led by Commander Rick Husband, and the mixed group I was in.

Our Heinz 57 "crew" contained two veteran space fliers— JAXA (Japanese Aerospace Exploration Agency) astronaut Koichi Wakata and former U.S. Air Force officer and chemist Catherine "Cady" Coleman—as well as four unflown Penguins from the class of 1998—Ken "Hock" Ham, Greg "Box" Johnson, Tracy "T.C." Caldwell, and me.

The two crews would be separated in the mountains, but we had a common goal: to successfully navigate the Wyoming backcountry and its majestic mountain range for ten days while learning everything possible from, and about, our crewmates.

The *Columbia* crew entered the range at a point opposite to where we started. The idea was that we would hike toward each other over the ten-day period, meeting in the middle at the top of Wind River Peak. After pausing to celebrate the moment on this mountain nearly three miles above sea level, each team would then initiate their descent, once again heading in opposite directions, targeting their respective exit points.

For two weeks in August my crew "survived" the absolutely beautiful Wind River canyon and mountain range, the weather picture-postcard perfect and the trip no more difficult than an expensive campout.

Temperatures were moderate, the skies a crystal-clear azure, and the nights cloudless, with the Milky Way galaxy beckoning to astronauts old and new. Aside from having to occasionally yell "Trowel ops!" to secure the garden tool when defecation among the flora and fauna was required, the ten days in the wilderness were trouble free.

Unless your name was Koichi.

Departure from Houston at sea level and the subsequent arrival in Lander yielded an altitude differential of nearly six thousand feet in less than eight hours. Having initiated our assaults on the mountains, we had risen to almost ten thousand feet in total altitude by our second day (our first day of actual hiking). As we set up camp that night, it was not surprising someone might experience the joys of altitude sickness.

Koichi was the lucky one.

It began with headaches and fatigue, then graduated to the more serious symptoms of stomach illness, dizziness, and sleep disturbance. Since exertion did nothing but aggravate the symptoms, constant rest breaks were required to accommodate his condition. With each passing hour, it became obvious the sickness was not going away.

In an effort to keep him functioning, we cut our daily doses of hiking short and made camp in early afternoon in the hope that adequate rest would allow him to recover in the expected two to three days. Koichi, destined to become the first Japanese commander of the ISS, was still far from well the day we were scheduled to climb the top of the 12,192-feet Wind River Peak.

Given this was a leadership training mission, we all took turns at the top of the food chain. T.C. and I shared command for the assault on Wind River Peak as we slowly climbed from our warm and toasty sleeping bags on a beautiful August morning. Our ever-present guides were silent partners, watching carefully as each of us dealt with the challenges of leading a team under stressful conditions.

The morning of the climb, observing our crew over breakfast and during the initial phase of our morning hike, my concern for Koichi increased. He wasn't getting better. He was getting worse. The best cure for acute mountain sickness is to descend as quickly as possible. As one of the leaders, I was seriously considering a request for helicopter evacuation to take him to a lower, and safer, altitude.

This situation was a tough test of my leadership ability. While envisioning the classic reunion moment at the summit, my heart and brain grappled with the reality of a sick crewmate. My conscience knew exactly what to do—get Koichi out of there—but having spoken with him almost constantly as his condition worsened, my heart knew how much he wanted to succeed. I thought I knew exactly where Koichi stood. He wanted to "save face" and achieve the goal with everyone else.

With the well-being of another person at risk, I had no choice but to admit my lack of confidence and turn to the instructors.

Our guides, Willie (Warner) and Scott (Kane), were calm, knowledgeable, and confident. They felt certain Koichi would be okay and ensured me they had seen this condition many times before. Koichi could safely attack the mountaintop at his *own* pace, with their oversight.

We would take whatever time was necessary to help him succeed.

Even though Koichi continued to consume headache and anti-inflammatory meds, it didn't appear to be helping his condition, and the slower travel rate put our scheduled rendezvous with the *Columbia* crew in jeopardy.

Short of breath, with fever, muscle aches, and blue, tingling lips, Koichi had a constant desire to just lie down and sleep. He was in bad shape. It looked as if even our goal of achieving the summit as a team was in danger.

Some two thousand feet below our high-altitude destination (about two more hours of travel at our pace), favorable winds brought the voices of Dave Brown and Willie McCool down from on high. They were perched on a rock high above, wildly waving arms and uttering unintelligible shouts from the top of the world. They flashed brilliant lights at us by positioning their signal mirrors to catch the sun's rays, signifying that they had won our inaugural and unofficial race to heaven's doorstep.

Losers only in the sense that we did not reach the top in conjunction with the STS-107 crew, our goal remained intact. We did reach the summit, where we were greeted by a bag of chocolate chip cookies wrapped in a blue bow, left by medical doctor turned astronaut Laurel Clark, and had our own celebration on the peak together as members in the unique fraternity of spacefarers.

Not to be outdone, we left a glass orb designed and blown by Cady's artist-husband Josh Simpson in the container dedicated for special deposits from all who reached her summit.

We basked in our success only briefly, relaxing in the brisk wind and ample sunshine, taking in the spectacular view. Koichi's condition dictated retracing our steps back to the previous night's campsite as quickly as possible. Our increased pace also allowed us to eventually catch up with the *Columbia* crew. Both crews exited the range together, one for all and all for one, to be greeted by the sight of the bus that would return us to Lander.

Koichi, feeling better with each decrease in feet of altitude, was again flashing his vibrant smile.

Our final day in the wild culminated at the original trailhead with a lunch of fresh food: sandwiches, fruit, beverages, and chips. It was a welcome change from the powdered, fat-laden foods of the wilderness.

The day was perfect. Clear blue skies, cool temperatures with ample sunshine, and a breeze kept us perfectly comfortable. We broke bread together in the trailhead parking lot, laughing and sharing stories of our trials and tribulations in the great outdoors. The mood was festive, and everyone, including Koichi, was feeling true satisfaction with our accomplishments.

Just before we were to load our gear onto the bus for the drive back, for some unknown reason Rick Husband, Box Johnson, and I began to sing a song from the popular 1970s TV variety show *Hee Haw*. The three of us in almost perfect harmony belted out:

Where, oh where, are you tonight?
Why did you leave me here all alone?
I searched the world over and I thought I found true love,
You met another and PFFFTHHPPT! you was gone!

In the end we would sacrifice "the moment" for our crewmate. We would reach the summit after all, but we did it together, as a crew, no matter how long it took. We were learning one of the key unwritten lessons I imagined someone hoped we would learn . . . that sacrifice in the name of mission success goes a long way in defining who you are.

It felt great to survive!

I returned to Lander in February 2006, still unflown but now officially assigned as a space station backup. In a serious lapse of common sense, I had agreed to participate in *winter* survival at the urgent behest of Suni Williams. As her Expedition 14 backup crewmember, I felt a sense of obligation to her as she prepared for her mission to the ISS.

Reluctantly, I again packed my bags for Wyoming and the mountains. This time it would be during the throes of a classic winter . . . cold and loaded with snow.

I couldn't wait.

Reenacting Yogi Berra's déjà vu all over again, we gathered our gear and stuffed our packs the first morning in Lander. This time skis, backpacks, and toboggans (we would each have to drag one wherever we went) were required, along with clothing, food, and cooking fuel for a ten-day stint in the mountain wilderness.

Snow was the wildcard this trip.

Our orientation briefings were short and specific. Most of our training—including the ability to recognize, avoid, and if necessary, survive in an avalanche—would be provided in the field, complete with copious amounts of snow.

This was serious business. The stakes had been raised in our survival game of poker.

Excitement was not a word I would choose to describe my feelings at the outset of our adventure. Fear, trepidation, and cold as hell were much more appropriate words. Having lived in Houston for more than half my life, my blood had thinned to the point where cold winters bothered me.

I was joined once again by my wilderness cohort JAXA's Koichi Wakata, along with fellow astronauts Suni, retired U.S. Air Force colonel Rex Walheim, solar physicist Ed Lu, and Canadian medical doctor Bob Thirsk. In this austere group, Suni and I were the only ones yet to experience the microgravity of space.

Exiting the bus for day 1 in the Wyoming tundra, I was not a happy man. We would be tackling the Absaroka Mountains in the northwest part of the state. Hearing the lectures from Mom about always honoring my obligations, I continued to tell myself to grin and bear it because, as *Columbia* astronaut K.C. Chawla loved to say, "We were training to fly in outer space!"

Our required skill set—cross-country skiing—was different for surviving in winter. We needed to learn how to maintain control on cross-country skis while toting a seventy-five-pound backpack and pulling a fully loaded toboggan. You have not really lived until you have attempted to pick yourself up from a four-foot snowdrift, a pack on your back and wearing the harness of a 150-pound toboggan. I'm just glad it was too cold to use a video recorder.

Critical to our skill development, and ultimately our survival, would be winter snow shelter construction. Techniques for setting up tents and building snow caves and snow "kitchens" would be extremely important.

Working in bright sunshine but bitterly cold temperatures, we were kept warm by the physical activity required for constructing monuments from snow. But it was also serious because we were learning the importance of proper construction technique to our well-being and survival. Our lives could depend on *our* ability to successfully construct these encampments and execute the procedures associated with living outdoors in the U.S. version of the Arctic Circle.

The first several days of hell on earth were blessed with clear weather, giving us ample chances to practice and perfect our newfound skills. As each day passed we became more competent, and our watchful NOLS leaders, Ian McCammon and Steve Whitney, continued to add more to our winter survival toolboxes.

Paramount in our skill development—as would be the case in the fast-approaching syllabus of honest-to-God station and shuttle training—we had to learn the appropriate way to defecate.

In the frigid wilderness, using a shovel handle for balance was required, with cleanup relying on Mother Nature's ample supply of organic toilet paper, a handful of snow. While performing a bowel movement in subzero temperatures does not lend itself to the quality reflection time that's available on my personal "throne" at home, my private poop-time in the snow, albeit brief, forced me to recall the NOLS motto "Leave no trace." I'm just glad I wasn't going to be there when the snow melted!

The ability to navigate through snow-covered mountains and to anticipate when conditions were ripe for a deadly avalanche did little to bolster my outdoor confidence, but it did go a long way toward me yearning to be back in the warmth of my living room in Houston.

We spent a full day crawling on the side of Two Oceans Peak performing avalanche training. Using homing beacons to locate imaginary bodies buried in the snow, we practiced as a high-functioning team focused on rescuing one of our crew. It was valuable training, but I prayed it would never be needed.

Approaching the final phase of our time in Wyoming's purgatory, the instructors monitored our ability levels and performance as teammates, leaders, and followers. Having performed well together during the week, we hunkered down in our double-snow-cave encampment affectionately referred to as Camp Dolly Parton. Our leaders decreed we were now capable of survival on our own, and they would no longer allow us to benefit from their tutelage.

With two days to go we were given our final instructions.

The following morning we were to close out Camp Dolly and move two kilometers farther west (toward our exit point) and establish a new campsite. Directed to spend the night there, we were to wake up and hike the remaining short distance to the exit point, whereupon our mission would be complete.

It sounded simple enough, and it would only be for two days. The next thing I knew, our instructors had disappeared. It was now up to us to survive.

Suni was serving as our leader. Relying on her NOLS training and the skills honed through years of work as a helicopter pilot in the U.S. Navy, she established radio contact with our vanished guides. She then reprogrammed the radio's dark orange LED dial to display the frequency that provided weather updates for the Absaroka Mountains.

As the radio crackled, the entire crew moved in next to Suni, mostly for warmth but also to hear better. With rapt attention to the detailed forecast, each of us tried to formulate our thoughts on what we were hearing.

Suni formally asserted her position as leader by affirming that everything looked good and that we would break camp in the morning and hike to the new site. Anticipating being ever-so-much-closer to my living-room recliner, I accepted her assessment and prepped for what I hoped would be a warm and comfortable final night's sleep in the right breast of Camp Dolly Parton.

Morning came in like a lion.

As I poked my head out of the tiny entrance to our snow cave, ready to move quickly to the spot where folks pooped and peed, I saw something that made my stomach turn. It was snowing hard . . . and sideways!

Being a boy from Nebraska, I had seen my fair share of snowstorms, and although it had been awhile since I'd seen one, this looked to be a doozy. Alarm bells were going off in my head.

Completing my daily ablutions (as my friends in Cold Lake, Alberta, taught me to say), it was time to return to camp to aid in cooking breakfast and closing out the campsite.

With the weather weighing heavily on my mind, I began to gently suggest that today might not be the best day to break camp and head back out into the wilderness. My comments were met with the expected type A astronaut responses of "This isn't so bad" or "We'll be fine out there."

I was not convinced.

Following breakfast and cleanup, we broke camp. Everyone

worked diligently to ensure all gear was accounted for in backpacks and toboggans while the snow continued to come down at a near-horizontal angle.

I continued my verbal assault on our plan, a sense of obvious urgency in my voice's volume and pitch. "We are astronauts, not mountain men," I pleaded with my colleagues. "If we want to do spacewalks someday, it probably won't help if we have had frostbite on our hands," I argued.

Walheim, having spent sufficient time in Colorado's Rocky Mountains in his youth, assured me he had skied in weather much worse than this. Bob Thirsk, one of the Canadian Space Agency's elder statesmen and a medical doctor, continued the "group assurance plan" by letting me know he dealt with weather like this all the time in Canada.

I was still not convinced.

For daily departure, we formed an avalanche line. This time it was my turn to go first, so I set off from the campsite with my personal equipment and established a position about fifty yards away. Then the campers activated their avalanche beacons and skied by in sequence at a pace allowing me as the "homing beacon" to monitor the communication signals between the beacons and establish them as acceptable or not. The closer each camper moved toward the homing beacon, the more rapid his or her individual beacon would beep. Once the final member of the party skied past the monitor's stable position, the camper with the homing monitor would take up the final spot in the single-file line of cross-country skiers.

Standing alone in the blowing snow, braced against the driving north wind, I used this opportunity to lobby my colleagues against our decision as they skied past. Choosing my words carefully (not one of my best attributes), I argued the folly of our ways with each skier.

Suni was steadfast in her decision to move forward to our next site. Rex, a solid military man, again citing his experiences in the mountains of Colorado, backed up Suni. Dr. Bob, as we called him, with the reassuring voice of an incredibly good bedside manner, restated his confidence that all would be well. Ed Lu, educated at Stanford in California and fellow lover of warm weather, was slightly less confident than our colleagues but not yet ready to side with the whiner from Nebraska.

Much like a senator filibustering on the floor of Congress, I continued to plead my case. "We have a perfectly good shelter right here," I reasoned. "It doesn't make sense to leave in uncertain weather and hike for most of the day, and then still have to build new shelters wherever we end up!"

Everyone turned a deaf ear. When Koichi, the final avalanche line participant, skied past, I was feeling less and less comfortable with where we were heading.

One of the more positive aspects of the site known as Camp Dolly Parton was that it was in a small valley in Moccasin Basin, sheltered somewhat from the driving winds and snow. Departing camp required we trek away from those homey confines on a path where the terrain began to rise.

As we followed one of the snowmobile paths that lined the basin (which we did whenever possible because it was easier than skiing across open country), my anxiety mounted with the rising terrain and my pleas became louder—mostly to allow me to be heard over the howling of the wind. My comments became less diplomatic: "This is stupid," I yelled. "We have no business doing this when we have a perfectly good, safe shelter right here. We are astronauts, not Grizzly Adams," I emphatically reminded the group. "This could destroy our careers!"

We continued to trudge up the hill, following delineator posts placed along the snowmobile route every twenty to thirty feet. Out of the protection of the small valley, the snow and wind became debilitating, requiring us to pull our scarves over our faces to minimize the amount of skin exposed to the cold.

Head down, I focused on the two narrow troughs etched in the snow by the skis of Ed Lu. I concentrated on following his path so I wouldn't have to look up; I could tuck my chin deeply into my jacket and sweater in hopes of generating more warmth. My legs already weary, I concentrated on my thoughts, forcing my brain to push each leg forward and slide it back in a monotonous, rhythmic pace that would keep me from falling too far behind.

Suni paused at the top of the first big hill, allowing the group to huddle together for a short rest and conference. It was now or never. I risked my astronaut reputation for perhaps the first (but not last) time in my career, continuing my verbal assault on what I now *knew* was an ill-conceived plan.

I pleaded again, repeating everything that might serve as adequate rationale. Ed, an experienced spacewalker, appeared as if he was ready to change his tune. For the first time in our morning's journey I had a potential ally. As we continued to talk about the situation, I was forceful in my stance that we were not using sound judgment.

Dr. Bob was the next to see the sanity of my words and join in the growing coalition for returning to base. Standing there in the freezing cold, horizontal flying ice pellets slapping us in the face, Suni pulled out the radio. We assessed the situation with our guides, informing them of our new (and smarter) conservative decision to return to Camp Dolly Parton and ride out the storm. At their suggestion, they would meet us there, spending the night in what would become very crowded "breasts." In the morning, they would lead us out on what we hoped would be a safer and smarter—but longer—journey back to civilization.

I learned a lot about myself on that trip, and it would have an impact on my career as an astronaut. I wasn't afraid to speak up anymore.

Believe it or not, Russia's version of winter survival training is easier. First of all, it's only scheduled for two and a half days. Second, and perhaps most important, they don't mind if you—in fact they encourage you to—build a raging fire to keep warm!

When cosmonauts are assigned to a spaceflight, they must undergo winter survival training—no matter how many times they've done it before. Their version also begins with two preparatory days of training, one in the classroom and one in the Russian outdoors.

On an assigned crew this time, I would be in the field with retired U.S. Army colonel and helicopter pilot Jeff Williams and

Russian cosmonaut Alexander "Sasha" Lazutkin. Sasha was our Soyuz capsule commander, and for this survival exercise the crew commander.

On day 1, we spent eight tedious hours in the classroom covering the Soyuz basic emergency kit (Наз, pronounced *nahz*), our survival clothing, how to build shelters (wigwams and lean-tos), and basic winter survival techniques.

Then it was time for a trip to a garage-like building on the Star City training territory of the Gagarin Cosmonaut Training Center. Here we executed a practice exercise, donning our Sokol space suits as if we were preparing to leave the space station in a Soyuz spaceship bound for Earth.

Fully clad in poorly fitted training versions of our Sokol suits, we climbed into a real, once-flown Soyuz capsule. As evidence, its hull was covered in seared burn marks and a black charred heat shield that had protected its crew from a fiery death during reentry.

Agreeing we had executed a successful simulated landing, we remained inside the cramped chamber. Three grown men sitting side by side as if occupying the front seat of a Volkswagen Beetle, we prepared to change into our winter survival gear.

The Texas phrase "three pigs wrestling in a burlap sack" came to mind as my body temperature climbed inside the heavy suit and as a result of the incredibly high heat being put out by the building's thermal control system. It was extremely important to monitor our body temperatures during the sim.

After discarding our Sokols and donning our Russian survival gear, we finally emerged one at a time through the overhead hatch (imagine the Volkswagen Beetle with a moon roof) the same way we would have to do in the field.

The simulation was over. It was time to do it for real.

The definition of what constituted "the field" has changed dramatically since U.S. astronauts first started training with the Russians. A substantial drop in space budgets in post-Soviet Russia caused them to rethink many of their space program's requirements. What used to be winter survival trips to more desolate (and perhaps more dangerous) locales were now short trips to a forest just outside Star City. Unfortunately, our survival training exercise with our cosmonaut colleagues happened at a time when a drop in temperature rivaled the drop in their budget.

We would not leave the woods for two and a half days.

The training site was a heavily wooded area near a popular Moscow resort about eight miles outside Star City. Arriving in the late afternoon, we were placed in a clearing covered with about four feet of snow trampled down during a previous crew's training exercise. With daylight decreasing by the minute, it was imperative work begin immediately.

Sasha Lazutkin, a Mir space station veteran, began organizing our minimalist gear while Jeff initiated construction of a lean-to shelter. It was my job to search for building materials and firewood; we were going to need a lot.

Construction of a lean-to shelter is much simpler than building a full-fledged wigwam or tepee. I had already heard about some of my astronaut colleagues who tried to build a wigwam. Because the wigwam didn't have adequate ventilation for the fire they built in it, one of the crew had to be removed from the exercise after suffering from severe carbon monoxide poisoning. I was glad we were building a lean-to.

The shelter need only be enclosed on two sides, with a sloping "roof" that connects to the sides. This results in a shape reminiscent of one half of a Boy Scout pup tent. The frame is constructed using whatever sturdy sticks one can dig up in four-foot Russian snowdrifts. Strips of the Soyuz parachute cloth are used to lash the sticks together.

More parachute cloth and pine boughs are interweaved to create the ceiling and walls whose primary purpose is to shelter the inhabitants as much as possible from chilling winds. Trying to satisfy environmentalists around the world, we kept the cutting of tree limbs and pine boughs to a minimum; we didn't want to cut more than we would actually need.

We covered the floor of packed snow with more boughs and parachute cloth in hopes of insulating our bodies from the cold ground when we lay down to try and sleep. Let me tell you, we didn't have nearly enough insulation.

Key to our survival would be a fire. According to our training regimen, we would need a signal fire if a rescue force came near and a second constantly maintained fire to warm us in or near the shelter. The signal fire is designed to burn fast, hot, and bright, illuminating the area to aid in our location, and it's not lit until a search team is almost directly overhead.

The shelter fire was closer to a traditional campfire designed for warmth and for heating water and food. Life in the frozen wilderness became much better with a roaring shelter fire.

The dubious distinction of sitting first watch over the shelter fire fell to me, and I was to remain awake and alert from ten at night until one in the morning. The arrival of nightfall—dictated by the now-setting sun—meant the air temperature would continue downward and I would be getting sleepy.

The first night's cloudless skies helped drive the temperature down to a balmy minus twenty-six degrees Celsius. The forecast was for temperatures to be in the minus twenty degree range, so the Russian meteorologists were (unfortunately) right on.

Sitting on one of the Soyuz seat liners that I had removed from the capsule in hopes it would insulate my bottom from the cold, I moved it as close to the fire as safety precautions would allow. I fully enjoyed the toasty warmth provided by the roaring inferno while my crewmates tried to catch a few fitful hours of sleep. Struggling to remain alert, my freezing cold body was pushing me toward sleep. Fearful I would not be able to keep the fire going, I focused my mental and physical energies on maintaining a constant flame.

Most of the wood I had collected was frozen solid, buried in the snow for days if not weeks. Using it in the fire necessitated a three-phased approach—first I had to melt the snow and ice from the log. Then I would let the fire dry the wood enough to allow it to start burning, initiating the final phase—its burning up. For very large logs, it was necessary to gradually feed them into the fire, allowing the three phases to be completed as if burning incense at home.

My watch passed uneventfully, the fire still ablaze. I was relieved by Jeff, and it was my turn to try and sleep. Fighting to find the perfect distance from the fire that would provide ample warmth and keep my survival suit from bursting into flame, I squirmed and wiggled incessantly until it seemed I had arrived at comfort.

But after thirty minutes of lying on an inadequate layer of pine boughs and parachute cloth, even with the fire's help my body could simply not stay warm. My threshold of pain had been reached, and no more sleep was to be had.

Whether tossing and turning on the ground or rising to wander through the forest, I was fighting to stay warm the entire time. Staying close to the fire most of the night, I was glad to see morning finally arrive.

I ate for the first time since the previous day's lunch. The food was similar to army C-rations (according to Jeff, and he should know), consisting of freeze-dried *tvorog* (yogurt), freeze-dried chocolate, a fig bar on steroids, a pack of small sugar cookies, and two tea bags with sugar and lemon. I devoured every bite, never thinking this stuff could taste so good. Unfortunately, I had consumed my entire day's rations.

Day 2 was a rerun of day 1. Gather firewood, improve the shelter (we added two more walls and a door but had no time to finish the rec room), stay warm if at all possible, and freeze your ass off when you tried to get some sleep. With a second night of subzero temperatures, I felt I did well with everything the day required, especially freezing my ass off. I was really good at that.

Upon waking on our final morning, the Russian training team arrived to survey our work and throw one final trick at us. We were instructed to gather our gear and prepare to march to the (pretend) helicopter 250 meters away (there were too many trees for it to land near our shelter). However, unbeknownst to Sasha and Jeff, I was to fall and feign a broken leg only thirty meters into our trek.

With all modesty I must say it was a performance worthy of an Oscar. The only difficulty was lying in the snow for forty-five minutes while they splinted my leg, built a stretcher, covered me with their coats, and dragged me to the chopper. That's when the exercise ended, and not a moment too soon.

Throughout those days early in my career as an astronaut, I was challenged physically, mentally, and psychologically. Each time, there were levels of anxiety I knew I needed to overcome exactly as I would need to do on a long-duration spaceflight. And at the end of each episode, I was able to look back with relief and pride exactly like I felt that day in the snow.

I had survived once again.

11

Sign of the Times

Symbolism exists in many forms in our world. Throughout history, symbols have provided recognizable icons by which we can identify persons, places, and things. Consider the Nike "swoosh," one of the most recognizable symbols on our planet. According to Wikipedia, it was created in 1971 by Carolyn Davidson, a graphic design student at Portland State University in Oregon. She met Phil Knight while he was teaching accounting classes and started doing freelance work for his company, Blue Ribbon Sports (BRS).

For seven years after its founding in 1964, BRS imported Onitsuka Tiger brand running shoes. In 1971 BRS decided to launch its own brand, which would first appear on a soccer cleat called the Nike, manufactured in Mexico. Knight approached Davidson for design ideas. She agreed to provide them, charging a meager rate of only two dollars an hour.

In the spring of 1971 Davidson presented a number of design options to the BRS executives, who ultimately selected the mark now known globally as the swoosh. Apparently, when asked about the logo design, Knight said, "I don't love it, but I think it will grow on me."

In June 1972 the first running shoes bearing the swoosh were introduced at the U.S. track and field Olympic trials in Eugene, Oregon. The rest is history. Today, can we find anyone in the world who couldn't identify this classic brand?

Then there's the classic symbol of the smiley face, which first appeared in 1963. Again, Wikipedia says it was created by Harvey Ball, an American commercial artist. As the story goes, he intended to create a happy face to be used on buttons for an advertising company. Ball's rendition of this happy face is considered to be iconic, with its bright yellow background, black dot eyes, and creases at the sides of the mouth. We've all seen it, and for many of us, it brought a smile to our face.

The NASA logo has three main official designs: the NASA insignia (known as the meatball), the NASA logotype (the worm), and the NASA seal. (The worm, consisting of the word NASA in a unique red curved text, has been retired from official use since 1992.) *Wikipedia* says that the NASA seal, approved by President Dwight D. Eisenhower in 1959, was slightly modified by John F. Kennedy in 1961.

According to NASA's website, the meatball design is credited to Glenn Research Center employee James Modarelli and dates back to 1959, when the National Advisory Committee on Aeronautics metamorphosed into the agency that would advance both space *and* aeronautics: NASA. Modarelli, asked by the executive secretary of NASA to design a logo that could be used for less formal purposes, simplified the seal, leaving only the white stars and orbital path on a round field of blue with a red vector. Then he added white N-A-S-A lettering.

In the easily recognizable meatball design, "the sphere represents a planet, the stars represent space, the red chevron is a wing representing aeronautics (the latest design in hypersonic wings at the time the logo was developed), and then there is an orbiting spacecraft going around the wing."

First known officially as NASA's insignia, this round logo was not called the meatball until 1975, when NASA decided a more modern logo was required and switched to what would eventually be dubbed, due to the heated rivalry between the factions of supporters, the worm.

Richard Danne and Bruce Blackburn were hired to create this new, more modern-looking NASA logo. When ready for its initial unveiling, it is rumored that NASA's administrator, Dr. James Fletcher, and deputy administrator, Dr. George Low, discussed the proposed design:

Fletcher: "I'm simply not comfortable with those letters, something is missing."

Low: "Well, yes, the cross stroke is gone from the letter A."

Fletcher: "Yes, and that bothers me."

Low: "Why?"

Fletcher: (long pause) "I just don't feel we are getting our money's worth!"

According to the NASA website, the meatball was the most common symbol of NASA for sixteen years. But when the modernized bright red worm came onto the scene in 1975, the meatball was abandoned until 1992. At that time, NASA administrator Dan Goldin reinstated the classic meatball insignia to invoke memories of the "one giant leap for mankind" glory days of Apollo and to show that "the magic was back at NASA." It has been the most common agency symbol since.

In addition to the insignia, NASA has another official symbol. If the meatball is the everyday face of NASA, the NASA seal is the dressed-up version. The NASA administrator uses the seal for formal purposes such as award presentations and ceremonies. Like the meatball insignia, the seal also includes the planet, stars, and orbit and vector elements, including the words "National Aeronautics and Space Administration, U.S.A.," inscribed around its circumference. It appears on the face of a formal document and on the front of the podium during important press conferences.

Astronauts are also fond of symbols. For example, a distinctively salient symbol was created by the astronauts of the Apollo era which identifies us as spacefarers. The symbol includes three vertical pillars, the outer two angled inward toward the center pillar, with all three intersecting at the apex, giving the appearance of a triangular shape. The pillar junction apex blends into the image of a single star. Each pillar represents one of the early NASA mission programs: Mercury, Gemini, and Apollo. A horizontal oval, representing an orbital path, encircles the three pillars near their midpoint. Taken altogether, it creates a simple but uniquely powerful design.

This symbol is presented to every astronaut as a lapel pin. Astronauts receive their first pin, minted in silver, after the completion of their initial basic training regimen. The presentation of these pins is often (but not always) a part of the once traditional but now somewhat sporadic ASCAN graduation ceremony. This graduation is a rite of passage for the rookie and unflown astronauts as they move from the status of being a true newbie to that of a flight-assignable astronaut.

Arguably, the symbolic pinnacle of an astronaut's career is the receipt of a second astronaut lapel pin, this one minted in gold. This precious metal symbolizes that the astronaut has officially flown in space and is typically presented to crewmembers at an award ceremony following a successful mission. The Astronaut Office sees to it that your gold astronaut symbol lapel pin is flown on your initial mission, and astronauts have the opportunity to fly their gold pin on all their subsequent missions, no matter how few or how many missions they receive. Rumors say that some commanders presented astronauts with their gold pins while in space, once the official "astronaut altitude" of sixty-two nautical miles (100 kilometers) had been reached. That did not happen in my case.

The Astronaut Office, like the NASA agency, employs many symbols. Since the early days of spaceflight, beginning with the Gemini program, for each and every mission flown a mission patch is used to symbolize the combined efforts of the many individuals required to successfully carry out the goals of our space agency.

Some individuals and organizations create a patch to represent an experiment or a specific payload being readied for flight. Others simply want to capture the focus or legacy of their organizations. For the astronaut mission crew, it is the official mission patch, a simple but revered piece of embroidered cloth. A collector's item and a huge source of pride, its cost is typically borne by the American taxpayer.

Today the process by which an official mission patch becomes reality is interesting and highly complex. In the big picture view, once a crew is assigned to their mission, the commander is given an inordinate number of administrative tasks. Mission-specific assignments must be made. Who will be seated on the flight deck? Who will serve as the lead spacewalker? Which of the crew will operate the robotic arm as prime and as backup? Who will be the loadmaster, the individual responsible for ensuring the accurate transfer of cargo to and from the spaceship? And no less significant in this pile of objectives is naming the astronaut who will be responsible for the design of the mission patch.

I have been at one time or another a member of at least six different crews. I was initially assigned to STS-118 as a shuttle rotating expedition crewmember, or shREC, the crewmember who flies to the station on a space shuttle, is dropped off, remains for four to six months, and then returns on a second space shuttle. (While the ISS was being assembled, the shuttle often carried ISS crewmembers to the station, leaving one and bringing another home. This concept of rotating crewmembers was discontinued as the retirement of the shuttle loomed and the Russian Soyuz rocket became the sole method of crew transfer.) When I moved from STS-118 to STS-117 my ride home to Earth would still be with the crew of STS-120; that's three crews. My five months on ISS would span two expeditions, or increments, so that I served as a crewmember of both Expedition 15 and 16. That makes five. Then I was fortunate to serve as a full-time member of the STS-131 crew. That is six separate yet intertwined missions, and each and every one of them had an official mission patch.

I was not directly involved in the patch design for any of the six missions. Nor was I intimately involved in the design of the STS-117 or STS-118 patches or the class patch for astronaut selection group 17. Most of my contributions were for the patch designs of Expedition 15 and STS-131.

The astronaut awarded (stuck is probably the better word) with the patch design is usually tremendously popular. However, that tide can turn in an instant when a member's input to the patch design is summarily dismissed or ridiculed. Crewmembers often exhibit unique personality traits during the patch design process that heretofore may have gone unnoticed.

Typically gung ho and often a rookie space flier, the person serving as the lead for patch design, or patch leader, must bring enthusiasm to the process and sufficient ignorance of the hassle involved in the mission icon's development.

It has been my experience that most crews have an "I don't care" person, usually (but not always) a male. This is the person who has a consistent response to the changes in patch design: "I don't care. Whatever you all want is fine with me." Yet this is often the same person who, when consensus is near, suddenly has a decided opinion. Like the proverbial turd in the punchbowl, they offer up their untimely input of "I don't really care, but why don't we do such and such?" Or "Why did we do it *that* way?"

The rookie leader must choose his or her words carefully at this critical juncture, acknowledging the crewmember's comments by initiating a discussion aimed at unifying the crew. Heated arguments and strategic posturing between crewmembers may result, usually requiring the commander's help to achieve an acceptable solution. After this, the "I don't care" person invariably abstains from all subsequent discussions.

The crew may also include an assorted combination of wafflers. These are the folks who always see a weakness in the current design. They disagree with some aspect of the design or the color but don't readily offer any concrete suggestions for improvement. This type of crewmember may also be heavily involved in the selection of matching crew shirts, both for training and for the onboard mission, but that's a discussion for later.

It is an exciting time indeed when the patch leader collects all the initial ideas from the crew and begins to formulate the general patch theme. At that point a NASA graphical designer is assigned to the team. He or she is a trained professional who assimilates and "fleshes out" key ideas using high-tech design tools.

Crewmembers head into this portion of the design process with one of four philosophies. First, they may rely heavily on the fact that the assigned graphic artist is a true professional born with artistic abilities. Second, they may assume the role of mother hen and tell the designers exactly what to draw and where to draw it. Third, and perhaps the most effective strategy, they utilize a combination of the first two. Finally, some crews enlist a third party, perhaps a crewmember's son or daughter, a friend who designs patches for a living, or a random space enthusiast.

After everybody has had their say, the patch leader and the graphic designer work free of input, investigating shapes, colors, and layout. Each crewmember's last name must grace the patch in some form, and when the name Metcalf-Lindenberger is to occupy a significant position on your patch's border, shape is a big consideration!

Reviewing the patch's rough draft is a much anticipated milestone. Several draft designs are produced, giving the crew some options in choosing a visual they hope will tell their mission story. The drafts are also useful in illustrating how the design team progressively moved from one design to the next.

The use of color becomes significant. Because a patch can incorporate only those colors that the manufacturer is able to reproduce, the patch leader has to go through several rounds of input as suggestions are made. Concerns from vigilant commanders begin to arise when the patch design process seems to be taking on a life of its own.

Yet when it all comes together and everyone is pleased, it is a proud and defining moment for the crew. Now the powers-that-be must formally approve the final product. If everyone has been reasonable and the rules, unwritten or otherwise, have been followed, the result is a symbol that will forever represent the crew and its mission, and NASA.

The Expedition 15 patch design began with me when Fyodor Yurchikin, the Expedition 15 commander, asked me to come up with the patch for our mission . . . or at least that's what I thought.

My idea originated at home as I was addressing a birthday card for my brother's oldest daughter, Taylor. As the "crazy uncle," I traditionally provide a sketch on the envelope's front. My sketch was like the puzzles I used to try and solve on the television game show *Concentration* when I was a kid. In Taylor's case I decided to draw something related to space and my preparation for the upcoming mission to the ISS. I started with a single arced line representing the curved surface of the Earth's horizon, angled slightly upward from left to right. On the line at the lower left, I added a partially risen sun to symbolize a new day beginning.

In my days as a trajectory design engineer developing products for shuttle and station rendezvous and proximity operations, we would often head to the chalkboard and sketch the relative positions and motions of the space vehicles involved in order to better understand what was going on in the world of orbital mechanics. Thinking along those lines, I drew a second arc on Taylor's card, originating below and toward the center of the first, rising up vertically and crossing over it to represent the trajectory of the space station orbiting the Earth. Then I added to that arc two black dots with a horizontal line through them and eight short vertical dashed lines at each end, two above and two below the horizontal line and four on either side of the dots. I had created a stylized but recognizable space station.

While the sketch represented my work as a space person and the family's crazy uncle, the more I looked at the image, the more I began to see how the two arcs made a beautifully fluid X. Hmm . . . the gears in my brain were churning. Our expedition number can be represented in roman numerals with the letters X and V. I was onto something.

In my attempt to emulate the great artists of history, I paused to contemplate ways in which I might be able to create that second, and necessary, V. Soon it came to me. I was to arrive at the ISS via the space shuttle while my Russian colleagues and crewmates would come by Soyuz—two rendezvous trajectories ultimately arriving at the same destination.

With two more gentle strokes of my pen, I had created two more arching orbit traces, both originating from the same point as the space station's. By adding cartoonish drawings of a shuttle and a Soyuz, one on each arc, I had created exactly the look I was seeking. With proper use of colors, we could highlight the X and V and with some technical and artistic refinement create one of the most unique mission patches in the history of the station program (see color plate 23).

In conjunction with our graphic artist, Sandra Wilkes, our patch was well on its way—at least until Fyodor and Oleg returned to the United States for their next training session.

I had already provided Fyodor with a computer JPEG image of the patch proposal while he was in Russia, so he was familiar with what Sandra and I were trying to go for. Upon his arrival at JSC, he immediately requested a meeting to discuss "our" patch design. As we entered the conference room of Sandra's building at the space center, Fyodor already had in his hand what he, the Expedition 15 commander, considered to be our near-final design.

While not being anything like what I had composed with Sandra's help, Fyodor and Oleg's version still had the single theme I was trying to capture—orbital traces forming the expedition number for our mission. They had essentially borrowed the Mercator projection of the Earth from the screens of Mission Control and depicted the orbital traces in two dimensions versus the three that my oblique representation tried to capture.

I couldn't really argue with their version, especially once we brought Suni Williams into the discussions. She was quick to agree to Fyodor and Oleg's design with just a few minor changes. I wasn't disappointed in the least, as the resulting patch was beautifully designed and clearly unique when compared with many of the previous station patches. As the patch got more and more visibility among the rank and file of the astronaut office, it got more and more kudos for its unique appearance. It looked like we had a winner!

The patch design efforts for STS-131, led by former high school science teacher turned astronaut Dottie Metcalf-Lindenberger, went even more smoothly. Despite the fact there were seven of us trying to reach consensus on this design, it was for the most part (thanks to Dottie's personable leadership style) an easy and timely process. While we had our wafflers and "I don't care" people, it all came together nicely. My contributions to the STS-131 design were to add the ISS graphic toward the bottom right of the patch (nearest my name, as I was the only station long-duration flier) and to make the star of the astronaut symbol serve the dual purpose of representing our corps *and* a sunrise at the top of the patch.

Once approved by NASA, the mission patch's final two milestones are the creation of a logo for embroidery on crewmember mission clothing and the word description explaining what the patch design represents.

The logo gets worked out with Judy Rasmussen and the folks at Lands' End Business Outfitters. With Judy's guidance it is a relatively quick process to isolate a few key components in each patch that leave the best and easiest design to embroider, leaving a clearly recognizable shirt logo.

The actual word descriptions are most often the responsibility of the patch design leader, so for Expedition 15 that responsibility fell to me. Since our crew was comprised of both Americans and Russians, I would have to get the English version translated into Russian. Thus it would be important to write the description with the goal of maximizing understanding and carryover from one language to the other. Not an easy thing to do when dealing with Russian.

The official descriptions of these two mission patches—perhaps significant only to those who were intimately involved—reflect the specific meaning of their designs:

ISS *Expedition 15*: The operational teamwork between human space flight controllers and the on-orbit crew takes center stage in this emblem. Against a backdrop familiar to all flight controllers past and present, and independent of any nationality, the fifteenth expedition to the ISS is represented in Roman numeral form as part of the ground track traces emblazoned on the Mercator projection of the home planet Earth. The ISS, shown in its fully operational, assembly-complete configuration, unfurls and then reunites the flags of this Russian and American crew in a show of continuing international cooperation. Golden spheres placed strategically on the ground track near the flight control centers of the United States and Russia serve to symbolize the joint efforts from each nation's team of flight controllers and the Shuttle and Soyuz crew vehicles in their chase orbits as they rendezvous with the ISS. A rising sun provides a classic touch to the emblem signifying the perpetual nature of manned space flight operations and their origin in these two spacefaring nations.

STS-131: The STS-131/19A crew patch highlights the Space Shuttle in the Rendezvous Pitch Maneuver (RPM). This maneuver is heavily photographed by the International Space Station (ISS) astronauts, and the photos are analyzed back on Earth to clear the Space Shuttle's thermal protection system for reentry. The RPM illustrates the teamwork and safety process behind each Space Shuttle launch. In the Space Shuttle's cargo bay is the Multi-Purpose Logistics Module (MPLM) Leonardo, which is carrying several science racks, the last of the four crew quarters, and supplies for the ISS. Out of view and directly behind the MPLM is the Ammonia Tank Assembly (ATA) that will be used to replace the current ATA. This will take place during the three Extravehicular Activities (EVAS). The 51.6 degree Space Shuttle orbit is illustrated by the three gold bars of the astronaut symbol, and its elliptical wreath contains the orbit of the ISS. The star atop the astronaut symbol is the dawning sun, which is spreading its early light across the Earth. The background star field contains seven stars, one for each crewmember; they are proud to represent the United States and Japan during this mission.

You may or may not agree as you look at the final patch and logo designs, but in my humble (and unbiased) opinion, I think the E15 and STS-131 logos turned out wonderfully.

12

Sixty-Two and Counting

The space programs of the world keep records for documentation, for competition, and maybe even for fun. Records provide a historical reference of successes and failures in the daunting pursuit to unlock the secrets of our universe. The United States Space Program is no exception. Records are maintained for the number of astronauts flown and on how many flights. We track hours of spacewalking time and who performed them. We even worry about which flight had the largest assembled mass in orbit. (My last flight, STS-131, held that record for a while.) Numbers abound reflecting the greatest and the most mundane achievements of spacefaring nations.

To be granted official status as an astronaut, you don't even have to orbit the earth. You need only achieve a specific altitude. What that altitude is depends on your reference. According to *Wikipedia*, the criteria for what constitutes human spaceflight vary. The Fédération Aéronautique Internationale (FAI) Sporting Code for astronautics recognizes only flights that exceed an altitude of 100 kilometers (62 miles). In the United States, professional, military, and commercial astronauts who travel above an altitude of 50 miles (80 kilometers) are now awarded astronaut wings.

Whether you choose the reference point of 62.1 statute miles (the exact equivalent of 100 kilometers) or 50, I maintain you must reach and stay in orbit to brag of astronaut status. But I'm prejudiced.

The day I first achieved that cherished milestone was beyond belief.

Trying to sleep the night before launch was hard enough. Trying to do it in the tiny, hotel-like room of astronaut crew quarters was worse. The itinerary had been laid out for us, as usually happens with a NASA event, especially something as significant as a launch. Breakfast was first, and per the commander's directive we were to all wear matching navy blue short-sleeved button-down crew shirts with khaki slacks.

On launch day, much of what you do is photographed or videotaped, even eating breakfast. We dined quickly, following our commander's lead, and smiled graciously for the cameras. Because the video was being aired live on NASA TV, we also provided obligatory waves. I found it interesting that for both of my launches, a beautiful cake was prepared with our mission patch proudly decorating the top. And both times not a single member of either crew ate a piece of that cake!

The kitchen support staff took orders for lunch—our last meal, if you will. I listened intently as the veterans chose simply—basic sandwiches with little to no condiments—to protect their stomachs from the potential nausea of zero gravity. Visions of my medium-rare steak and loaded baked potato departed quickly, replaced by the blandness of a turkey sandwich on wheat, with lettuce and spicy mustard.

Medical checks followed breakfast. These are mostly a formality. The flight surgeons looked us over, patted us on the back, and wished us good luck. If someone was sick at this point, after spending the last seven days isolated from family and friends, it could throw a serious monkey wrench into the mission planning process. Fortunately, we were all given a clean bill of health.

The commander, pilot, and mission specialist 2 (shuttle flight engineer) busied themselves with briefings throughout the morning. Discussions about weather dominated, the meteorological experts checking current conditions and forecasts for the launch-pad and emergency landing sites around the globe.

I didn't have much to do. I was like a sack of potatoes, mere cargo to be delivered by the supplier to the buyer somewhere in orbit. I made sure all my landing clothes were packed appropriately. Multiple bags were required. One was for Edwards Air Force

Base in California in case bad weather in Florida pushed us there. Another was for a normal return to the Cape. A third bag was necessary to cover an emergency landing site, potentially outside the United States. It seemed strange for me to be thinking of landing, because mine wouldn't come for at least five months!

The timeline called for me to suit up shortly after our quiet lunch. With launch time scheduled for late afternoon on June 8, 2007, it felt like our pace was easy, almost leisurely.

Returning to my room, I noticed that I was beginning to feel nervous about what was coming. Thinking about where I would be sleeping at the end of the day, I had the expected feelings of excitement and anticipation mixed in with a boatload of anxiety.

Each of us had been given a target time to begin to suit up. That meant one last trip to the restroom, followed by the donning of your diaper.

Known as the MAG, or maximum absorbency garment, our launch-day diaper is a pull-up, not the "taped" version I used on my children when they were infants. For the same purpose, many astronauts (especially males) strategically place feminine hygiene pads within the MAG to help prevent "free flow" during the two-plus hours of idle time on your back in the prelaunch countdown. Useful in my preparation for this exact moment was an informal training session held months earlier in Cottage 3 back in Star City, Russia. During dinner, one of our female (and veteran) astronauts was discussing the subject of MAGs for those of us designated as first-time space fliers. She mentioned the use of feminine hygiene products but failed to use the word "pads." I spent most of the session trying to imagine where and how I was going to place tampons in my diaper. Pretty naive, huh?

MAG-donning complete, I added the remaining layers of underwear and cooling garments, grabbed my Ziploc bag of personal items (pens, pencils, duct tape, and wedding band), and began an undignified, skivvies-clad trudge to the suit-up room.

Assisted by a United Space Alliance suit tech, I slipped into my bright orange astronaut crew escape system (ACES) suit and black boots. Its major pieces (boots, helmet, and the suit itself) all bore tags with a single letter of the alphabet—my personal identification symbol. My ACES suit could save my life in the event of a contingency. Proper donning was critical.

Securing our gloves and helmets to our suits, we initiated the crucial preflight pressure check. With the order to close and lock my helmet visor, air flowed into my now-inflating suit, stretching its bladder until I looked like an orange Pillsbury Doughboy. No leaks found, the hiss of releasing air lasted only a fraction of the time it took to inflate. I now had time for some well-earned relaxation in my faux leather recliner.

As in many of our training exercises, multiflight veteran J. R. Reilly was the final piece of the suit-up puzzle, being the last to don his gear. With completion of his pressure check, launch was drawing near. It was time for a well-rehearsed and time-honored astronaut tradition.

We gathered around the equipment table in the front of the room, clearing a space to play cards. Chief astronaut Steve Lindsey dealt seven poker hands, one for each member of the launch-ready STS-117 crew.

The poker game is played for good luck. As each hand is dealt and played, the lowest hand is eliminated from the game. No one departs for the pad until the mission commander has lost and is out of the game, signifying his bad luck is gone. Once that happens, the crew can confidently head to the pad.

Objective complete, bathed in an aura of good luck, we assembled in proper two-abreast order for departure from the suit room and crew quarters. Destined for launchpad 39A, we were led by our commander and pilot. I would march with my Penguin classmate John "Danny" Olivas. J. R. Reilly, the seasoned veteran—and the extra member of our odd-numbered crew—brought up the rear.

Waving to well-wishers assembled behind barricades in front of the crew quarters exit, we boarded the sleek, silver (and old) Astrovan for the ride to the pad. The conversation in the van was strained. Several jokes were made, which were met with polite laughs.

We were encouraged to hydrate with bottles of water from a cooler at the van's aft end. Though it was a steamy June day in

Florida, few dared to down even a swallow or two, fearing the need to urinate during strap-in.

I took everything in, watching carefully the moves of shuttle-flown veterans, searching for clues to make my inaugural journey go smoothly. No jokes were played on the rookies, as in the past when seasoned crewmembers pulled fake boarding passes from their spacesuits, leaving the neophytes scrambling to find out why they had none.

The enormity of what was about to transpire was beginning to set in, probably for all of us but certainly for me. As we passed the Vehicle Assembly Building and made the turn onto Crawler-way Road, the Space Transportation System and *Atlantis* stood tall against the background of a near-cloudless sky. I swallowed hard and said a silent prayer.

Standing on the pad in the shadow of the launch support structure, we were dwarfed by the two-hundred-foot-tall stack of raw power. I had heard it many times, and now I understood. She really did seem to breathe, as if alive. Ultracold liquid hydrogen and oxygen audibly seethed through her propulsion system pipes, prepared for their eventual explosive meeting in the shuttle main engine combustion chambers. Performing a dual role, the frigid gases cooled the now silent main engine bells. Like a rodeo bull awaiting its break into the arena, *Atlantis* groaned under the strain of being locked to the pad.

We climbed into the elevator as a crew, carrying the bags protecting our gleaming white reflective-taped helmets. Accelerating quickly, as evidenced by popping ears, we arrived at the 195-foot level, towering above the swamps of the Kennedy Space Center.

Even our order of ingress into the white room and subsequently onto the decks of *Atlantis* was preplanned. Assigned to the windowless middeck for launch, I would enter in the sixth slot, a blessing for someone needing to pee.

I took the walk past the emergency escape baskets, following the path to the famous 195-foot-level toilet. Its door wide open, I tentatively stepped inside. Exercising the care that my life-preserving launch-and-entry suit deserved, I unsnapped my zipper and pulled it back far enough to expose my crotch. Manipulating my layers with nervous hands, I finally voided into the lidless stainless steel bowl. Milestone achieved!

Still awaiting my call to cross the metal gantry and enter the white room, it was time to perform what would turn out to be an incredibly emotional task. I needed to call my wife.

Situated near the gantry entry point, bolted to an iron stand, is a black telephone. Dialing "8" for what had to be the world's most heralded outside line, I punched in the numbers for Susan's cell phone.

From somewhere in the Launch Control Center, she answered the call, or so I thought. I could hear her voice on the other end, but for some reason she could not hear me. I called to her, "Susan? Susan, can you hear me?"

I heard the panic in her voice as she literally screamed to those around her, "It's Clay! I know it's Clay! I can't hear him, I can't hear him!" She began to cry as I tried to decide what to do. Feeling the pressure of my rapidly approaching ingress time and my crewmates' desires to use the phone, too, I took a chance and hung up. I prayed that a quick redial would be the answer.

After only a partial ring, Susan's voice captured the line. "Clay?" she pleaded. "Are you there?"

I spoke, hoping she would hear. Caught up in the same fear and anxiety she was experiencing, I could never have anticipated the critical nature of what started out as a simple phone call. This would be the last time we would talk before launch, and unthinkably, perhaps forever.

"Hi, honey, it's me—can you hear me?"

She cried again. But this time, through tears of relief she struggled to push out her words. "Yes, yes! I can hear you," she cried.

Realizing I had very little time, I told her that everything was going to be okay. Holding back tears of my own, I said, "I love you, Susan," and I thanked God for the precious call.

Inside the white room, the waiting suit techs positioned my parachute harness on the floor in front of my feet. I stepped through the leg straps and threw on the shoulder straps as if donning a tight-fitting jacket. It was damned uncomfortable, just like in training. Contorting my body like a performer in Cirque du Soleil, I wiggled and stretched and pushed and pulled, anything to relieve the pressure points.

Knowing everything going on in the white room was beamed to any TV tuned to the NASA Channel, I wanted to signal my family. This was often done with hand-drawn signs, but our staunch marine commander had emphatically said "no signs." Resorting to the hand signals we used with our kids, I pointed to my eyes, pounded my fist against my heart one time, and then pointed directly at the camera lens. Hoping that Susan and the kids would see it, either live or on some replay, I had sent the message, possibly for the last time, to those dearest to me: "I love you."

It was time to take my seat.

Fully clothed in a bulky space suit, I crawled through the orbiter's tiny middeck hatch, having much difficulty with the gymnastic maneuvers required. With *Atlantis* pointed skyward, the change of ninety degrees made the simple act of getting strapped into a seat seem totally foreign.

J.R., already strapped in, smiled broadly and welcomed me aboard. The strap-in process, when executed by the experts, took little time. Lying on my back, not really comfortable at all, I had lots of time to wait and to think . . . and to pee again.

As I half-listened to the crackling conversations carried on in my communication (comm) cap, the passing of time, coupled with me being on my back, put my bladder in the mood for a discharge. While it may seem simple, peeing while lying on your back is a practiced art, and I had not practiced. I was now regretting my failure to heed the advice of my predecessors who had suggested a practice session or two, wearing a diaper, lying on my back in a bathtub at home.

So I began picturing mentally the thundering power of Niagara Falls and the flow of the Platte River near Nebraska's Lake McConaughy. I was just about there. Focusing next on a vigorous flow from the tap in my bathroom, I sensed the coming experience of orgasmic proportion.

And then it happened!

No, I didn't pee. Commander C.J. Sturckow called me on the intercom.

It was an innocuous call, just to see how I was doing. He totally broke my concentration. Answering him with "I'm okay, thanks," I went back to my hydraulic daydreams.

I was having no success, but soon it wouldn't matter.

All communication checks were complete, and the countdown clicked steadily backward. More than two hundred miles above Earth, the International Space Station was moving at five miles per second through its ninety-one-minute-long orbit. We would have a scant five-minute window to lift off or risk missing my future home.

Inside the Launch Control Center, a cadre of some two hundred launch controllers, led by NASA test director Steve Payne, methodically moved through their checklists making damned sure everything looked good.

Through the hard work of thousands of people, we were ready, holding at nine minutes before launch, the final time to decide whether the shuttle is indeed ready to go.

The person making that decision would be the launch director, Mike Leinbach.

My attention was now solidly on the communications pulsing through my headset. Listening to every word, without a hint of needing to pee, I heard Payne initiate the launch status check. Polling his team of controllers, he asked for their readiness to resume the count and whether they were "go" for launch. Unanimous calls of "go" preceded Payne notifying the launch director that his team was indeed ready to proceed.

With that, Leinbach conducted his own poll, pinging the engineering, safety, weather, payload, and operations management teams. Hearing nothing that would preclude an on-time liftoff, he informed Payne that we were "go for launch." The countdown resumed with the test director's call, "In three, two, one, mark!"

With only minutes until liftoff, I opened my small Ziploc bag that contained my antinausea meds. I popped the pills and took a swig of water from the bag precariously strapped to my right knee. They would enter my system in ample time to aid my first interactions with zero-g.

The crew was silent. Commander and pilot responded only

per the checklist in the performance of switch throws and calls to the launch team. Essential electrical circuits were connected to the electricity-generating fuel cells. Auxiliary power units were started, giving life to the vehicle's aero-surfaces being counted on to help steer this powerful stack of rocketry. The caution and warning database was cleared of all previous errors. We had a clean slate. Focus was on the coming liftoff.

I wiggled and squirmed to find comfort. I was feeling like a multilayered deli sandwich on flatbread. Hard on my back for over two hours now, on layers of parachute, harness, spacesuit, and bladder, stacked on an aluminum-backed chair with a puny half-inch pad, I was ready to be free.

It wouldn't be long now.

Listening to the constant chatter of the launch director and his team, I drew a mental picture of the passing milestones leading to ignition. My excitement continued to build as the shuttle's onboard computers took control of *Atlantis* and the clock continued its downward trek to 00:00.

At T (time of ignition) minus two minutes, the orbiter test conductor called: "Close and lock your visors. Initiate O2 flow." We replied collectively, through the voice of our commander. "*Atlantis*, Roger," was all C.J. needed to say. Now that my visor was locked, the breathing sounds in my headset reminded me of Darth Vader. It was time. We were going to space!

Hours of simulations had me ready for the cadence of the flight deck crew. With the commander's first call of "Nav Init," we had less than ten seconds. I prepared to become a spaceman.

My body tensed with the roar of the shuttle's main engines rapidly coming to power. The vibrations from these mighty nozzles coming to life in the six seconds prior to liftoff shook the entire shuttle and filled our comm-cap-covered ears with thunder.

"Engine Start . . . three at a hundred." Pilot Lee "Bru" Archambault confirmed what the shaking and noise had already told me— our engines were purring at 100 percent.

"One-oh-two, one-oh-two, auto, auto," came the simultaneous calls from Commander Sturckow and flight engineer Steve "Swany" Swanson, matched exactly with a countdown clock of 00:00. The shuttle flight software was correctly doing its thing, and the solid rocket motors were fully ablaze. We were going somewhere!

As C.J. called, "Clear of the tower," Bru chimed in with, "Three at one-oh-four." We were traveling 120 miles an hour, the shuttle's main engines working together at 104 percent capability, essentially full power and then some, cranking out nearly 394,000 pounds of thrust each!

In less than a minute, we were accelerating faster than the speed of sound and burning propellants at the rate of ten tons per second in our highly controlled explosion.

The call of "good digitals" came solidly from Swanson, indicating the primary flight control software was seeing the same thing as the ample but less capable backup lines of code.

C.J. contacted Houston. His voice vibrating, akin to talking while riding in a helicopter, he offered, "Houston, *Atlantis*. Roll Program."

Houston acknowledged the computer-driven roll of the multi-element stack to a "heads down" attitude, meaning that the antennas mounted on the orbiter's roof could now contact ground stations with stronger signals. "Roger Roll, *Atlantis*," CAPCOM and C.J.'s fellow marine Tony Antonelli replied.

"LVLH on the left."

"LVLH on the right."

The sequential calls from commander and pilot signified completed switch-throws on the cockpit's front panels. Shuttle displays would now show attitude data in a local-vertical, local-horizontal reference frame, which is much easier for us earthlings to comprehend.

It was the greatest roller-coaster ride in the history of man. We rumbled, we shook, and the sound was overwhelming. Anything not solidly tied down fell to the floor as high fives and fist bumps passed through the middeck. It *was* the experience of a lifetime!

We waited intently for the imminent throttling call. Heard only in part by the *Challenger* crew, the disastrous milestone still brought chills to the heartiest of souls.

"Throttling," Bru noted. "Three at sixty-seven." Already seven miles from the pad and five miles high, the shuttle computers had dialed back her thrust level to two-thirds of her capability, slowing us down as we passed through the regime known as maximum dynamic pressure, or "the bucket," so named for the shape it forms on a computer plot printout of thrust versus time. Reducing our speed would keep anything from snapping off the orbiter due to our ever-increasing speed and the high levels of pressure in the lower atmosphere.

With concurrence from the ground, we were "go" at throttle up. Lee's intercom call, "Throttling back up; three at one-oh-four," confirmed we were back at "full" (104 percent) speed.

Swany made good on his required call of "Ninety seconds," informing the crew that at this point, if needed, we could fly her manually, but nobody wanted that.

The next major milestone, two minutes into the flight, was separation of the solid rocket motors. Almost twenty-five miles high, the sleek, white boosters separated using explosive charges, small rockets pushing away from big rockets. We were in for a jolt! We heard it and felt it, and the flight deck crew would actually see it. At the requisite two minutes and five seconds, the expected thump occurred. The solid rocket boosters were destined for a parachute-aided splashdown in the Atlantic Ocean.

Safely onto our programmed trajectory, we could open our visors. The ride was smoother now. Dropping the solid rocket boosters left us running on engines gulping copious quantities of liquid fuel, fed from the bowels of the external tank, fast enough to drain an Olympic-sized swimming pool every minute. We were getting lighter and faster with each passing second.

I breathed a sigh of partial relief. Heading into my third minute as a real astronaut, I was feeling as if I was just along for the ride. I told myself to enjoy it, as the CAPCOM and commander began to exchange the first of several calls known as mode boundaries.

"*Atlantis*, two-engine TAL, Zaragoza," called Antonelli.

With Sturckow's "Copy, two-engine TAL, Zaragoza," we knew we could land in Spain with only two of our three main engines functioning, a transoceanic abort landing.

"Single engine, Zaragoza, one-oh-four." CAPCOM let us know we could reach Spain with only one remaining engine operating at full thrust.

Everything was going like clockwork. Approaching the astronaut-significant milestone of sixty-plus miles in altitude, we began to level off slightly. Because we were accelerating rapidly, the g-forces made each of us weigh three times what we do on earth.

The onset of g-forces was not painful. It was, however, extremely uncomfortable. But because we were prone, the increased force was focused through our chests rather than our heads, helping us maintain our internal equilibrium and reducing the possibility of puke filling our helmets. Even breathing was forced, fighting against the weight added by our continuing acceleration.

The call of "Press to MECO (main engine cutoff)" signified we were approaching our orbit, where the engines would no longer be needed.

A mere eight-and-a-half minutes since the thunderous roar began, I heard a gentle hissing sound of the engines shutting down. Flying from the base of my chair, held in place only by my seatbelt, I was weightless.

We were in space!

I glanced to my right to see J. R.'s now-empty chair. Looking left to ask Danny where J. R. was, I saw his chair was empty, too. Embarrassed and feeling like I'd better do something astronaut-like, I decided it was time I removed some of my gear and started into my orbital insertion checklist.

Gloves removed and tethered to my kneeboard, I went for my helmet. I lifted it gently over my head and placed it in front of my chest. Letting go with both hands, it floated there, barely moving, as if suspended from some sort of magician's invisible wiring system. Man, oh man, was this ever cool!

There was no call of sixty-two miles that day. I didn't need one. The silence of the shuttle's main engines was the only call I needed. I was in orbit and I was official.

13

Dark Days of Summer

As a kid I read a lot of comic books. My favorite hero was Super-man. I dreamed often of having his unbelievable super powers and living life as a beacon for all humanity. I wanted to be the "Man of Steel."

For nearly six months in the summer and fall of 2007, I was as close as I would ever come to *being Superman*. I wasn't indestructible, and my vision remained pretty pitiful without my contact lenses, but I *was* faster than a speeding bullet (flying around the Earth at 17,500 miles per hour). I *was* more powerful than a loco-motive. (Spacewalking in zero gravity, I tossed two pieces of junk hardware into outer space: a two-hundred-pound table-sized alu-minum camera support structure and an unused tank of ammo-nia the size of a refrigerator, weighing almost seventeen hundred pounds.) I *was* able to leap tall buildings (and anything else inside or outside the space station) in a single bound.

So when people ask me what it was like living and working in space, my answer is straightforward and simple: "I was Superman every day. I flew to breakfast, I flew to work, I flew to the bath-room . . . I even flew while I was *going* to the bathroom!" I *was* *Superman* every single day.

One hundred fifty-one days, eighteen hours, twenty-three min-utes, and fourteen seconds. In most elementary schools, that's nearly the time from the start of Christmas break until the cov-eted last day of school. No matter how you calculate it, it's a pretty long time. That is especially true when you are 215-plus miles away from the Earth, living in a pressurized can, isolated from most of humanity. You can't even go outside and play without days of intense preparation.

Make no mistake about it, the time I spent in outer space was nothing short of incredible. It was a time I will cherish for the rest of my life; I would like nothing more than to go back. I had more fun than any normal person has a right to expect. (Some would question using the word normal in a sentence describing me.) Yet just as in life here on Earth, there were times when things didn't go well and the outlook was not so rosy, when the crew got down, a little frustrated, even angry. These times account for me applying the introspective label "dark days of summer."

The first week in space passed quickly. Having just arrived via the space shuttle *Atlantis*—whose crew would remain at the station for a scant nine docked days—we pushed hard to accomplish the massive set of shuttle and station objectives. When the shuttle crew ultimately departed, we had little to no time to relax, as our first spacewalk was only a few weeks away. But as focused as I was on getting the jobs done safely and successfully, I simply wasn't prepared for what happened in late June, only three weeks into my spacefaring journey.

I had just finished up the many jobs and tasks essential to cleaning up after the visit of STS-117 and was preparing our ISS crew for July's upcoming spacewalk, our first. I was putting away tools, stowing spacewalking gear, and resizing space suits in an effort to clean up the airlock for what was to come. In my now near-normal modus operandi, when my workday was complete, I flew to my onboard personal space station support computer and cranked up what had quickly become my favorite software program of all time, a Cisco Systems application known as the IP (Internet Protocol) phone. The IP phone has to be one of the biggest assets to long-duration space travel in the history of the world. Through this simple, easy-to-use software, crewmembers have the capability to call Earth as simply as you can dial your cell phone to speak with Grandma. Just like E.T. the extraterrestrial, astronauts can phone home.

I popped on the Bose noise-canceling headphones, ensured their connection to the computer sound jack was secure, and that the on/off switch was correctly positioned. Now a seasoned IP phone veteran, I opened the software application's dial pad keyboard with a double-click of lightning speed, quickly locating the number to my wife, long since saved into speed dial. My index finger smashed the computer keyboard's enter key in anticipation of another live voice-hookup with Susan via her NASA-provided cell phone.

The software sent electromagnetic waves from transponders on the outside of the space station, which were then bounced off the nearest tracking data and relay system satellite floating in geostationary orbit twenty-three thousand miles above the earth, and back toward the Earth. Meanwhile, I played in my head the ring that I anticipated Susan would hear. She had programmed her phone's ring tones so when the ISS called, she would know who was calling. It was sort of a science fiction caller ID.

My euphoria was shattered when, after the four-second delay, my standard opening phrase of "I love you, I love you, I love you" was not returned by her sweet "I love you, too!"

I was in my very first month as a space alien and my wife was in tears.

To relate the story of this—the first truly dark period of my time on ISS—requires some background information.

The day prior to the launch of STS-117 I was honored to receive a surprise phone call. Lauren Lunde, an administrative support staff person at astronaut crew quarters in Florida, had given me a yellow "telephone call missed" sticky note from U.S. senator Chuck Hagel of Nebraska asking if I would please return his call. Although I had been a Texas resident the same amount of time as I had lived in Nebraska, I was still thrilled at the possibility that a U.S. senator from my home state would be calling me personally.

So I dialed his number. I was feeling pretty damned special. Hey, I was gonna be talking to a high-brow senator from Nebraska! After waiting through "please hold, Mr. Anderson" and "one moment, Mr. Anderson," Senator Hagel's voice commanded the line. Along with the usual chitchat, he wished me good luck and Godspeed and he told me how all of Nebraska was proud of me. This marvelous conversation enhanced the feelings of pride and accomplishment that I enjoyed as I prepared for my first trip into space.

Finally in orbit, and settled by my first couple of weeks of life on the ISS, I realized it would only be proper for me to return Senator Hagel's phone call. We had the technology. Being the only American on board the station, the IP phone was mine for the taking. (The station had three dedicated IP phone lines, but because my crewmates were Russian, it was rare not to have an open line available—the time difference between Russia and the United States meant their friends and relatives were sleeping while mine were awake. The station now has six of these coveted phone lines.)

This time, though, it wasn't going to be so easy. In order to return Senator Hagel's call I was going to need his phone number—imagine that. Having never flown before, I lacked forethought. I had neglected to add the phone listings for the senators and congressmen from Nebraska to my crew notebook's telephone book section. How selfish of me to only have phone numbers for my friends and family.

After sending a couple of earthly emails, my beautiful bride, Susan, came through, as she would so many times throughout my five-month increment. Within a single day I was dialing my special long-distance call to the senate office of Chuck Hagel in Washington DC, knowing exactly when to place the call because Susan had had a preparatory conversation with the senator's staff.

The senator was on the line within seconds. He sounded a bit taken aback . . . perhaps I was his first call from outer space.

We chatted casually, as if we had been friends forever, discussing the views from space through the station's inadequate number of windows, the beauty of the Earth, my first look at the state of Nebraska from 220 miles above, and of course, our beloved Huskers' prospects for the coming football season.

I subsequently learned that Senator Hagel mentioned our phone conversation as a part of a special news conference the next day. This long-distance phone call from "Nebraska's astronaut" was a big hit for him. For me it was a good morale booster, and helped to combat the homesickness that had accumulated during my so far short stay.

During our next IP phone call, Susan and I discussed how the contact seemed to have been a benefit for NASA, Susan's educational programs, and the wonderful folks in the state of Nebraska. We considered the idea that in the spirit of political equal opportunity, perhaps we should attempt to contact *all* of Nebraska's state senators, congressional representatives, and the governor.

Another email to Susan flew through the ether asking her if she could check out websites that might have the contact information for these key players. Once again, she was way ahead of me. Susan made a single inquiry to Ms. Peggy Wooten, then head of the Protocol Office at the Johnson Space Center.

What Susan and I assumed was a simple contact request caused hell to break loose within JSC's gates.

The Protocol Office immediately made a panic-stricken phone call to the head of the Astronaut Office, Steve Lindsey, demanding to know "What is Clay Anderson trying to do? What is his motivation? His agenda? Is he planning on running for office after he leaves NASA?"

Susan reassured them: "Clay just wants to tell them all 'hi,' thank them for their support and leadership, and let them know how proud he is to be a Nebraskan." No hidden agendas. Nothing of the sort.

The next thing Susan knows, Mr. Lindsey wishes a private meeting. Arriving at his office, not knowing what was about to transpire, Susan took the seat across from him behind his brown laminated barricade—also known as a conference table. Even before Steve had finished questioning my motives, he made it crystal clear to Susan that "everyone involved" had decided these calls were not going to happen.

Eventually, when cooler heads prevailed and they finally figured out we weren't trying to pull a fast one on anybody, "everyone involved" was all about helping us make NASA look good, going so far as to offer me official NASA "talking points" for each of the elected officials! However, by this point my earthbound wife, working full-time while being a solo parent to two young kids, exhibited nerves that were beginning to fray badly.

While Susan was still reeling from this snafu over contacting politicians, NASA management again stepped in to put a damper on my family while they were trying to support me in my long-duration space travel.

The Houston Astros baseball organization has a long-standing tradition of supporting the Astronaut Corps. Their partnership with NASA has led to the creation of an annual event deemed NASA Night at Minute Maid Park. During the summer of 2007, my old crew of STS-118 was asked to make an appearance at the game and throw out first pitches. Scott Kelly, commander of the STS-118 crew, asked Susan if our son, Cole, would like to represent his "off the planet" dad by throwing in a first pitch with the crew. Susan logically thought this was a win-win scenario for family satisfaction as well as good publicity for NASA.

Understandably, Cole was elated at the prospect of being on the field at Minute Maid Park, throwing a first pitch to one of the 'Stros. He would be ready!

Unfortunately, the JSC Legal Office, led by Mr. Bernie Roan, decided that Cole would not be allowed to throw. He was not an *astronaut* and they would not allow a child to throw a first pitch, period. It wouldn't "look right." We graciously asked for further consideration from the leadership of the Astronaut Office and were summarily informed, via Steve Lindsey, that NASA "wouldn't even let (JSC Center Director) Mike Coats's son throw a first pitch."

And this is why, the day that I called down to Earth expecting to have a simple, loving chat with my wife, I found her sobbing at her desk, and I could not help her. I was in outer space.

The second of my "dark episodes" was between me and Mission Control and was about technical issues. My recollection is that Fyodor, Oleg, and I were preparing the station for the arrival of the STS-118 crew. The men and women of spaceship *Endeavour* had key robotic arm operations and four spacewalks scheduled in order to attach the S5 truss segment, the fifth connecting element to be attached on the right (starboard) side of the station. The S5 truss would further prepare the station for the addition of more solar arrays and the Harmony module (Node 2) later that year.

Prior to their arrival and docking, I was performing standard but critical iss activities. These included disposing of trash and prepacking supplies and equipment we no longer needed so that the *Endeavour* could return them to Earth and the station would have more stowage room for the thousands of pounds of supplies *Endeavour* was to bring us.

I was also gathering tools and prepositioning the items the *Endeavour* crew would need when they exited the airlock on Flight Day 4 for Rick Mastracchio and Dave Williams's first spacewalk of the mission.

My goal as the only American station crewmember was to offload as much work for them as possible so that when they arrived on station, they could immediately focus on the robotics tasks and their excursions outside.

The trouble started on the morning we were to have a visit from a Russian Progress cargo ship. I was tasked to be in the airlock when the ship was scheduled for docking, gathering the space-walking tools that Rick and Dave required. I was sorting tools and equipment into several mesh bags for them, according to speci-fications sent to me in advance of their arrival. I would also pre-pare the mini-workstations (mws) that attached to the front of their spacesuits. These mws's held various tools, a small trash bag, a portable drill, metal wire ties, and various other gadgets they needed to have easy access to while they crawled around outside.

Fyodor and Oleg were handling the docking activity in the Russian segment. The arrival of another unmanned cargo ship was an operation that happened frequently on board iss and they didn't need my help.

The standard for Progress arrivals was that two crewmembers (always Russian if there were two on board) performed the moni-toring functions, ready to take over manually if an "off-nominal" event were to occur.

The airlock contains a simple yet clever piece of equipment mounted above the lead spacewalker's space suit. It is a foldout bag made from special white Nomex fabric, and is used to stow extravehicular mobility unit equipment—spacewalk gloves, mole-skin, eyeglasses, and the like—in its various pockets. The bag both protects the items and prevents them from floating away in the absence of gravity. It had been in its prescribed location since my arrival with sts-117 and was in perfect condition, having suffered little damage from its time in the shirt-sleeve environment inside the airlock.

One of my tasks for the day was to take that bag down and stow it in another. Then, when *Endeavour*'s crew delivered the new bag, I was to dig out the old bag and give it to them to stow back in the shuttle. As I worked I began to think there had to be a more efficient way to accomplish this. I called Mission Control via the space-to-ground loop 2 and cleverly suggested it would be more efficient to leave the current bag in place, use it for all four evas with sts-118, and then have Rick and Dave give me the new bag just prior to their departure. At that time I'd give them the old one for return.

My plan was not exactly embraced by the folks down on Earth. I got considerable pushback for that and several other time-saving suggestions. My frustration level was growing significantly.

The situation came to a head hours later when I received an email from the ground. Forwarded to me by our lead flight director, Bob Dempsey, the note related clearly that while I may have been frustrated with the ground, the ground was growing frustrated with me. The comments were, to say the least, acerbic.

"Why doesn't he just be quiet and do what he's told?" was the response to my numerous questions regarding task protocols. One comment was more to the point: "Why don't they just bring him home with the sts-118 crew?" It was obvious I was not winning any popularity contests.

Bob Dempsey was trying to help me see things from the perspective on the ground, hoping to further my understanding of the negative impact I was having on them and to perhaps get me to back off a bit.

At first, I blew them off. I told myself I was strong enough to overcome the insensitivity of their remarks. Just let it go, I thought. They're just venting.

But I couldn't let it go. It festered inside me like a bad order of sushi.

"Who the hell do they think they are?" I thought. "I'm the guy living here. Who has a better understanding of the best way to do things than me?"

For two days I struggled. I now knew how some of the Skylab 3 astronauts felt. Having read Robert Zimmerman's *Leaving Earth: Space Stations, Rival Superpowers, and the Quest for Interplanetary Travel* in 2004, I knew of the Skylab crews' difficulties with the ground control team. Like those astronauts, I felt a growing undercurrent of tension between the ground and me. I was depressed and upset with how I was being treated. I quit talking to the ground. If I was required to speak with them, it was short and to the point—very unlike me.

I did not share my situation with my crewmates. I'm sure they knew something was going on, but I couldn't open up to them. In what may have been a totally incorrect assumption on my part, I felt that as Russians, they would interpret my emotional swings as a sign of weakness.

Fyodor, receiving backdoor information about the situation from flight controllers in Russia, offered some simple yet sound advice. "Clay, remember," he would say with a mischievous grin, "smile and patience."

Though still feeling I was in the right, I committed myself to change. I asked myself, "How can a guy who has a really good heart and tries so very hard still be misunderstood? Why couldn't I just do things their way and shut up?"

My only answer is that it's not in my nature. Blame Nebraska and the farm. When I think something can be fixed, made better, easier, faster, more efficient, I can't stop myself from trying to do it. Then, when my good advice is snubbed, for the life of me I can't understand why it isn't as obvious to them as it is to me!

Relating the situation to Susan and my flight psychiatrist, Dr. Gary Beven, I told them, "I guess I'll have to leave NASA when I land. . . . Apparently we (Susan and I) have upset so many folks that I will probably never fly again and my reputation is soured." Scared, mad, and confused, I asked Dr. Beven via email, "This is not what's supposed to happen when you go into space, is it? When you are just trying to do the right thing and enjoy some time in the limelight? I am starting to feel down again."

Dr. Beven responded, "As a man of faith, you already know that God put you in this situation for a reason. Maybe it is to later make improvements for others who venture into space—especially the ones who might be afraid to speak up and change the status quo."

He told me, "It is way too early for you to think about leaving. Don't think that far into your future yet. I predict that when the STS program ends, and the ISS and long-duration crews are finally in the spotlight, things will greatly improve, and most, if not all, the changes you envision will come to pass. I predict a big CB (astronaut office) culture shift at that point."

His words were prophetic. That shift is going on today. With the shuttle program now museum fodder, the space station is the focus of renewed attention, process improvement, and a huge NASA presence on the social media websites.

Fighter pilots often talk of their ability to compartmentalize, to focus on the task at hand, holding bad thoughts or difficulties at bay. I got a lot of practice with that while living on the station. I would have been a good fighter pilot.

Dr. Beven advised me to use the same technique in dealing with critical remarks from the ground: "This is one of those occasions you will really need to compartmentalize your disgust and anger so you can focus on the mission's day-to-day events, maintain your physical health, get enough sleep, and finish the last portion of the increment safely—that is the most important thing. The time will arrive, when you return, to deal with what occurred in debriefs and via other means. Let it go for now—otherwise it will tear you up inside during the mission."

He told me not to get discouraged but to focus on the positives. I had two good Russian friends, I was doing awesome with EVAs, friends were coming for a great mid-increment STS mission (118) with good science and lots of hard work being accomplished, and I knew that my family would be waiting for me with open arms.

I tried to follow this excellent advice, but the situation still ate at me. I felt some sort of olive branch was needed. The STS-118 crew was due at the station in a few days and I simply couldn't remain in this mood. So in an effort to make things more collegial with the ground, I wrote them an email. Entitled "Warts and

All," it was my personal apology for any untoward behavior thus far in the increment.

I asked Bob Dempsey for his approval: "If you are okay with this, I would like it to go to all of the flight controllers here and in Huntsville. It comes from my heart. Many warned me before launch that I would be this way. It has taken me too long to wake up and smell the coffee."

The letter was addressed to "All Members of the Flight Control Teams at JSC and MSFC (Marshall Space Flight Center in Huntsville, Alabama) supporting E15." It read:

This message is overdue. I hope everyone can understand that it is written in sincerity and with positive intent and that it is necessary . . . at least it is for me.

When I arrived in space I adapted very quickly physically. I don't think, however, that I adapted very well mentally. During my first 42 days or so in orbit, I have grown . . . unfortunately for some of you, you had to observe and deal with that growth. This growth did not happen as rapidly as it needed to . . . because of that, I have been unfair to you and that is wrong. To that end, I would like to apologize to you all and hope that we can now start with a clean slate.

You are truly the best and brightest that NASA has to offer. You ARE the tough and competent flight controllers of MOD and the POIC. The folks that work long hours, pull terrible shifts and yet, through it all you provide us, the on-orbit crews, with your best efforts, 24/7. In spite of the fact that I came from MOD and sat in the very rooms that you toil in, I forgot part of that dedication. I forgot what it really means to do your job, do it well and then head off to another 4 hours of meetings! I was too focused on me. And that is not my nature.

You have kept me honest, given me information that I should have already known and you have helped me recover from my mistakes. You have done it all with the professional demeanor and graciousness that I am sorry that I didn't always provide to you. From today on, I will endeavor to not make those errors again.

Please understand that I will have my good days and my bad days . . . hopefully more good than bad! ;-) For those that know me well, you probably understand that my mantra has always been about improving life on ISS for those who will follow after me. That is indeed a good goal, one that I will continue to honor. I will just do it in a better way.

Keep up the great work, and take some time to enjoy the ride . . . for if not for you and your efforts, I would be but a passenger on this journey. I want to be your contributor, your eyes, ears, and hands in space.

I signed off with, "All the best, Clay."

I can never be sure if my words did anything for anyone but me, but I felt right again. Much like Superman first struggled to find his place on Earth, I struggled to find my place in space. But once I found it, I felt good. I could focus, and I could smile again.

I had a grand mission and that grand mission would go forward. I had much more work to do.

After all, I was preparing for visitors from another planet.

14

Crime and Punishment

As children, most of us learned about the "good guys versus the bad guys." Those of us who grew up in the sixties amused ourselves for endless hours playing cowboys and Indians, Superman against Lex Luthor, Huskers versus Sooners. Today, while those games have largely been replaced by video games for the Xbox and Wii, they're still typically based on the theme of good versus evil.

That good and evil might relate to the space shuttle and International Space Station programs would probably seem like a stretch to most. Yet it is possible for folks in those programs to be perceived as evildoers—persons that I, as a kid, would have done everything in my power to bring to justice and put behind bars. It is disappointing to admit to you that I became known as one of those evildoers, but here, within the pages of this book, I can proclaim my innocence for all time. Perhaps you'd like to hear of my crimes?

My slip to the dark side started early in my astronaut career. As newly decreed astronaut candidates (ASCANS), our Group 17 Penguins were headed to Washington DC to receive the standard ASCAN briefing from the leaders at NASA Headquarters.

Peggy Wilhide was the director of public affairs at NASA Headquarters. Her job was to explain everything associated with our role as NASA's newest ambassadors and spokespersons. She covered science and payload experiments, visits to Capitol Hill, prelaunch and mission activities, and the public affairs office's proclivity for hammering us with "talking points." They didn't trust us as far as they could throw us.

Following an enlightening discussion with the head of the NASA HQ Science Department centering on the quantity of methane gas produced by bovines of the world compared to that emanating from termites, self-appointed ASCAN Group 17 funnyman Garrett Reisman of Parsippany, New Jersey, provided sufficient comic relief on the subject to earn his call sign "Mite."

That conversation segued into the question and answer period, highly anticipated by the thirty-one neophytes in the room.

Not at all bashful, and naive about the impression it might make on my colleagues, my hand shot up quickly. "Why is it that every time I turn on the television, I have to watch Kobe Bryant or David Schwimmer or some other talking head tell my children to stay in school or stay away from drugs? Why can't astronauts do public service announcements? Why can't it be me—astronaut Clayton Anderson—wearing my orange launch-and-entry suit telling the kids of Nebraska to stay in school, study math and science, dream big, and reach for the stars?"

My proposal was met with several seconds of total silence. The reply that I wanted but in all honesty was surprised to get was "You know, that's a really good idea! We need to work on that. We'll get back to you and we'll keep you apprised of our progress."

Barbara Zelon, also in attendance as our NASA Johnson Space Center public affairs director, nodded vigorously in agreement. I was smugly confident I had scored big points with my new friends from the public affairs office while also impressing my astronaut colleagues.

Six months passed in our ASCAN training flow without a word about how the astronaut PSAs might be progressing. Not being one to sit on my hands, I fired off an email to Ms. Wilhide—copied to Ms. Zelon—asking for a status report on how my idea was progressing. Peggy replied politely that the idea was still in the works. She thanked me for asking and let me know that the public affairs office would keep me apprised. Satisfied once again that the wheels were turning on my wonderful take-the-world-by-storm idea, I returned to my training confident that one day soon

I might be on TV. (I had little experience dealing with bureaucracy, so a bit of naiveté on my part was normal.)

Six more months passed. No communication, no emails, nothing. My virgin status with NASA HQ was turning into full-fledged gigolo mode as I began to sense I might be getting it directly in the backside. Once again I got on my laptop and fired off a second email whose subject line was my self-perceived brilliant idea. This time my message was not quite so professional in its composition. It was laced with pent-up frustration.

Again the reply was cordial and timely. "We continue to work on it." I sensed where this might be going: nowhere, fast!

I mostly forgot about my idea until I was working a shift in Mission Control as capsule communicator (CAPCOM) for the Expedition 4 crew (Yuri Onufrienko, Carl Walz, and Dan Bursch). During a period of slow activity on the space station and boredom in Mission Control, I decided it was time to check on my outside-the-box idea once again. After all, it had been almost two years. The only problem was that my contact person, Ms. Wilhide, was no longer director of public affairs at NASA HQ.

Undaunted by this minor setback, I changed tactics and turned to the JSC director of public affairs. Disappointed to learn that Ms. Zelon was no longer with that office either, I targeted my ire at the *new* head of public affairs at JSC, a gentleman named Dan Carpenter.

This time my email note was simple. It explained the history behind my forward-thinking idea and my disappointment in not hearing anything from anyone. I related how difficult it was for me to imagine that no one was working on this win-win NASA scenario with the gleeful fervor of a cat shredding a roll of toilet paper!

The response timeline was longer this time. When Dan did finally reply, it was clear he had done his homework. He was a fan of my idea. His reply stated that his office had thoroughly discussed the idea and in fact they had discussed it with the Astronaut Office. But at this time it wasn't going to be implemented. He explained that he had very little control at his level.

He went on to say that the Astronaut Office told him that no astronauts had shown any interest in the idea whatsoever. This is the part that gave me heartburn. Excuse me, who the heck did they think I was—an astronaut impersonator? Here was an astronaut right in front of them—ready, willing, and able to take the plunge and do NASA's first astronaut PSA. What was going on? It was entirely possible that the Astronaut Office didn't have any *flown* astronauts who were interested. There are those at JSC firmly entrenched in the camp who think if you haven't flown in space, you aren't really an astronaut.

On my personal astronaut scorecard, I was nearing my first mistake. Totally missing the concept of "keep your head down and keep coloring," I assumed that as a brand-new astronaut and longtime NASA employee, I was much worldlier in the ways of NASA than I actually was. Thinking that I might even have control over something, I felt like Luke Skywalker battling Darth Vader on the Death Star. I could hear Lord Vader's raspy baritone saying, "Luke, join me and I will complete your training. Then your transformation to the dark side will be complete."

I stood poised and ready to launch my first turd into the astronaut punchbowl, a skill that unfortunately I would perfect with time. Given an unsatisfactory local response, I was growing increasingly impatient. Once locked and loaded, this turd's target would be at a much higher level.

At the time of the *Columbia* accident, the head of NASA was Sean O'Keefe. Having served as a family escort for the *Columbia* mission, I had attended funerals, gatherings, and numerous meetings during which Mr. O'Keefe and I had struck up a friendship. I felt comfortable taking my PSA idea to Sean.

Having absolutely no idea how to contact Mr. O'Keefe directly, I turned to the magic of NASA's "x500" website (a virtual telephone and email address book). With the World Wide Web doing its high-speed electron thing, it took only seconds for Sean's email address to appear, waiting to be copied and pasted in the "To" line of my opportunistic electronic correspondence.

Beginning with a standard greeting and a "How ya doin'?" I quickly got to the point of my now-stagnant PSA mantra. Composed in just minutes, my fully formed turd was on its way to Washington DC in seconds, ready to perform a splashdown worthy of the Apollo program.

The results were almost instantaneous. The next day I received a voicemail message from one of Mr. O'Keefe's NASA representatives in Washington. "We love the idea," he exclaimed. (Maybe it was just stated, but to me it *felt* like an exclamation.) "Please call me back." I tried to call back multiple times that day, leaving messages each time, but my efforts were apparently in vain. Near the end of the day the "astronaut police" were sent to apprehend me—the criminal. I received a call from Andy Thomas.

Andy, a veteran astronaut and native of Adelaide, South Australia, was serving as the deputy chief of the Astronaut Office. During the short trip to his office, I felt as if handcuffs had already been slapped around my wrists

Entering his private room, I knew I was busted and that my sentence was forthcoming. "What's going on with NASA HQ and Sean O'Keefe?" he asked. I passionately related my story, every single detail. I told him about my clever idea and all the promises I had received along the way. I explained how I was simply trying to do good for NASA, apologizing profusely for any errors in judgment I may have made.

Andy remained calm and appeared to take everything in stride. His first question seemed to be totally off the wall. "How'd you get O'Keefe's email?" he asked.

When I told him about the x500 website, he seemed impressed that I would know how to find it. He didn't seem too bent out of shape about what I'd done, but he did warn me of the perils of "doing an end run" on astronaut management. I apologized and said it wouldn't happen again. I had no idea my career was to be laced with troubled episodes—some intentional, some accidental.

(As a matter of record, almost ten years after my initial idea was sprung on NASA HQ, the first astronaut PSAs were filmed and released. The first was released in Wisconsin with "cheesehead" astronaut Jeff Williams. The second was aired in Nebraska with yours truly.)

My first report from the Astronaut Evaluation Board reflected my standing within the Astronaut Office and contained a gentle warning to tread carefully.

Rated "eligible (for a flight assignment)," the board stated:

> Clayton is a very, very strong performer. He was a great expedition crew support astronaut, was well regarded by the flight director, and is a good Mission Specialist (MS) 2 candidate. He did well in the ASCAN Extra-Vehicular Activity (EVA) skills programs, and his T-38 skills are very strong. Clayton is motivated, shows initiative, and does not need to be told what to do.

The board also signaled clearly, however, the following under the heading of "Special Issues or Considerations":

> As Clayton progresses in his career as an astronaut, which is expected to be highly successful, he should continue to promote organizational values and work through the FCOD [Flight Crew Operations Directorate] management chain.

I should have heeded those words of advice more carefully.

Apparently, the NASA Astronaut Office has a parole board. I say that because after my mission performance on Expedition 15 it was decided that I "had difficulty working and playing well with others."

As the sole U.S. crewmember during my time with Expedition 15, I was completely responsible for operations in the space station's U.S. segment. My Russian crewmates, Fyodor and Oleg, were more highly trained than most Russians in the operations of the U.S. systems, due in part to the long length of their training template. They had ample time to prepare. This was a distinct resource for the U.S. Mission Control Center team of which they took full advantage.

It was a normal day of station operations. I was headed for the Unity node to remove one of the module's panels and perform a straightforward task behind its wall. Removing the panel had to wait while I moved numerous bags of equipment and supplies that were bungeed to its outer surface. (In a place desperate for storage space, Unity's other role was as an "open-air" closet.)

I quickly moved the bags one by one away from the panel and

secured them within an empty space, or "hole," on the deck of the node where a rack had once been. Once the bags were secure, I began the tedious but simple process of removing each and every one of the forty-four captive fasteners that held the panel firmly in place.

With the work area completely exposed, it was easy to move in and execute the task. The node was full of environmental control equipment ranging from fans to valves, but the job was easy and quickly performed. I spent most of my time exposing the parts to be worked on and then covering them up once again.

Two days later I was knee-deep in spacesuits, cleaning and organizing the airlock for spacewalks to come. As I merrily worked my way through some of my favorite activities, Fyodor floated into Node 1, tools in hand.

"What's up?" I queried my Russian commander.

"I have task," he replied in understandable but grammatically incorrect English.

I thought nothing of it, expecting his usual perfect execution. But as he began to remove the very same stowage bags I had so carefully returned to their place two days earlier, my focus turned to his timeline. "Fyodor, what are you doing there?" I asked.

"Task behind panel here," he informed me.

"Show me," I ordered, flying to a station laptop displaying the daily timeline.

He showed me the task and its location. As always, he was correct. He needed to be behind the exact same panel I had opened just days ago, but the task he was to perform was totally different. I was making a premature assessment, but at that point my gut was beginning to boil as my frustration grew with the ground control team's poor attention to detail. Fyodor successfully navigated the stowage, and the panel and hardware behind it, and all returned to normal.

As the end of the workweek approached, I was once again staged in the airlock. I had nearly completed preparing the space suits for the STS-120 crew's upcoming walks when I glanced up to see Oleg performing the Russian version of a Superman impersonation as he flew through Node 1.

"What's up with you today, Oleg?" I offered.

"I have a task here in Node 1," he replied, with English as good as most Americans'.

"What is the task?" I inquired further.

"I will be working on the electrical patch panel, behind this wall here," he replied as he pointed to the now infamous panel covered with stowage bags hiding the fingerprints left previously by Fyodor and me.

Now I was pissed! Exhibiting a level of anal-retentiveness not part of my character on Earth, I fumed at the inefficiency infecting our timeline. Why didn't the ground have us do all three tasks the very first time we pulled down the stowage and removed the damned panel? What the hell were they thinking?

Frustration peaking, I grabbed the handheld microphone of the auxiliary terminal unit, hit the button for space-to-ground line 2, and keyed the microphone.

"Houston, Station on Space-to-Ground 2 for inefficiency," I called.

"Station, this is Houston. Go ahead on two," came the friendly callback of veteran astronaut, fighter pilot, retired air force colonel, and now CAPCOM Jim "Vegas" Kelly.

"Yeah, Vegas. Clay here. Just wanted to let you know that the three of us all did separate and distinct tasks this week in Node 1. Each task was behind the exact same panel. They all required removal and temporary stowage of the exact same set of bags; they all had us remove the same forty-four fasteners and then we had to put it all back in place. Three separate times. I just wanted to let the ground know that we did it, but we are not happy about it."

A pause in the conversation, lasting nearly thirty seconds, was broken as Vegas's voice came back on the line: "Clay, we copy and concur."

The line went silent as I floated weightlessly above the airlock floor, trying to calm the frustration that had undoubtedly raised my blood pressure. I had launched another turd, this time a weightless one, but it would have the exact same impact on its target.

The total number of weightless turds I launched from ISS escapes me, but no doubt it was substantial. Safely back on the ground after a sometimes combative five months, I was sentenced to what I would call the astronaut version of "community service," otherwise known as the astronaut penalty box.

The words used by the Astronaut Evaluation Board to describe my 152 days of service on board the ISS were, in part: "Although Clayton is thoughtful with his peers, he needs to improve his communication skills and attitude towards other teams with which he interfaces. . . . He tended to be a bit too casual with Mission Control, and sometimes too frank, and he could have been more patient during stressful times." They went on to say that "Clay will need to rebuild his relationship with Mission Control if he is to fly again." The recommendation for my flight status, as developed by my office peers, was listed as "conditionally eligible."

It's tough to admit, but on some of this they were right. While my intentions were always aimed at making things better for those who would follow me into space, I had not heeded the advice I'd been given and I let the frustration build to a point where it affected my work and my interactions with the ground.

Yet I wasn't totally at fault. The situation on ISS where we were all assigned work behind the same panel in the same week was ridiculous. As a crew support astronaut for the Expedition 4 crew, I participated in the weekly planning meetings where these types of situations were discussed. On numerous occasions I was the "elephant in the room" who complained when the technical team failed even then to grasp the concept of "proper planning prevents poor performance." To direct a crew to waste that amount of identical (and expensive) crew time on orbit was the highest form of government waste. It was inexcusable.

Even though my family and I had some legitimate grievances, I could have handled myself better. I did not follow the unspoken rule that no matter what, the ground is always right and they should be treated with kid gloves.

I took to heart the "community service" recommended by the Astronaut Evaluation Board "that Clay would benefit from leadership/followership and teamwork training," that "he be put in a leadership role, perhaps as a branch chief, to satisfy this development in part," and that "he consult with his Human Resources representative for additional development classes."

Still, it was tough getting dressed down like that.

To help repair the supposed damaged relationships, I would need to rely on the management within the Astronaut Office. Unfortunately, they continued to rely on my being a self-starter and didn't provide any guidance. While they did task me with the role of lead CAPCOM for the Expedition 18 crew (Mike Fincke, Greg Chamitoff, and Sandy Magnus), it was not really a true leadership or management position. I would have no employees to supervise and lead, no budget to manage. It would, however, provide me with an excellent opportunity to restore my image. Working as a cog in a solid technical mission machine would allow me to showcase my integration, communication, and people skills, along with my ability to truly be a team player. In addition, there would be ample exposure to key players and well-placed leaders who might one day help me return myself to good standing.

My efforts were totally sincere. I worked hard to be the best lead CAPCOM on the planet. No details were left undone. Communication was considered paramount. Assistance was offered at every turn. Like a Boy Scout helping a lady cross the street, I tried to be everything for everyone. I maintained my sense of humor, exhibiting it when appropriate and throttling it back when necessary. In short, I felt like I was performing exactly as I always performed—I was doing nothing differently than I had done in my previous twenty-five years with NASA.

When I got the opportunity to return to space as part of the STS-131 crew, it appeared my astronaut management team agreed with me. But old habits die hard.

It started with a simple and caring thought. Rick Mastracchio and I were just trying to help.

We had just found out that there would be an opportunity to see some of the hardware we would be working with during a spacewalk on the STS-131 mission. The hardware was being prepped at

Kennedy Space Center for its installation into the space shuttle *Discovery*'s payload bay. The next time we would be able to see it would be through the visor of a spacesuit helmet in the unforgiving vacuum of outer space.

Our crew secretary, Suzanne Singleton, was preparing our travel orders. As veteran astronauts, we preferred one of the sleek white-and-blue NASA T-38 jets and a pilot to fly us to the launch site. No hassle with the Transportation Security Administration, no one frisking us and grabbing our junk—just a quick jaunt at seven hundred miles an hour, then a rental car, and within twenty minutes we'd be looking at hardware. Since ghastly weather and/or lack of a pilot would leave us grounded, it was paramount that we have an alternate form of transportation, known in astronaut-speak as "backup commercial air."

Using Fed Traveler, a new agencywide travel booking system, Suzanne intended to book two round-trip seats on Southwest Airlines from Houston to Orlando and reserve a rental car for Rick and me. It should have been a simple matter. Yet, as with most government programs, though the *intent* of the Fed Traveler system was good, the *implementation* left something to be desired. In fact, I think our secretaries, if pumped full of sodium pentothal, would say that Fed Traveler sucked!

Rick and I are not known for our patience, tact, and diplomacy; we just look for the most efficient way to do things. While Suzanne was in the midst of her bureaucratic struggle, Rick and I decided to help speed up the process of securing our backup travel accommodations

We pounced on our government-issue laptops and with a few simple clicks found ourselves in a virtual world of hell and damnation, full of nonintuitive user-interface traps.

Our goal was as simple as Suzanne's: we wanted to secure seats on a jet from Houston to Orlando. We didn't care which airline. Navigating the website was not for the faint of heart. Nothing was straightforward or clear; dead ends and confusion reigned.

As I struggled to get somewhere, I kept running across a dialog box that wanted my PNR. As a NASA aerospace engineer and a steely-eyed astronaut raised on a steady diet of NASA acronyms for nearly thirty years, I thought I knew them all. But my cerebral cortex couldn't cough up the meaning of PNR.

Stated as a mathematical equation, the function of Fed Traveler difficulty to use was directly proportional to my temperature and inversely proportional to my patience! I searched every inch of their web page for some kind of clue. I tried "Frequently Asked Questions." I clicked on anything that moved.

It didn't come.

We dialed the special Fed Traveler phone number. We got elevator music. Five minutes into our serenade, the line went dead. We redialed that same phone number four more times, each time receiving the same result. Our patience (or at least *my* patience) was running out.

Finally, all other options exhausted, ignorantly thinking I had nothing to lose, I slid my mouse over to "Contact us." A single click and a blank email screen appeared, offering a catapult from which I could launch yet another enormously smelly (as it would turn out) turd, this time destined for the punchbowl of Fed Traveler.

The "To" line contained a readymade address, a cryptic conglomeration of letters and numbers that gives you no clue where your note is headed. I assumed whoever was on the other end was some schmo, perhaps a college student trying to earn a few bucks on the side.

With little thought, I typed quickly into the subject line: "What the F*** is a PNR???"

You would think I'd be smarter than that.

Beautiful, I thought. Short, clear, concise, and to the point, it went right to the heart of the matter with a tiny bit of flair thrown in. Cleverly, the subject line gave my sentiments just the right emphasis, clearly conveyed in my graphic representation of that classic vulgarity, "Fuck."

I leaped to the composition area, "To Whom It May Concern," and typed a description of our ongoing dilemma, thinking all the while just how professional I was being. The words flowed from my charged brain through my fingers to the keyboard: "Whoever invented Fed Traveler should be fired. It is the worst use of federal funding in the history of our government!"

Oh, baby, I was on a roll! I was so proud of myself that it took only seconds for me to review my classic composition, smile in reverent acknowledgment of a job well done, and hit the "enter" button, sending a thousand electrons flying through the wires of the Internet.

My turd was zeroing in on its punchbowl target at the speed of light. Where and upon whom it would splash were only moments from revelation. Impact was eminent.

On the heels of clicking "send," my mind began racing. Oh my God . . . what have I done? Can I call it back? No . . . it's too late now. I rationalized internally that it just went to some weird in-box address. No one will think anything of it, just an email from another satisfied customer.

In forty-eight hours I was swimming among the turds, treading water like my life depended on it. I was in deep shit!

What started as an ordinary day was changed in an instant by an office visit from an excited Suzanne. "We heard about your email," she gushed.

"Uh-oh," I thought. "This can't be good." If Suzanne had heard something, it had permeated through the entire astronaut support staff. Apparently this time I had gone and *really* done it; I had returned to the darkness of my criminal past. As I sat at my desk digesting the implications of Suzanne's words, I could only think that this could be really bad. So bad, in fact, that my wife and I would become concerned for our careers. It was obvious the word was out when our STS-131 mission commander, Alan "Dex" Poindexter, cornered me in the office and said, "You need to go to the principal's office, take your lumps, and forget about it."

Forgetting about it was going to be tough to do. I knew what was coming. The only question was when and how it would manifest.

This time it would not come from the deputy chief. It would come from the head of the Astronaut Office, four-time shuttle veteran Steve Lindsey.

The punishment phase for my second offense began at the Kennedy Space Center during the launch countdown for shuttle mission STS-127, the travel plans to which had started this whole episode. As well as reviewing hardware, Rick and I had volunteered to assist the JSC public affairs office by serving as interview subjects for the various media outlets that miraculously appear in droves for each shuttle mission.

Our travel plans to the Cape would be altered when the mission, with minimal pizzazz, gained increased media attention when the first launch attempt was scrubbed. A dangerous hydrogen leak had been observed during prelaunch tanking operations.

To accommodate the rising interest, more astronauts would be needed at the Cape to meet with the press, further enhancing our justification for being there. T-38 seats were immediately authorized for Rick and me to fly to Florida.

When technical problems postponed further launch attempts (it would be delayed five times, launching on its sixth attempt), Rick and I were unable to remain. We were placed in the unenviable position of having to find rides for the return to Houston. It was our responsibility to check the NASA flight manifest to determine whether there were any open T-38 back seats or, better still (because you can sleep!), slots with the bigwigs on the shuttle business jets.

Because we were not on the official mission manifest, we were not the highest priority of those who had to fly back. Every single seat was taken on the two NASA Gulfstream business jets; I was going to have to fly back in the back seat of Commander Steve Lindsey's T-38. I was not looking forward to the ride.

During our preflight preparations, Commander Lindsey made no mention of the email, but I was sure he was aware of it.

Our flight time on the first leg was an hour and a half. We were flying one of the T-38s outfitted with new avionics, the high-tech electronic flight instrumentation system (EFIS). I didn't have much experience using EFIS (I had just a few flights under my belt), but it turned out to be a blessing in disguise.

Feigning that I knew less about EFIS than was actually true, I encouraged Steve to fully brief me on the various nuances of the system for the entire flight.

There were no worries regarding any email to Fed Traveler.

As we landed at our first stop on the Gulf Coast not far from

Biloxi, Steve informed me I would be at the controls flying the final leg back into Ellington Field.

Apprehension leaped to the fore again. This could give him the perfect opportunity to dress me down. He would be free of most responsibilities while I piloted the jet; he could take me to task at thirty thousand feet.

Again my fears were unwarranted. Lindsey apparently decided he wasn't going to do much talking on the forty-minute zip into Ellington.

I focused hard on my flying duties. A neophyte with all the jet's new bells and whistles, I still wanted to fly well. I figured that if I could dazzle him with my flying prowess—staying on altitude and speed to within a few feet and a couple of knots, navigating concisely and with no errors, balancing fuel flow and the like—I might be able to impress Steve enough that he might forget all about that damned email.

Yet deep in my heart I knew it was a futile effort. We would have to have the conversation eventually. I could do it now and get it over with or just keep nursing the hopeless dream that it would all just go away. I opted for the former, taking my sweet time when we landed at Ellington, piddling at every opportunity, giving Steve every chance to bring it up.

I loitered near the parachute room for what seemed like an eternity.

Nothing.

I continued to drag my feet heading to the locker room. It took me more time to change out of my flight suit than it takes Susan to do her hair. Still nothing. I sat on the bench in front of my locker, making noises to signal I was still there. I stayed for as long as I could stand it. Finally, I couldn't take it anymore. I decided the time was now. But I was too late; he was already gone, heading home for the weekend with his family.

I would hear absolutely nothing from him until the following week.

I arrived at work on Monday to find an email sitting in my inbox. A meeting had been scheduled between me and Steve Lindsey. I buoyed myself for the confrontation, knowing full well I was in the soup. Having punched the "send" button that fateful day, I was pretty much caught red-handed. I could do nothing but plead my case and await my sentence.

The meeting was short and to the point. He began by praising my work in the T-38 jet the previous weekend, elaborating on how sharp and smart I was and how quickly I grasped the intricacies of the EFIS. Then came the *but*.

It was time to be dressed down.

He explained that my behavior was unacceptable and how pretty much the entire JSC senior staff was pissed off about my email. Several people said that he should remove me from the STS-131 crew. He then let me know how he stood up for me, how he had decided I would remain on the crew, with one condition.

Yeah, there's always a condition.

I was to call each and every person who was offended by what I did; I was to apologize to them and profess my wrongdoing.

The hell with that, I told him. I said that if he told me who each and every one of those people were, I would personally set up a one-on-one meeting with them and apologize to them in person!

Those names never came. Though he promised they would show up in my email in-box, the names never came. Hmm. Was *he* the only person who was truly pissed off at all? Was *he* the one who wanted me removed from the flight but couldn't justify it within his own soul?

While I will never know the answers, I do know that a couple of weeks later, when I ran into Natalie Saiz—the head of human resources at JSC and one of those who was supposedly upset—I said, "I heard some of you on senior staff were upset about my Fed Traveler email."

"Oh no," she replied. "Nobody cared at all."

A letter would be placed in my astronaut file. Authored by Commander Lindsey and fully documenting the email incident, it would remain there until June 2011, assuming there were no further incidents. When June 2011 arrived, I asked for it to be removed. Lindsey, no longer the head of the astronauts but preparing for his final shuttle flight, agreed.

The summation of my criminal endeavors would ultimately end my astronaut flying career. Allowed to fly with the crew of STS-131, I would be called into the office of the chief astronaut again in November 2010. This time the person seated behind the mahogany desk would be Peggy Whitson, my former crewmate and NEEMO 5 and Expedition 16 station increment commander.

As I seated myself in one of the chairs at her circular conference table, she initiated the conversation with a simple question. She asked my intentions regarding my future within the office. I replied that with the current ages of my children, I was not yet ready to reenter the flight line (take a flight assignment to ISS). She responded with a proposal for making me a management astronaut. I would no longer be considered active. It would mean the loss of T-38 privileges; I would no longer receive health-care benefits from the onsite flight medicine clinic—for myself or my family—and no more formal Russian language or robotic arm training. I could work shifts in Mission Control as CAPCOM; I could serve as a crewmember in simulations for the control center team. I would be expected to provide meeting support, participate in a spacewalk runs in the Neutral Buoyancy Lab, and—oh yes, provide meeting support.

Giving her an emphatic response of "No, being a management astronaut sucks," I asked, "What are my flight opportunities?"

"There are not many," she said, nervously twisting the end of the scarf she wore around her neck. Noticeably uncomfortable, she pulled out the hard copy of her crew assignment template so we could review the potential flight openings. After a few seconds, she began to stumble and stutter as she tried to come up with the proper words.

"Does the office want me to fly again?" I asked.

Her reply, while not unexpected, stabbed me to my heart. "Honestly?" she said. "I have much better choices to fly in space than you."

I sat there dumbfounded, as if I had just been told that I had terminal cancer.

"You don't have the temperament for long-duration spaceflight," she added.

Having no idea how to respond, I just sat there. It seemed as if time had stopped. Finally, in an effort to minimize the sting of her words, I tried for lightness, asking, "Do you like your job?" She replied that most of the time she did but not when she had to have meetings like the one we were having.

Fighting back tears, I stood and moved toward the door. Turning to address her one final time, I said quietly, "I'm sorry I let you and the office down."

Punishment received.

15

The "Void" of Outer Space

I was gently floating in the U.S. lab module, my feet firmly anchored to the clever but overdesigned foot restraint device most typically used by astronauts when operating the Canadian-built robotic manipulator known as CanadaArm2.

Positioned on the lab module's starboard side adjacent to my sleep station, I was working at my laptop computer catching up on overdue emails when my jovial, strapping crewmate, Russian cosmonaut Oleg Kotov, sailed through the center of the connection module known as Unity (Node 1).

He was not exhibiting his usual brilliant smile (often mistaken by me for a smart-ass grin). I acknowledged him as he continued his Superman-like flight to the sixty-foot-long laboratory's center. In a move worthy of Spiderman, he snatched a handrail and with a turn of his formidable wrist dropped gently onto the deck, aft of the single American segment window that gazed on the Earth.

The look on his face did not necessarily indicate concern, so I felt certain this was not a big deal. All was still well on the ISS.

Then he muttered in his native Russian the words a space station astronaut never wants to hear:

"Clay, АСУ не работа" (*ah-SOO nyeh rah-BO-ta-yet*).

It took a second for my weak Russian language skills to kick in. He said, "The toilet doesn't work."

"Clay, не есть (*nyeh YEST*)," he followed. ("Stop eating!")

Now, I don't know about you, but anytime someone tells me the toilet is broken and to stop eating, the situation is very grave.

It suddenly occurred to me, floating there staring at Oleg in disbelief, my mind churning, that I had just eaten a *very* satisfactory lunch.

For me and Russian food, this spells regularity.

I had only a few short hours. Oleg tried to explain to me the technical details as to why the toilet would not work. It had to do with a sensor inside the system that measures the amount of chemical pretreat disinfectant (akin to Tidy Bowl) that mixes with water to form the liquid that disinfects the urine prior to pumping it into the holding tank.

I didn't care why it happened; I just needed it fixed—and fast!

When we realized it was Friday afternoon, the seriousness of the situation began to look dire indeed. The Russians in the control center in northeast Moscow near Korolev leave promptly at five o'clock on Fridays. It was uncertain as to when and if they would be able to diagnose the problem and tell us the corrective procedures. My day—hell, my weekend—might be totally ruined if we couldn't use the crapper. For a person with regular bowels, this was causing panic to set in.

As it turned out, the ISS ACY was nonoperational for a period of over sixteen hours. When I simply couldn't hold it any longer, I had to use the toilet in the Soyuz docked to the ISS. Thus I am a proud pooper in four separate spacecraft: space shuttles *Atlantis* and *Discovery*, the International Space Station, and Soyuz TMA-10. I believe this may be some sort of record, but so far NASA has failed to exhibit a willingness to confirm this dubious distinction.

One of *the* most frequently asked questions I get during my travels comes from both adults and children. They raise their hands, some literally leaping from their chairs, waiting to hear me say, "Go ahead."

Sheepishly, and usually with a sly grin, they ask, "How do you go to the bathroom in space?" The room then erupts with giggles, and eventually the squirming and snickering quiets down to a lesser buzz.

"We go to the bathroom in space the exact same way you do on Earth. It's just that we need . . . (I pause here for effect) . . . a vacuum cleaner," I tell them.

The room erupts a second time with laughter and giggles from young and old alike. Grinning children provide the standard cat-calls of "Yuck!" "Ewww!" and "Gross!"

In space, the basic waste-depleting functions of the miracle we call the human body are exactly the same as on Earth. The biggest difference is how your body signals your brain that it's time to go, and the way you collect and dispose of the nasty byproducts.

In the Russian-designed and -built toilet of the ISS, called the ACY (ah-SOO), urination ("tee-tee" during my speeches) uses a long collection tube with a plastic yellow funnel and cap attached to its business end. (The Russian word for hose is schlongk—no kidding.)

A suction device resides in the bowels (ha-ha) of the hardware system under the floor at the aft end of the Russian service module. This fan provides the pull that moves the urine into and down the tube to subsequent system components. There it is mixed with the liquid pretreat disinfectant and collected in a metal can containing small blocks of a absorbent material that functions like kitty litter.

While simple in concept, it works quite well. Once a can is full it is swapped with an empty tank and the full one goes into temporary stowage near whatever Progress cargo vehicle is going to eventually transport it away.

The process of having to change the urine tank is referred to by American crewmembers as "Winning the Red Light Lottery."

Your body signals to you it is time. You must perform a personal wastewater dump. You drop everything you are doing (actually, you just let it float or you tack it down with duct tape or Velcro) and fly at warp speed toward the haven of relief known as ACY.

Your brief flight time is spent praying that when you arrive at said destination it will be available and not exhibiting the feared "occupied" signal of a tightly closed door.

Slamming on the brakes by grabbing a handrail alongside the doorjamb of the potty, you lift your knees to your chest and shift your center of gravity to a higher position. Perfectly timed after weeks on the station, the result is a graceful acrobatic turn and a final slide down into the narrow confines of the toilet compartment.

Putting your back to the crapper, with legs fully reextended, a quick push against the starboard wall produces a pirouette of

180 degrees. The front of your pants directly facing "ground zero," you are nearly ready.

With the smoothness of a seasoned zero-g veteran, you slide your sweat-sock-covered toes beneath the positioning rail on the service module compartment's floor.

Directly in front of the waste can, speed now of the essence, you unzip your trousers. Critical appendages fully deployed, stable position assured, you reach for the hose and remove the yellow plastic funnel's tethered cap.

You prepare to flip the "stop-cock" (fan activation) lever located just below the funnel to the ON position. Ready to execute this simple task, honed during countless training repetitions, your focus shifts momentarily from the task at hand (or in your hand) to the toilet's control panel lights to ensure all LEDs reflect the emerald green hue of "all systems go."

A lone red LED blazes brightly its message of negativity like a neon sign in Times Square. Forced to squint to be able to read the tiny text etched (in both Russian and English) beneath the miniature glass diode, the message is clear: "Waste tank is full."

You do NOT move the stop-cock lever to the ON position because the waste tank is full. Congratulations, you have won the RED LIGHT LOTTERY!

Trying not to think of the roar of Niagara Falls, you must now swap out the wastewater tank.

First, you "safe" the system by flipping a couple of the ACY panel's switches. This allows you to continue the maintenance task by lifting a bulky floor panel just outside the toilet compartment to gain the access needed to remove a tank chock full of urine and replace it with a new, empty one.

If only the execution of all bodily functions was that simple.

In performing "number two"—pooping, defecation, crapping, sending the Browns to the Super Bowl—the aforementioned scenario may *still* be applicable. However, astronauts learn early on in their spacefaring careers whether they are "simo" (for simultaneous) or "serial" performers in the toilet. Serial is best (in my humble opinion) as it gives you the opportunity to concentrate on one thing at a time, eliminating the need for multitasking.

Assume that we are serial performers and our personal pre-mission process analysis has shown that we urinate first. Following the successful conclusion of our efforts to "tee-tee" (and there were no lottery winners), we may proceed to the more "concrete" activity of pooping.

It is *extremely* critical for everyone to have accurate aim. Imagine yourself on a camping trip, ready to perform this critical bodily function, but your target is a hole about the size of the opening on a jar of spaghetti sauce. Further imagine that when you do poop, it won't fall to the ground. It won't fall at all. Gravity is essentially absent and there is no "separation factor."

Without gravitational pull the process of executing number two relies on near-perfect body position and flawless technique.

My preference (learned only after a few bouts of trial and error) was to totally remove my lower body clothing and stuff it behind the handrail opposite the "throne." That made it easier to position my cheeks to maximize the possibility of success.

The ACY toilet is very much like those used for camping: an empty can with a hole in the top. A small plastic bag with tiny holes in the bottom is inserted into the hole and attached to the rim of the can with an enclosed rubber band. Holding the urine hose and funnel, then turning the stop-cock lever to the ON position, gives not only suction for urine but also a small tug that fully extends the plastic bag (by virtue of those small holes).

An additional benefit of the fan is it sucks the nasty odors into the system where they are effectively absorbed by filters.

If our aim is successful and our diet is sound, a long, smooth, brown "cobra" will snake its way into the very bottom of the bag.

The fan's pull in the toilet is less than that of the urine hose (and much less than in the space shuttle's toilet), making it highly unlikely the "snake" can break free on its own. Separation factor is key. By donning a rubber glove and executing a scissoring motion with your index and middle finger, you slice through the offending feces and gently push it down where it's supposed to go.

Some astronauts have reported (bragged about, actually) the innate ability to execute a floater. This is done by hovering slightly above the can and using their internal musculature to impart a small separation velocity to the turd. In a classic illustration of Newton's second law, the pooper gently floats toward the ceiling while the snake breaks free to move slightly lower into the plastic bag.

Not an advocate of floating, I feared even one attempt with this unreliable technique could lead to a nasty mess I would be required to clean up!

I did investigate alternative techniques to the "scissor," hoping to create ways to not have to venture too close to the *E. coli*–rich substance.

The first I termed the "wiggle." While hovering only slightly above the can (thereby disqualifying me from claiming a true floater), in a move akin to a Miley Cyrus twerk, I wiggled my cheeks while giving an extra push from my abdominals. If I performed the wiggle in rapid succession, I was sometimes able to break the snake free.

A second technique was a slight variation on the floater. This involved maintaining a tight cheek seal on the can while pushing hard with my abs. Then, exit force at its maximum, a quick upward thrust pushed my body a few inches above the can. At that point vertical movement must be abruptly stopped and the head is craned downward to visually verify a successful separation. If the stars were aligned, given the greater distance between buttocks and can, I could see "air" between my waste contribution and my rear end.

The job is not yet finished. Any protrusion of poop must be forced into the bag fully beneath the level of the rubber band. On really tough days that meant having to fold down the Play-Doh-like tormentor that was poised like a striking cobra at the top of the can.

Cleanup operations are as on Earth. Personally, I did not use normal toilet paper, as Huggies wet wipes and Russian gauze pads sufficed nicely.

The next step was disposal of the rubber glove, pulling carefully from the wrist to turn it inside-out, keeping everything of importance squeaky clean.

The final act was pulling the rubber band free of the waste can's rim and giving the now-sealed bag one last push into the can. Logically, the more bags in the can, the more difficult it was to push the bag in. When a waste can was nearly full, it was time for extra caution to ensure no disasters occurred. With no running water on board, a second Huggie, followed by a disinfectant wipe, was the main way to defeat uncleanliness in the "post-op" phase.

Replacement of the used bag with a fresh one for the next "operator" was a great way to score points with your crew. Not to say this ever happened, but imagine your newly arrived female commander streaking from the toilet, cussing like a sailor and wanting to know "Who in the hell forgot to replace the damn bag?"

16

The Doctor Is In

The Mission Control Center team is made up of talented and dedicated individuals. Led by the flight director—an individual of uncanny intelligence who is much smarter than the average astronaut from Nebraska—the team consistently functions at a high level. In fact, many flight directors have submitted applications to become astronauts. Perhaps it is to NASA's advantage that those who achieved the level of flight director did not get selected to fly in space. If they had, it would have been a tremendous loss to the Mission Control teams.

Known within the hallowed halls of Mission Control simply as Flight, they know more details about every ISS system than perhaps the system experts know themselves. They are in charge, and in total control, of the team on the ground.

On all issues that arise, Flight makes the final decision, which is based on inputs from their local team of experts, and in this modern era of spaceflight, from teams around the world. After they analyze all available data, more often than not their decisions are spot-on. Yet every once in a while, as governed by the laws of statistics, they will not choose wisely.

I believe that is when they reveal their character. Are they willing to listen further, gather more data, and perhaps alter their decision, or do they remain steadfast, confident they are ready to move forward regardless of the situation? Responsible for the safety of both the crew and vehicle, true leaders know when to take risks.

Pressure, stress, and uncertainty come with the territory.

I experienced them, too.

Being willing to listen and then readjust is a key characteristic of a successful long-duration space flier. It is a lesson I sometimes struggled to grasp. I was often impatient, expecting things to change right away. But the space program is an aircraft carrier. To turn her requires more than the push from a mere tugboat like me.

But I had help on the ground. Some of the most important members of my Expedition 15 support team were doctors. The medical team, comprised of both flight surgeons and psychiatrists, worked diligently to keep me healthy on board—physically *and* mentally.

My flight surgeons were Dr. Cedric "Ric" Senter and his backup, Dr. Joe Dervay. The psychology team was led by Dr. Gary Beven and his able-bodied substitutes, Drs. Frank Carpenter and Walt Sipes. Further support came from child psychiatrist Dr. John Marcellus, who had spent time working with Cole after the *Columbia* disaster.

Medically I was solid. A certified gym rat, I spent ample time in the astronaut workout facility. I lifted weights, performed aerobic exercise, anything to give me an edge heading into my long-duration flight.

Preflight medical preparations called for a multitude of specialized tests designed to find anything that might prevent me from honoring my flying commitment. Single percentage points in the wrong direction from the norm could keep me from living my dream.

With an unenviable family health history, my flight docs focused on two specific areas of concern: my heart and my rear end. With heart attacks, strokes, and cancerous polyps in my family's past, key tests were needed. Full-body MRIs determined the level of potential blockage around my heart and arteries. Stress tests calculated my heart's ability to drive highly oxygenated blood throughout my body. And then, as the childhood space joke goes, the flight docs said, "We also need to check Uranus."

Before being considered for official assignment to a space station flight, you must be certified for flight by the Aerospace Medicine Board. A U.S. entity much like the selection committee that picked you in the first place, this board requires appropriate data be gathered and evaluated in order to understand your capabilities and, more important, your limitations. To that end, NASA puts you through a battery of tests, most of them physical in nature but some of them mental.

Eventually, your data is presented to the Multilateral Space Medicine Board. An international alliance, this board carries the power to deny you a trip to space if your medical situation is at all questionable. Typically, any issues you do have are dealt with and have a plan for resolution, leading (you hope) to nonconfrontational acceptance from the international community.

Space fliers with health problems can be limited in performance capability and thus be costly to the U.S. government. Consider for example a potential astronaut with a history of kidney stones. This is not a malady an astronaut wants to suffer during a six-month stay aboard the International Space Station. While the excruciating pain of a kidney stone incapacitates the sufferer, the fact that it will likely cause some crewmembers' abrupt and immediate departure from the orbiting platform is by far the larger consequence from NASA's point of view.

Additional screenings are necessary for potentially cancerous polyps in the colon and intestines—another situation NASA tries to avoid. Hence you are obligated to participate in the proctosigmoidoscopy, or "procto," exam. I like to call it the original Silver Snoopy. (The real Silver Snoopy, awarded to NASA and contract employees for outstanding achievements, depicts the famous cartoon character Snoopy created by Charles M. Schulz. Because it represents the astronauts' own recognition of excellence, the Silver Snoopy is awarded by the astronauts themselves.)

Far from any type of award, my version of the Silver Snoopy is more of a curse—a curse for those wishing to orbit the Earth.

I remember fondly that eventful day in the spring of 1996 when the schedule for my initial interview week (year thirteen of my infamous fifteen annual attempts) called for me to drop by Building 8 and the JSC Space Flight Medicine Clinic.

As always, I was appropriately greeted by their highly professional staff, then led to a small preparation room. I was handed two green-and-white cartons, each containing a bottle with a smooth insertion nozzle, a kit for the self-infliction of an enema. Apparently a little preflushing was required before a steely-cold video camera would be sent to a place where no camera had been before.

"What do I do with this?" was my first question to the nurse. "I am still a virgin when it comes to enemas." She chuckled only briefly, letting me know I had given her a line she had heard a million times.

Her clever reply included instructions to strip down, lie on the bed on my side, and insert the nozzle of the bottle inside that area typically occupied (according to some, anyway) by my thumb. I sensed her empathy for amateur comedians like me when she said, "The pointy end goes in first."

"Squeeze vigorously," she said, "and squirt away until the bottle is completely emptied." "After that," she continued, it would be up to me to "squeeze those cheeks together and fight like crazy to not give in to the urge to 'fire away.' Hold it in for at least fifteen minutes" was her final piece of unsolicited advice.

Piece of cake, I thought. My naiveté was soon replaced with actual experience. I felt I was holding back the Niagara River just above the falls.

After what seemed like an eternity but was probably only five to ten minutes in "mission elapsed time," I could stand it no more. I leaped from the fetal position I had so confidently assumed on my cardboard bed, threw down my boxer shorts, and deposited my hiney on the smooth black toilet seat with speed that rivaled electrons flowing through copper wire.

Out it came, as if the Hoover Dam itself had opened every single one of its flow-release gates, gushing with the full force of Obi Wan's light saber, in a laminar flow only an aerospace engineer could love.

The force of entry from my intestinal deposits into the commode's pool of now-polluted water was vigorous to say the least. Droplets of water splashed upward, adhering to the pink flesh of my backside as if I were enjoying a French bidet. A sense of calm began to envelope the lower half of my body. Feeling much better if not a bit overconfident, I was thinking, one down and one to go!

Round two proved to be even more difficult. Knowing the

expected outcome, it was a near life-and-death struggle to pinch my cheeks together tightly enough to hold back the raging torrent. Redirecting my focus, I bit (ever so lightly) my right forearm, hoping to stave off the inevitable for a few more precious seconds to allow the chemicals to do their job. As sure as the humidity rises in Houston, and in a manner nearly identical to my first release, I lost the battle against a chemically enhanced Mother Nature.

Hoping against hope that I had done enough, I threw on my hospital gown, then trudged into the exam room. There I was greeted by Nurse Mona and Dr. Walt Hein (no kidding).

Dr. Hein must have been pushing seventy, tall and lean with slightly hunched shoulders and a set of gray whiskers that followed his jawline in a clean half-inch strip. Nurse Mona could have been one of those classic character actresses from a World War II movie—full bosomed and clad in white with the demeanor of a drill sergeant. They were quite the team for heading up an expedition through my colon.

Dr. Hein began to speak first, Nurse Mona by his side. I really don't remember much of what he said or did until he calmly reached above my head, just past the video monitor, and removed an eight-by-ten framed picture from the wall.

The color picture, faded from years of fluorescent light exposure, was a graphic representation of the human intestines both large and small. With his long, thin index finger, Dr. Hein proceeded to show me that "we" would be going from "here" (a point near the exit of my derriere) to "here" (a point that appeared to be somewhere in the neighborhood of my left shoulder).

I performed a mental analysis of his statement. Using Dr. Hein's graphic as a guide, my mind computed a distance corresponding to that between Cairo, Egypt, and the headwaters of the Nile. It was not a pleasant proposition.

I was going to be there awhile. Dr. Hein slowly donned his pale yellow plastic coveralls, ready to ward off anything not eliminated during my virginal enemas. As he paused to don his rubber gloves, making sure to snap each of them at the wrist, I imagined I was feeling the way someone facing a firing squad must feel.

I tried to relax, per the advice of ever-vigilant Nurse Mona, by gazing at the video monitor and telling myself how cool this is and that I really did want to be an astronaut. The monitor's views did nothing but make me feel like I was performing the lead role in a remake of the Dennis Quaid movie *Inner Space.*

Dr. Hein in a monotonous voice continued to remind me that it was okay to "pass gas." (As if I needed any encouragement. Gas was expelling from my backside at a rate akin to that of a pot of boiling oatmeal.) My comfort factor continued to decrease at an astronomical rate as the "Silver Snoopy" plowed its headlight and video camera deeper into the flexible tubing of my bowels.

Even concentrating on the video didn't help. Seeing a squeaky clean tunnel of pink corrugated tubing eventually got boring. My insides became so uncomfortable that my mind couldn't focus on anything other than the metal intruder invading my innards.

When Dr. Hein finally said we had "gone far enough," I wanted to kiss him. While I'm not sure if the probe reached its physical limit, I had most certainly reached mine.

The exit of the video probe was quicker than its entrance, but its outbound path of travel still felt as if someone was pulling out my insides. I was certain I heard a loud "pop" when the business end of the probe saw daylight for the first time in over twenty minutes.

The cruelest part of the entire exercise was that it was only the preliminary event. Once I had become a full-fledged astronaut, the tests became even more detailed. Given my family history on my father's side, the flight docs were hell-bent on sending me off for graduate training in the intestinal field. You guessed it: the dreaded colonoscopy.

I was cursed. And I was damned glad.

They tried to prepare me on the ground. They gave me briefings about long-duration spaceflight, including a two-inch-thick notebook entitled *Practical Planning for Long-Duration Missions.* For my personal readiness, they gave me checklists on finances, insurance, and legal matters. They provided suggestions for disaster readiness. They offered helpful tips on separation, reunion, and stress management. "They" were my Behavioral Health and Performance Group and the Astronaut's Family Support Office.

For a first-time flier, my fears and concerns were very real. Words like depression, loneliness, isolation, separation, and death—words that rarely entered my consciousness before I became an astronaut—appeared there now. The unknown loomed large in front of me, and my ability to deal with it by myself was iffy. It was possible (yet highly unlikely) I wouldn't survive. And I could only imagine the fears of my family.

I received individual coaching from my psych team. I recall a specific preflight briefing provided by Dr. Sipes that hinted what was to come. I'm paraphrasing but he basically told me, "You're on your own. Don't expect much help from anyone."

Comforting words to be sure. He would later tell Susan in her advance private briefing that she needed "to grow thicker skin." We were in for some fun.

Before our mission, the Russians gave us their version of psychological training.

As part of our winter survival syllabus, the Russian psychologists provided me with a set of ten colored cards. The only instructions were that we were to "put the cards in order." What kind of order was not specified. Upon completion, the instructor evaluated the order we chose as he made a series of thoughtful sounds. Apparently it had something to do with reflecting our mood and attitude. Beware those who had black or brown on the top of their deck. They would be watched carefully. Weird.

They also asked us to perform a reaction drill using a stopwatch. Without looking at the face of the stopwatch, we were to estimate various time intervals (five seconds, thirty seconds, one minute) by starting the watch, counting internally (or however we chose to do it), then stopping the watch at the prescribed interval. Before I started my training, I was able to do the task accurately, estimating the time increments nearly perfectly.

However, after spending two and a half days in the Russian wilderness without sleep, I was asked to perform the same test. I found this comical. The longer the interval they asked me to time, the faster I fell asleep holding the stopwatch. That had a lot to say about my mental state, like, maybe I was tired.

Teamwork exercises were also important to our Russian colleagues. In one instance I was asked to stand on the top of a rick-ety table facing away from my crewmates. With eyes closed and my hands folded across my chest, I was instructed to fall off the table backward. Trusting that my crewmates would be there for me, I took the leap of faith. Weighing two hundred pounds, I was a hefty load to catch. My trust in my crewmates was rewarded with the absence of the sound of my skull hitting the floor.

We also did a classic team-building exercise using two long pieces of wood. With each of us standing on the planks in single-file "parade" formation, our feet loosely affixed to each board, we were required to move a given distance together under various restrictions such as no talking. A bit old-fashioned and not diffi-cult to complete, this exercise must have proven us to be a good team, because we were only asked to do it once.

Dr. Beven and his associates also administered several tests for challenging and assessing the mental well-being of astronauts.

An expensive endeavor like the space station aims to provide a big bang for the buck. The human performance of astronauts is key. We are expected to work hard during our time in space, max-imizing the return on the taxpayer's dollar. In order to do that, folks on the ground monitor our sleep, psychological adaptation, how we interface with the station's systems, and our behavioral and cognitive health.

Both preflight and on board we participated in an experiment called WinsCAT (Spaceflight Cognitive Assessment Tool for Win-dows). I took the test six times before I flew and then every thirty days in orbit, with one final test after thirty days back on the ground.

The tests originated in 1996 after the disastrous fire on Rus-sia's Mir space station. The psychologists and medical folks real-ized that in situations like that fire, they had no way to judge how memory, concentration, focus, and other cognitive abilities were affected during long-duration missions. They needed to have a way to quantify a crew's workload (too much or too little), their response to emergencies (fire, depressurization, and toxic spills), and their levels of depression.

Experts on the ground, using existing assessment tools, compiled a suite of cognitive tests. Designed to look at how we think, reason, and remember during our time in space, these simple tools were computer-based, took less than fifteen minutes to perform, and provided us with immediate feedback on our mental state.

The tests could also be used to assess a crewmember's medical condition. For example, in the event of a head injury or after exposure to a toxic gas or an adverse reaction to medication, test results could tell doctors on the ground if further treatment was required.

They were also touted as effective measures of a crew's readiness. Whether in preparation for performing a high-risk activity (such as spacewalking or docking) or during periods of heavy workload or less-than-optimal sleep, the tool could help show if we were at less than peak performance.

Many astronauts considered the tests frivolous. I was a fence-sitter. I considered the tests credible, but having never lived off the planet, I wasn't sure how well they could measure my mental state.

After six reps on the ground to baseline my performance envelope (and to make sure I wasn't cheating), I took my first test in flight. The tests were varied and short, and actually kind of fun.

For me, the hardest was called code substitution.

Nine unique symbols were individually matched with the numbers one through nine. In the first test you had a short time to memorize the pairs. All nine number-symbol pairs appeared on the screen. You had to remember the code, that is, which symbol went with which number. Then, as the pairs popped onto the screen at random, you had to decide whether it was correct per the code. The symbols ranged from the Greek letter omega, to the yen sign, to a checkmark, to a left-facing triangle. To make it even more difficult, after the initial presentation of the memorization screen, you took two totally different tests prior to returning to this one. No fair!

The test for continuous processing, or "running memory," could be challenging, too. Faced with a changing single-digit number projected on the screen every second or so, you had to decide if the current number was different or the same as the number previously presented. If I wasn't careful, or if I was the least bit tired,

I could be lulled into a coma, totally forgetting the previous number. It took concentration to score well on this one.

The mathematics test was pretty simple. Equations were presented and you had to calculate the result. For example, the equation of $4 + 7 - 3 + 2 = ?$ has the answer of 10. But during the test the proper response was to hit the key for an answer greater than five or less than five.

My favorite test was called "Match to Sample," a test of pattern recognition. It reminded me of playing *Tetris* on the computer. A square divided into sixteenths appeared on the screen. Two different colors were used to create a distinct pattern within the sixteen squares. After a couple of seconds, two sets of sixteen appeared. My job was to decide which of the second patterns matched the first. I tried to note if the patterns of squares were similar to a number or letter. I would also mentally recite phrases like "three top right, one bottom left" to help me recall the patterns.

While this battery of tests may have provided the ground-based team with what they would consider a scientifically accurate indicator of mental health, they did nothing to help me with frustration.

My personal experience with aggravation may not even come close to those of other long-duration astronauts. As my time in space grew, so did my buildup of stress and feelings of "You want me to do what? Really? Are you kidding me?"

For example, we have all heard the joke "How many (fill in the blank) does it take to change a light bulb?" Consider that aboard the station, a light is called a General Luminaire Assembly. It is made up of the socket, called the Baseplate Ballast Assembly, and the bulb, technically known as the Lamp Housing Assembly. In order to change that light bulb, procedures require you to wear safety glasses and have a vacuum cleaner handy—just in case the bulb breaks. Yet the actual bulb is encased in a plastic enclosure, so even if the glass bulb did break, the pieces of glass would be completely contained. Once it is replaced, you are required to take a photo of the newly installed bulb before turning it on. I often teased the ground and training teams that we should give it the name of Long Incandescent Glowing Hot Thing, or LIGHT. Ah, the comic opportunities provided by the U.S. government.

While I was in orbit, situations seemed to happen to me at random. When taken singly they were not difficult to overcome. It was when incidents began to pile up on each other, or become impacted by little irritations, that my limits were pushed.

These situations were harder to tackle miles above and months away from home. It took the help of folks like Dr. Beven and my family support lead, Brooke Loofboro—and some cleverness on my part—to turn frustration into pleasure.

Floating in the U.S. laboratory module Destiny, I was working hard to replace some plant and worm experiment samples (yes, that's right—worms) on a payload called the Commercial Generic Bioprocessing Assembly (CGBA). It was a simple task, but I was running into trouble during verbal exchanges with the ground. Unable to locate specific pieces of equipment, I sensed my frustration level rising. Consulting the stowage note the ground provided (which told me where things *should* be) and having searched everywhere, I turned to the control center team to see if they had any other potential solutions.

I was asked, "Did you check the stowage note?" My temperature quickly increased and I fought the urge to bark at them, "Of course I checked the stowage note! Do you think I'm an idiot?" But instead of making an inappropriate comment, I held back. This time I sought alternative ways to change my attitude.

The idea came to me quickly. I flew into my sleep station and grabbed a pair of my clean white boxer shorts. Checking my Omega Speedmaster wristwatch, I noted that in Houston it was approaching ten o'clock in the morning.

Although it was early in the day in Houston, ten o'clock was nearing the end of my workday in space. It was also the time when the NASA television channel began to show live audiovisual images from the ISS. Less than five minutes from being live on TV, I hatched my plan.

Floating from my bunk back out into the lab, I concealed my boxers from the video camera mounted on the forward end of the module. As I passed my computer screen I checked the small window in the upper left, a graphic representing part of the communication system for the entire station.

This window let us know at a glance whether we could talk to the control team or whether the ground could see us through the station's video system. In the symbolism of colored lightning bolts, green meant good signals. Anything else meant a short wait for satellites to realign.

As I expected, there were no green lightning bolts, signifying no audio or video capability. The green "squigglies" would appear precisely at ten.

I flew beneath the lab's forward video camera. Noting the time to live video at less than thirty seconds, I donned the boxer shorts— but not in the conventional sense. This time, they went on my head! Microgravity was my ally, allowing the white underwear to puff out above my head so that I looked much like a professional chef.

Experiment samples in each hand, I anticipated the countdown to my live appearance.

With five seconds to go, I repositioned myself with my back toward the lab's aft end. This would allow me to float straight up, looking directly into the camera. I was ready. I slowly rose to fill the camera's lens.

Waving and grinning mightily, I flashed my pearly whites to all the folks back on the ground and mouthed the words "Hello, Houston!"

Oleg, flying into the back end of the lab from somewhere in the Russian segment, began laughing uncontrollably, simultaneously grabbing a camera from the wall. Similar to an ESPN sports photographer, he rapidly snapped away, capturing multiple images. Chronicled for all eternity, Clayton Anderson, United States Astronaut, floating in space with boxer shorts on his head!

Later, after landing I would learn that my escapade did not have the expected result in Mission Control. Flight director Kwatsi Alibaruho, the first African American to hold this position, was leading the team that morning.

As my image was captured by the camera in space, it also appeared on the massive control center TV screens on the ground.

"P-A-O, Flight," Alibaruho called the on-console officer for public affairs.

"Flight, P-A-O," came the expected reply.

"What the hell is he doing?" queried the MIT graduate-turned-leader of Mission Control.

For seconds, silence filled the airwaves, until Alibaruho ordered, as only a flight director can, "Cut the feed, NOW!"

Thousands of viewers (or maybe only hundreds, if you've actually seen NASA TV) were greeted with the classic multicolored vertical bars on their television screens as the public affairs officer cut the signal.

That's the kind of stuff Dr. Beven had to deal with.

As it happened, I wasn't the only one dealing with psychological issues during the summer of 2007.

With some fellow astronauts making "poor choices," rumors were flying fast and furious around the space program.

Lisa Nowak, involved in a love triangle with my astronaut classmate, former test pilot and naval officer Billy Oefelein, had taken her now-famous diaper-clad journey to Florida a few weeks prior to our launch. In this episode, an embarrassment to the entire corps, Lisa was arrested after accosting Billy's girlfriend in a parking lot at the Orlando airport. Furthermore, someone had leaked information stating that astronauts had been drunk or hungover at the pad on launch days. An official government investigation was launched and a report written, NASA's Astronaut Health Care System Review chronicling the incidents and pushing NASA to defend its Astronaut Corps.

Living off the planet, I got word of these crazy events in a surprising conference call with Steve Lindsey, the head of the Astronaut Office.

I received word from the ground that I had a call on space-to-ground 3. Those were code words for "someone wants to speak to you privately."

Steve was cordial but his first words went directly to the recently released report. He outlined its contents and the efforts the space center had taken to "circle the wagons." Asserting nothing off-color had actually transpired, he tried to assure me all would be well.

I was familiar with the diaper caper; it had been splashed all over the news while I was still training. The drunk astronaut story was news to me. My first response was "I'm not mentioned in the report, am I?" I knew the answer was no, but I wanted to hear it from him directly.

Steve laughed and assured me I was not part of the problem (at least not *that* problem). But the alleged shenanigans would have other psychological impacts on my five-month tour.

As a result of the perceived astronaut scandal, NASA's Public Affairs Office, in conjunction with NASA Headquarters and the Astronaut Office, decided that several of my "personal choice" video conference events would have to be canceled. The fact that one of those choices was to be on *The Dr. Phil Show* was probably what put them over the edge.

Because one of our astronauts had flipped a gasket, and others allegedly imbibed too much at the wrong time, I would miss out on an opportunity to represent NASA in what I felt was a positive light. Management thought that with all the press coverage now focused on astronauts, something from my videoconference with *The Dr. Phil Show* might be taken the wrong way—as if Dr. Phil was counseling me.

I thought it would be cool to commiserate with Dr. Phil. We could discuss the psychological aspects of being cooped up in a tin can with two Russians for six months, endlessly boring holes through the sky. We could talk about the pursuit of childhood dreams and the almost-certain need to overcome adversity somewhere along the way. It seemed a good way to put some positive spin on the situation and show the world that astronauts are human beings, too. If nothing else, it gave Dr. Phil a decidedly different topic to discuss, one that had nothing to do with adult temper tantrums, girls faking pregnancy, mother-in-law mayhem, or the best celebrity babysitters.

With all of this happening in August, my time in space grew short. Attempts were made to line up my backup choice, NBC TV Weatherman Al Roker, but there simply wasn't enough time. Through Roker's agent, I would end up in a videoconference with Russian funnyman Yakov Smirnoff instead. He was a good boost for my psyche and morale, telling me in his heavy Russian accent, "It is very bad situation when astronaut funnier than comedian!"

Most days, morale aboard the ISS was good. The three of us meshed well, and we took turns serving as unofficial morale officers for the crew, making sure the mood stayed light.

One night early in the increment I was awakened from sleep by the crackle of the station communication system. Blasting through the speakers came the sounds of conversations from the ground—and all of them were in Spanish. The chatter trailed on for over twenty minutes, which I would learn the following morning is about the amount of time it takes the station to traverse Mexico and South America from northwest to southeast.

At breakfast, I explained to Fyodor and Oleg (they might say I bitched) about the interruption in my sleep. They both broke into wry grins. Turns out that the previous day they had misconfigured the Russian communication system after a routine test, leaving the network perfectly tuned to pick up matching frequency audio transmissions from the ground.

We had a good chuckle that day. Later in the week the situation ramped up. Working hard in the lab, I suddenly heard a burst of loud music through the intercom speaker around ten fifteen in the morning. Hearing mariachi music, I wondered what the hell was going on. I thought we were passing over Mexico again! My question was answered in seconds when Fyodor in a fatherly voice chuckled and said, "Clay, *chai-ku.*" It was time for our coffee break.

For the rest of the mission, Spanish music became our standard coffee-break signal. Each time I heard it, I grabbed the microphone. With a tongue trill worthy of Spanish American comedienne Charo, I called out *¡Ándele! ¡Ándele! ¡Arriba! ¡Arriba!* and floated down happily to my friends.

Laughter was always an important part of our psychological toolbox for life in space. Flying into the Russian service module for dinner one evening, I was greeted by a heated conversation between my Russian crewmates.

I listened intently, trying my best to decipher their fast-paced emotional Russian exchange. As I struggled to pick up on the thread of their argument, the only thing I could make out was the repeated use of the word "bobs." That's strange, I thought. I don't remember learning a Russian word *bobs.* Perhaps they're referring to something having to do with our lead flight director, Bob Dempsey.

After a few more minutes, I couldn't take it any longer. In my limited Russian, I told them I didn't understand their conversation and asked them to please slow it down a little so I could try and figure it out.

Fyodor smiled and said, "Clay, you know. Bobs. Big bobs, little bobs."

Laughing, I now saw the light!

"You mean boobs," I corrected. "You're talking about boobs!" Providing them with the standard male gesture of cupped hands held up to the chest, indicating a well-endowed female, I said, "Breasts, right?"

Repeating himself excitedly, but now with the proper pronunciation, Fyodor gushed, "Yes, boobs!" As if back in junior high school and participating in a round of potty talk, he chuckled, "Little boobs, like Suni."

Oleg, not to be outdone, jumped in. "Yes, little boobs, like Peggy," he chortled.

Fyodor, not missing his chance to pile on a high-profile U.S. astronaut—one not revered in most cosmonaut circles—added, "Little boobs, but BIG penis!"

What is it they say in *Reader's Digest*? Laughter is the best medicine? In space, it's the cure.

17

The Hard Thump of Reality

The journey that began in earnest in December 1968 with me glued to a black-and-white TV set culminated in part on November 7, 2007, aboard the space shuttle *Discovery*. Orbital mechanics dictated that upon completion of my first jaunt into outer space—five months on the International Space Station—I must now face the prospect of my first homecoming from outer space. After 151 days in microgravity, *Discovery*'s touchdown at the Kennedy Space Center was scheduled for the late morning hours of November 7.

Prepping for landing day is almost as hectic as launch day and orbital insertion. There are so many things that must be completed to get everything (and everyone) ready for coming home. Equipment used during the mission must be carefully packed for return to Earth. When NASA says "packed" they mean *packed*; equipment must be stowed in such a manner as to avoid any damage upon return to Earth's gravitational field or from the hard thump of the orbiter's main landing gear when the tires strike the Shuttle Landing Facility's fifteen-thousand-foot-long concrete landing surface.

That morning the crew awakened on schedule, downed a quick breakfast, and donned navy blue cotton long underwear made by Patagonia. The long underwear was comfortable against our skin and performed the critical function of covering our maximum absorbency garments, more commonly known as diapers.

Heavier, less comfortable liquid-cooling garments would be put on at the very last possible minute over our diapers and long underwear. Over everything we would wear our Advanced Crew

Escape System (ACES) spacesuits. The highly visible and recognizable orange "pumpkin" suits serve as our first level of protection in the event of a high-altitude emergency bailout like that contemplated by the crew of the *Columbia* tragedy.

The crew was busy on the flight deck checking the shuttle's navigational systems, test-firing her reaction control system jets and manipulating all her hydraulically controlled aerodynamic surfaces—parts absolutely critical to the "one shot only" entry of this 215,000-pound spaceship, a hunk of tiles, insulation, and metal that must land with the lift of an aircraft. Just prior to landing, all jets are turned off and the shuttle must land as a glider. And with no go-arounds, there's only one opportunity to do so safely.

Flambo, Longbow, and Husk-Bo were packing up sleeping bags, experiments, trash—all the supplies and hardware—before the final thrust of the orbital maneuvering system (OMS) engines that would slow us down enough so gravity could gently tug us back into the Earth's atmosphere. (STS-120 was known as the "Bo" crew. Led by Commander Pam "Pambo" Melroy and pilot George "Zambo" Zamka, all crewmembers adopted "Bo" call signs for the mission: Doug "Wheels" Wheelock became Flambo for his difficulty lighting a fire in the rain, Scott "Longbow" Parazynski for his height, Stephanie "Robo" Wilson for her robotic arm genius, Dan "Bo-ichi" Tani for his Asian heritage, Paolo "Rocky" Nespoli because no one could think of a good Italian "Bo" name, and yours truly became "Husk-Bo" for my home state.)

Still, we managed to find time for zero-gravity play as we worked in the middeck. The gravitationally liberated Sony video camera was passed back and forth, videotaping "stupid astronaut tricks" as we launched M&Ms across the living quarters toward mouths stretched to their limits hoping for a successful capture of the tasty candies.

We gathered and filled drink bags for each crewmember, readying us for the process called fluid loading. Required of astronauts on entry day, fluid loading tops off the fluids in your vestibular and blood pressure systems. Taking in salt tablets and fluids on landing day helps you better withstand and respond to a force it hasn't experienced in quite some time—gravity.

After a couple of weeks in space, your systems learn that it takes less effort to push blood "up" into your brain than when you were back on the Earth's surface. With your bodily systems essentially running on idle, gravity has no trouble pulling blood away from your head and down to your feet. The results are potentially disastrous.

Being a rookie astronaut, my knowledge of the fluid loading process was purely theoretical. My choice of beverages to load on landing day was based on an earthbound set of taste buds and included hot chicken broth (two bags—a big mistake), followed by purple grape drink and ending with tropical punch. The fruit drinks were artificially sweetened, as sugar diminishes the body's ability to retain liquids, thereby lessening the benefit of fluid loading. Since my size and weight dictated that I needed sixty-four ounces of fluid over a two-hour period, I followed up my tasty combination of liquids with plain old iodinated water and the remaining mandatory salt tablets. The process began with a call from our commander to "initiate fluid loading." I was not prepared for the ramifications of that simple directive.

The choice of chicken broth stemmed from taste-testing sessions on the ground where it tasted like a bowl of Mom's chicken soup. In space the salty chicken taste was not nearly as appealing.

When Pambo called for us to load our second bag, I wasn't even half finished with the first one and I still had purple grape drink, tropical punch, and water to get down. Fluid loading was not as easy as I'd thought it would be.

With our preparatory tasks completed and three seats reinstalled in the middeck, our focus turned to the upcoming OMS burn.

Critical to entry if completed successfully, it would drastically reduce our orbit's altitude by slowing our orbital velocity. With the shuttle moving more slowly, the effect of gravity becomes more pronounced, pulling us toward Earth, which is the desired effect. The timeline would then begin to move at a breakneck speed, giving us less than sixty minutes before touching down.

Our work on the middeck accelerated to what seemed like an almost frenetic pace. The flight deck crew had to be suited up and strapped into their seats before Pambo and Zambo would initiate the OMS burn.

The mission's end would begin in earnest when Pambo's gloved index finger hit the execute button of her center-console computer keyboard. The shuttle's ancient software would then initiate the preset countdown to ignition of the two OMS engines.

One floor below the flight deck, we worked with the primary goal to get everyone into their launch-and-entry suits and strapped down in their chairs.

The suiting up of seven adult crewmembers is a task requiring forethought, planning, and teamwork. The order of suit-up was flight deck first: commander, then pilot, then mission specialist 1, and finally, mission specialist 2. Until they were strapped in, we couldn't even begin to think about the three of us on the middeck.

Middeck had an order too: returning ISS crewmember first, then Wheels (also a rookie flier), and finally the crew's veteran, Scott Parazynski. In the event of a last-minute problem, a veteran, experienced and familiar with the suits and hardware, is able to get suited up and strapped into position quickly and without as much help as a rookie.

Once Flambo and Longbow had strapped me in prior to deorbit, there was nothing for me to do but relax and take in the experience and the final activities performed by my crewmates. At touchdown, I was lying on my back, perfectly comfortable in my recumbent space shuttle seat. Being six feet tall, my booted feet extended into two open and empty lockers.

We hit the runway hard, the impact providing a jolt that clearly welcomed me back to my home planet. Much to my surprise, I was feeling like a million bucks.

Safely back on the ground, I was in hog heaven, contemplating seeing my wife and kids after five long months. KSC's astronaut support personnel opened the shuttle's side hatch, and veteran astronaut Jerry Ross poked his head in.

"Welcome home!" he said with a huge smile.

An orange corrugated hose, or "elephant trunk," was inserted through the hatch to pump cool air into the rapidly warming mid-deck. I could smell the scents of Earth, and it didn't even matter which smells they were. It was awesome to be home. At least it seemed that way from my comfortable vantage point of lying on my back.

Jerry coordinated the extraction of each crewmember in a clear and specific order. The "iss guy" would be last.

Scott and Wheels exited their middeck seats quickly and apparently readapted to Earth's gravity within minutes. They hurriedly departed *Discovery* in anticipation of doffing the bulky, heavy, extremely warm suits they had been perspiring in for the last hour.

Turning my head ever so gently to the left (now that I was back in the firm grip of Newton's second law, moving too fast would cause "stomach awareness"), I watched as my crewmates were brought down the ladder from the flight deck, starting with my good friend from Italy, Paolo Nespoli.

As Paolo slowly descended the short metal ladder under the watchful eye of Ross, I shouted, "Way to go, Paolo! Great job!"

He slowly turned his head toward me, and with great effort, uttered a quiet and unconvincing "Thanks." That was followed by the audible splat of a discharge of fluid from his stomach onto the middeck floor.

Daunted by this resonant and disconcertingly visual display of fluid unloading, I returned my head to neutral and concentrated on the switches and dials mounted on the ceiling in an attempt to get that puking out of my mind and to once again bask in the sense of complete success that had previously washed over me.

Finally it was my turn. Jerry Ross placed a calming hand on my left knee.

"Are you ready?" he asked.

"You bet!" I said, having no idea whether I was or not.

He undid my remaining parachute-to-harness straps. (I had already released my five-point seatbelt harness, as it's a simple device requiring only the turn of a knob.)

Watching for the telltale signs of uneasiness that only a veteran space flier could see, Jerry asked me to slowly sit up.

It took me a great effort to rise to the seated position, even with an assist from Jerry's strong arms. Upright for the first time on Earth in over five months, the entire middeck of the orbiter began to spin counterclockwise at an incredible rate. Fighting off nausea, I focused on one of the cream-colored lockers we'd opened and closed a hundred times as we packed up. The locker seemed to stare right back at me. Keeping my gaze affixed on my newly found reference point, I resisted the urge to turn my head as the shuttle support team shouted instructions to each other as they began to unload our personal gear.

It took only a few seconds for the spinning of the middeck to slow down and ultimately come to rest, presenting me with the view that any earthbound astronaut would have expected.

Jerry Ross asked again, "Are you okay?"

"Yes," I responded without much enthusiasm.

"I need you to turn to your left and get down on the floor. You will have to crawl to the hatch," he said.

I turned left ever so slowly, anticipating the moves needed to get myself to my hands and knees on the shuttle's middeck floor. I took a deep breath. Positioning my hands forward to catch myself should I lose control and fall in a pumpkin-orange heap, I made the move. The thickness of my launch-and-entry suit protected my kneecaps from the hard floor after 152 days of treading only on air. Success was achieved until I moved my head to look at the open hatch and freedom.

The spinning started. Once again, I held firm. My head remained as stable as the faces on Mount Rushmore. It took less time for the spinning to stop than before. Confidence washed over my tired and overheated body. With newfound vigor and the hope that I was going to be able to exit without puking my brains out, I allowed myself the fantasy that I might even be able to perform the shuttle walkaround with the rest of the crew.

It took a considerable amount of strength in my arms and upper body to pull my two-hundred-pound self into the opened hatchway. Nearly exhausted from the effort that took only seconds, I was greeted by two able-bodied flight surgeons. I gave them a weak but sincere smile as they hoisted my arms around their shoulders and lifted me from what was essentially a prone position. It was time to try and walk again. For the first time in over five months, my legs began to receive commands from my brain, the orders flying at the speed of light through a nerve system that seemed to be relearning everything from scratch now that gravity had returned. As if I were Tim Conway playing Mr. Tudball on *The Carol Burnett Show*, my size-thirteen black flight boots shuffled slowly across the gantry way to the door of the crew transfer vehicle (CTV).

My intestines were having even more difficulty making the transition to normalcy. I had gone from mostly Russian food on the space station to a diet of American food aboard the shuttle. Thus, my internal organs had been in a constant state of gaseous protest for the last two days of the mission.

While I was flatulating like a machine gun, I had not been able to have a successful bowel movement for two days. Coupled with the fact that landing day required me to don both a high-altitude g-suit and the Russian version of athletic compression shorts, my bowels were having a hard time fighting against the pressure.

Finally in the vertical position, the call of nature was coming in loud and clear to me and to anyone close enough to listen or inhale. The fluid-loading protocol we had successfully completed a few hours before was beginning to see results. Sixty-four ounces of liquid and a number of salt tablets contained in my stomach and intestinal tract had a tremendous desire to be uncontained.

So there I stood, fully clothed in my orange suit with polished black flight boots and all the requisite clothing and sublayers, and I had to take a crap!

"Could I please use the bathroom?" I asked politely.

There was only one toilet in the RV-sized CTV, and it represented everything pure and good from some porta-potty company.

"It's busy—the ladies are cleaning up," said NASA flight nurse Cathy DiBiase.

Desperate measures were needed. I had to focus on something to take my mind off my bowels. Unfortunately, after a long-duration space flight, my ability to successfully "head 'em off at the pass" using only the muscles in my buttocks was severely diminished. I was squeezing my butt cheeks together as if there were no tomorrow.

Finally my flight nurse suggested I could get out of my flight suit. Agreement came quickly. It was beginning to dawn on me just how hot I was with all those layers on. Being ever so careful to keep my head in a steady, upright, and stable position, I gingerly sat down in an imitation leather recliner. My flight nurse gently untied and removed the increasingly heavy black boots. Even the simple act of glancing down to watch her work brought me to the threshold of a regurgitory explosion.

Next was the orange suit. Critical to the successful doffing effort would be my ability to hold my head still while they pulled the rubber-lined helmet ring over my large and unstable cranium. A time ripe for puking, it would require precise teamwork for my helpers to ease the metal ring over my head. I was required to drop my head forward, then not jerk it right back up once the ring had passed over. Many a strong and steely-eyed astronaut has blown chunks during this key maneuver.

The overwhelming desire to hurl all over the floor was being trumped by my need for time in the toilet. With the orange suit now successfully removed I once again lobbied for some time in the crapper. My request was met again by what was now becoming an unacceptable response: "One of your crewmates is still in there."

The inability of this group to get me into the toilet was beginning to sound like a reason to drop trou and let it go right there in the middle of the floor. Continually returning to a "buns of steel" mentality, I squeezed my ass cheeks together with all my might. Failure was not an option!

A second and more nauseating wave suddenly overcame my sensory organs. My body temperature was continuing to rise. Extremely warm and uncomfortably clothed in my high-tech undergarments, I readily agreed to the suggestion that I get into more comfortable garb. My blue cooling garment top was promptly removed (I had chosen not to wear the bottoms because in training I had determined that my legs would not require much cooling), followed by my long-sleeved underwear shirt.

Facing the reality that removing my final piece of clothing—my

1. Taking air samples among the stowage in the Unity module (Node 1) of the International Space Station. (NASA, photo by Fyodor Yurchikin)

2. Author long jumping for the Hastings College track team in 1981. We wore our shorts much differently then! (ANDERSON FAMILY)

3. Author at age nine, the year he remembers first dreaming of becoming an astronaut. (His mother said they "discussed it" years earlier.) (ANDERSON FAMILY)

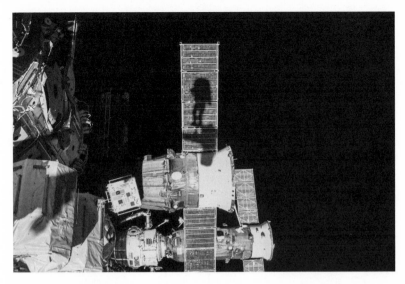

4. Author's self-proclaimed perfect selfie, captured while flying on the Canadian robotic arm during his first spacewalk in 2007. (NASA)

5. The physics of surface tension clearly illustrated on the middeck of *Discovery* during STS-131. (NASA)

6. Author, relieving some tension, has fun donning boxer shorts while performing the commercial generic bioprocessing assembly (CGBA) experiment in the ISS laboratory module Destiny. (NASA, photo by Oleg Kotov)

7. STS-131 and the space shuttle *Discovery*, with a multipurpose logistics module (MPLM) and ammonia tank assembly (ATA) in her payload bay, approach the ISS and an attached Soyuz vehicle in April 2010. (NASA)

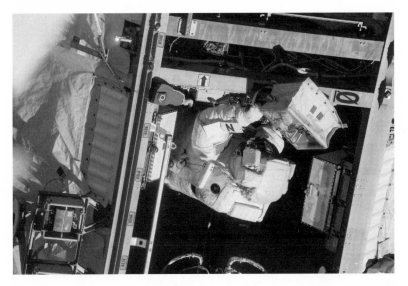

8. Using a symbolic cuff checklist to salute the author's home state of Nebraska while exiting the ISS truss structure during the first spacewalk of STS-131. (NASA, photo by Alan Poindexter)

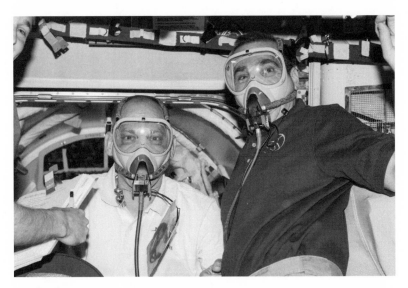

9. Author and fellow spacewalker Rick Mastracchio prebreathe pure oxygen from the ISS airlock under the watchful eye of crewmate Jim Dutton in preparation for one of their three spacewalks during STS-131. (NASA, photo by Jim Dutton)

10. (*Opposite top*) The Anderson kids. From left to right: brother, Kirby (age 1), the author (age 2), and sister, Lorie (age 4), pose for a family portrait in August 1961. (ANDERSON FAMILY)

11. (*Opposite bottom*) Author with the ISS Expedition 23 crew in the Destiny lab module. Back row (L–R): Tracy Caldwell Dyson, Russian cosmonauts Alexander Skvortsov and Mikhail Kornienko. Front row (L–R): Timothy "T.J." Creamer, Russian Oleg Kotov, and Soichi Noguchi (JAXA). (NASA)

12. (*Above*) Group 17 members of the astronaut class of 1998 (L–R: Commander Alan "Dex" Poindexter, Tracy Caldwell Dyson, T.J. Creamer, and the author) pose near the airlock hatch in tribute to their deceased classmate Patty Hilliard Robertson (photo near hatch window), who perished from burn injuries sustained in a private plane crash in 2001. (NASA)

13. (*Opposite top*) Author testing his Russian Sokol suit with Fyodor Yurchikin and Oleg Kotov after arrival on the ISS. (NASA)

14. (*Opposite bottom*) The only picture in existence of the entire ISS Expedition 15 crew. Clockwise from left: Oleg Kotov, Fyodor Yurchikin, the author, and Sunita Williams. (NASA)

15. (*Above*) Exhibiting some Husker loyalty in the Destiny lab module. (NASA)

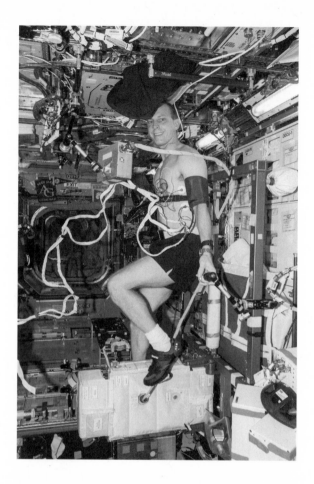

16. (*Above*) Author performing his monthly vo2 Max test that measures aerobic capability on the cevis stationary bicycle. (NASA)

17. (*Opposite top*) Author in the Russian service module playing with "malted milk balls" developed by the Iowa State University Food Lab. (NASA)

18. (*Opposite bottom*) Clad in his Russian Sokol space suit, the author and Expedition 15 crew prepare to undock their Soyuz capsule and redock at a new port. (NASA, photo by Fyodor Yurchikin)

19. (*Opposite top*) Author working out in the ISS "weight room" using the Interim Resistive Exercise Device (IRED). Note the shoulder pad harness. (NASA)

20. (*Opposite bottom*) Window view during the NASA Extreme Environment Mission Operations (NEEMO) 5 mission in the Aquarius habitat near Key Largo, Florida. (NASA)

21. (*Above*) The NEEMO 5 official crew photo in the Aquarius habitat sleeping quarters. Left (*from top*): astronauts Garrett Reisman and Peggy Whitson, and habitat technician James Talacek. Right (*from top*): NASA scientist Dr. Emma Hwang, the author, and habitat technician Ryan Snow. (NASA)

22. Author swaps a "Texas handshake" with President George W. Bush at Ellington Field after 152 days in orbit. (Official White House photo)

23. The Andersons pose with the president of the United States in front of Air Force One. (Official White House photo)

24. Prior to shuttle emergency egress training, the STS-131 crew pauses for a crew portrait. L–R: The author, Naoko Yamazaki (JAXA), Dorothy "Dottie" Metcalf-Lindenburger, air force colonel James "Mash" Dutton, navy captain Alan "Dex" Poindexter, Stephanie Wilson, and Rick Mastracchio. (NASA)

25. Author shares a reflective moment during a suited crew training exercise. (NASA)

26. (*Above*) Author practices shuttle water survival training in the Neutral Buoyancy Lab (NBL) near the Johnson Space Center in Houston. (NASA)

27. (*Opposite top*) Sample insertion into the minus 80 degree freezer (MELFI) in the station's laboratory module Destiny. (NASA)

28. (*Opposite bottom*) NASA "nerd" engineers pose in front of a cherry red Corvette for a group photo early in their careers at the Johnson Space Center. (CLAYTON ANDERSON)

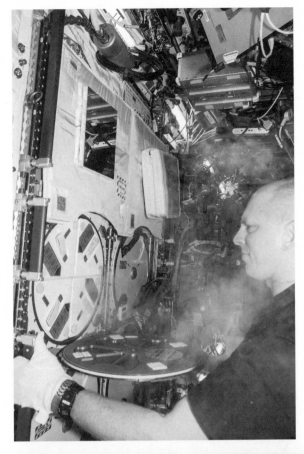

29. Posing in the U.S. airlock with two Extravehicular Mobility Units (EMU) ready to head into space or take the field for the Nebraska Cornhuskers! (NASA)

30. Author poses with his mother, Alice, in the NASA Conference Center beach house at Kennedy Space Center just prior to his first launch into space. (KIRBY ANDERSON)

31. Daily training session on the CEVIS stationary
bicycle aboard the ISS. (NASA)

32. (*Opposite top*) An Anderson family photo in the author's crew notebook is captured digitally on the shuttle middeck. (NASA)

33. (*Opposite bottom*) Final nighttime launch of a space shuttle. *Discovery* lifts off on April 5, 2010. (NASA)

34. (*Above*) Author's ride home—the crew of STS-120 poses in the newly delivered Harmony module (Node 2). Top row (L–R): army colonel Doug Wheelock, the author, Dr. Scott Parazynski. Bottom row (L–R): Paolo Nespoli (ESA), Stephanie Wilson, air force colonel (retired) and *Discovery* commander Pam Melroy, marine corps colonel George Zamka. (NASA)

35. After completing three strenuous spacewalks on STS-131, the author and Rick Mastracchio relax in the Harmony module (Node 2). (NASA)

long underwear bottoms—would have me standing there in front of God and everybody wearing only a diaper, I was extremely embarrassed. I asked if there were other clothes for me to wear.

Nurse Cathy, as if impersonating a magician with a top hat, pulled a pair of synthetic, lined, navy blue running shorts out of nowhere. They looked amazingly like those worn by Frank Shorter in the 1976 Olympics, and had the potential to fit over just one of my legs . . . maybe. Nurse Cathy sympathetically declared that the only other choice was my red Hanes boxer shorts, reminiscent of an astronaut Christmas party video skit starring ISS Expedition 9 astronaut Mike "Spanky" Fincke performing zero-g gyrations in a parody of an underwear commercial from the nineties.

My choices limited, and the privacy of the bathroom not available, I reached for the red cotton undies, then threw off my diaper, revealing myself to anyone within eyeshot. Hell, I simply didn't care anymore! Naked as a jaybird, I fastidiously pulled on the shorts, one leg at a time, carefully avoiding any rapid movements that would put my "no puking" record in jeopardy. After I successfully donned the underwear, the words I had been looking forward to hearing were uttered from somewhere within the CTV: "The bathroom is open now."

Elated, I grabbed the long silver bar mounted overhead to stabilize my weakened body. Resuming my deliberate Tim Conway shuffle, I was handed a white puke bag by Nurse Cathy: "You know, just in case."

The toilet door was wide open; I was going to make it. My vision was captured instantly upon entering the tiny room. Poised proudly on a shelf above the small sink were seven bottles, six of which contained recent urine samples from my obviously dehydrated crewmates. Not the best thing for my neural synapses to begin their earthbound processing. I grabbed my bottle and maneuvered close to the toilet to minimize any potential messes. Red boxers down around my knees, I began urinating into my personal sample bottle. The smell was overwhelming! Sensing this could be the trigger I was trying to avoid, I positioned my left forearm against the wall in front of my face. Leaning forward, while simultaneously voiding into an unseen bottle below, I buried my nose deeply into the crevice formed by my bicep and forearm hoping to offset the putrid smell from the dark yellow discharge with the more tolerable scent of my own sweaty skin. The smell of epidermis and sweat seemed to do the trick.

Having tightly screwed the lid back on its container, I placed it on the shelf. Crisis averted, my thoughts turned to a much needed bowel movement. I turned around slowly and lowered my backside until icy cold porcelain on naked skin informed me that I was now seated on the mobile "throne."

A torrential release ensued that was more welcomed than a raise in my paycheck. Confidence now bordering on arrogance, I thought nothing would get in the way of my successful no-puking return to Earth.

A few minutes into my bodily function, my skin became increasingly warm. The aroma of "number two" was entering my consciousness. I cupped both of my hands tightly over my face, hoping to replace the acrid smell with one slightly more favorable to my senses.

Breathing deeply, the sense of dread subsided and I was able to reason more clearly. Thinking that a flush of the toilet might be helpful, I twisted my body, reaching for the flush handle. As I was groping at the side of the toilet tank it become apparent that the flush handle was located down near the floor, for operation using one's feet. Knowing that moving my head toward the floor would have disastrous consequences, I turned to what I hoped would be a successful plan B. It was not meant to be. One more whiff of an already completed critical body function told my brain that finally I had had enough. An oral discharge was imminent. I grabbed for the pristine white barf bag.

I unloaded into that bag with a fervor not seen since my final sixteen-hundred-meter relay effort on the Hastings College track team. Volume quickly became a concern, as thrusts from my stomach muscles continued to push pale purple liquid from the depths of my gut. With a couple of final thrusts, complete with audible cues sounding like what one might hear after a successful frat party, my "Technicolor yawn" drew to a welcome close.

Then, with me sitting on the stool in a considerably compromising position, the door flew open. "Are you okay?" Nurse Cathy asked predictably.

"Yes, I'm fine," I yelled. "I'm just throwing up! Please close the door."

As the door swung closed, I figured it was time to finalize my efforts. Having made sure my body was completely empty, I cleaned each and every orifice from which nastiness had emanated. Still not feeling too great, but much better than when I originally entered this tiny stink hole, I mustered up enough strength to stand and get out of the bathroom, back into a more welcoming (and fresher smelling) environment.

Opening the door, I was greeted by a hospital gurney with a waiting IV bag, ready to replace the fluids I had so unceremoniously discharged only moments ago.

I welcomed the opportunity to lie down and relax. Sheer exhaustion was beginning to set in. I desperately needed some rest. The ride back to astronaut crew quarters was only twenty or thirty minutes in actual time, but it seemed like a blissful eternity to me, asleep on my newfound bed. As we approached the Office of Space Communication (OSC) Building at KSC, where I would be transferred from the recreational vehicle into the biomedical wing, I was awakened by the din of welcoming voices.

Emotion and excitement pulled me from my exhausted stupor. I was finally going to see my family! After 152 days in outer space—not to mention the week prior to launch spent in quarantine—I ached for the touch of my wife and kids. With the help of my good friend Mary Jane Anderson, a biomedical science investigator from JSC with Nebraska ties, the upper half of my bed was raised slightly.

At the back of the murmuring chorus, standing strong and tall but looking a bit tentative was my son, Cole.

As our eyes locked—in what for him must have been surprise at his dad's pale-as-a-ghost gaze—I began to weep. The emotional release was almost as if something tragic had happened. He looked terrific, appearing to have grown at least six inches since I left the planet! He began to smile and I was at peace; I was home.

With tear-blurred vision, I saw my wife, Susan, and daughter,

Sutton, emerge from the crowd. As they cautiously approached the gurney, my tears gushed, this time accompanied by gulping sobs the likes of which I hadn't experienced since the day after *Columbia* exploded, when I broke down and cried during church.

I reached for Susan's hand and pulled her tightly against my chest. We squeezed each other tightly for the first time in over 152 days. Between sobs of joy, hugs, and kisses, I whispered into her ear the words I had been rehearsing for months: "We did it, honey, we did it! We did it together! I love you so much!"

Our personal time was short-lived. It was time for all my post-flight tests. Sutton, now almost seven years old, watched with utter amazement as Mary Jane slid a newly opened catheter into a vein in my right arm. With rapt attention, Sutton watched her daddy's blood being sucked into multiple clear-glass test tubes.

"Daddy's face is really white," she said.

Drawing blood was not reinforcing my body's recovery from the weightlessness of space.

In only a few minutes, the powers-that-be instructed me it was time to move to where postflight experimentation on me could begin in earnest. As they wheeled me to the next location, Susan and Sutton on either side of the gurney and Cole following closely behind, I recognized Canadian astronaut Chris Hadfield. Dressed in his blue flight suit, he was moving along with our assembly. Destined to one day become the first Canadian to command the space station, I assumed he was there in some official capacity, although I didn't have a clue as to what that might be. The person I would have expected was my crew support astronaut, Chris Cassidy. (Chris would also fly on the station during the period Hadfield served as the commander.) Cassidy had been on the landing strip helping us get out of the *Discovery* in his capacity as a "Cape Crusader" (the nickname for astronauts who are assigned to support a mission's launch and landing operations), so it was possible Hadfield was acting as his backup.

Suddenly Hadfield grabbed Sutton by the arm and tried to pull her away from the gurney. Anger welled up inside me. In a firm voice he told her she couldn't be with her father because Daddy had to go do tests. Had I been possessed of any strength whatsoever, I think I would have punched him in the nose! I know he was trying to do his job, but this was important family time. Pushing my reconnection with them until later in the name of data gathering seemed inappropriate.

As I was whisked away from my family, Susan was consoling Sutton with the reminder that we would be seeing Daddy very soon. My sense of loss and anger was offset when the small crowd burst into a rousing chorus of applause and shouts of "Way to go, Clay! Welcome home, Clay!"

During the transit to where data collection would begin, I quietly suggested to Nurse Cathy that I needed to use the bathroom again. Helping me down from the gurney, she cradled my right elbow, giving me support as she directed me toward my destination. Her query as to whether I desired her assistance was met with my sincere "No, thank you." I felt up to tackling this challenge alone.

Nurse Cathy maneuvered me to the threshold of the restroom. It appeared enormous in size. In the room's center sat a solitary white pedestal sink. To its right was a standard flush toilet.

Reassuring Nurse Cathy that I was capable of doing this on my own, I began the daunting trek across the open tile to the desperately needed destination. Wiser since the CTV experience, upon reaching the toilet I removed all my clothing (t-shirt and briefs) for the upcoming discharge. It was not until I was far into my second bowel movement of the day that I realized a critical error had occurred. I had no puke bag.

Fearful that yelling for help would further compromise an already tenuous situation, I scanned the area for anything that could serve as backup.

There was nothing but the sink, and time was running out. It was time for MacGyver-like improvisation. Maintaining a steady head and posture, and stretching with all my might, I could not reach the sink.

Undaunted, I made my next move. Sliding my ass carefully around the back circumference of the seat, closest to the tank, I was able to maneuver my backside to the point where my left cheek was firmly positioned on the side of the seat closest the sink, while my right cheek was hanging in mid-air, performing its own version of Wicked's *Defying Gravity*.

With a desperate lunge, I reached for the edge of the sink. But my fingers, weak from my five months in orbit, began slipping free from the rim. My body began to follow. I was sliding from the toilet, slipping under the sink. Then I spied the only option I had left. Reaching below the sink and stretching for all I was worth, I grabbed for the bright silver P-trap assembly. With a solid grip on the pipe, I pulled my chin up to rest on the edge of the sink, still managing to keep one ass cheek on the toilet seat.

There was no time for further adjustments. A flood of fluids returned, accompanied by the verbal grunt of another Technicolor yawn.

"Are you okay?" came Nurse Cathy's dependable cry as she sprinted into the center of the bathroom.

"I'm fine; I'm just puking," I barked.

Nurse Cathy was staring at a totally naked, totally embarrassed astronaut, stretched almost horizontally between a sink and a toilet, puking his brains out.

Fatigue was wearing heavily on me by the time a group of Canadian scientists began prepping me for data collection for the Canadian Cardiovascular Investigation on ISS. They were studying the body's cardiovascular system and its ability to deliver blood to the organs in a weightless environment. By observing the human body's fluid system in zero gravity, they hoped to better understand how it works on Earth. A better understanding could lead to medical breakthroughs for folks with heart and circulatory problems.

As a willing preflight volunteer, I was pretty much stuck doing whatever they wanted or needed, and they needed data collected immediately after landing. I was so exhausted it was difficult to keep my eyes open, but every time I began to fade away, one of the investigators would push or prod me to move this way or that way. It took several hours before they were finally finished. Another session would be required first thing the next morning.

I didn't care. I was about to spend the night with my wife for the first time in over 152 days. I knew what I *wanted* to do that night with Susan, but I was not at all optimistic that my body would comply. It simply didn't seem possible that I would be able to stay awake. Unless I could get a catnap, my intimate night with Susan was going to consist of me lying down on the bed and greeting her the next morning.

Finally, at the room in crew quarters I was to share with Susan, I received a phone call. Sutton was in the condo on the beach imitating her father . . . she was throwing up, too. Susan felt it necessary that she stay there with Sutton rather than coming all the way back out to crew quarters at KSC.

While disappointed, I realized this would be best for all of us. I was fighting to stay awake and remain ambulatory. I hadn't eaten anything in hours for fear of puking it right back up. My rehabilitation specialist, Mark Guilliams, was hoping we would be able to get in a short rehabilitation workout before I fell asleep for the night.

Mark's plans had about the same odds of happening as my romantic evening with my wife.

I begged and pleaded with Mark and Nurse Cathy to just let me go to sleep. Mark negotiated; he would leave me be for the night if I agreed to a session on the stationary bike after my data gathering procedure the next morning. Willing to do almost anything in order to get to go to sleep, I quickly agreed.

As our negotiations ended, Nurse Cathy wheeled an IV tower into the room with antinausea medicine in the clear plastic bag.

I suggested, and they agreed, that it might be best if I ate something before going to sleep. My original plan for my first meal back on Earth was a medium-rare T-bone steak (Nebraska corn-fed beef) with a loaded baked potato and a good, hardy Cabernet Sauvignon (Silver Oak Cellars, perhaps).

I settled for two pieces of wheat toast with grape jelly that Mark graciously brought to me on a Styrofoam plate with a napkin, and I loved every bite.

With a hint of nausea and without my wife, the day of my triumphant return to planet Earth came to a close at 8:37 p.m. in that tiny room. It was my fifteenth wedding anniversary. Glowing faintly, a silent calculator marking my new earthbound pedometer, the numbers on the radio alarm silently clicked over from 8:36 to 8:37. My mind went blank . . . no dizziness, no thoughts of accomplishment, no regrets . . . just the restful peace of my first night's sleep back under the influence of gravity.

I slept for nearly nine hours. My body position had not shifted one iota from where it was when I crashed the night before. As I tried to roll over and get out of the bed to empty my screaming kidneys, I felt every ounce of my two-hundred-plus pounds. Every single movement required energy that just didn't seem to be there anymore.

I had to carefully position myself for each distinct movement, as if my body was a marionette and my brain a puppet master. Minutes passed before I reached the foot of the bed, my feet planted squarely on the floor. Head resting in my hands, I contemplated the scope and magnitude of the prospective journey to the toilet. My body insisted I had precious little time left. It had to be done.

Focusing all my energy on my upper body, I made a lunge reminiscent of my long-jumping days in college and gained the two feet between myself and the entertainment center near the foot of the bed. Grabbing the edge, I pulled myself into an upright position.

Leaning on furniture and walls I made slow, heavy progress to the door of the crapper, where I worked myself into a stable position within the doorjamb.

Feeling like a contestant on *America's Biggest Loser* or *Extreme Makeover: Weight Loss Edition,* I rotated 180 degrees, then forced my gym shorts down as far as I could push without bending over. Privates liberated, goal in reach, I released my death grip on the door jamb and pushed every so gently. Gravity slammed my ass down on the toilet seat with the subtlety of an anchor hitting water, but the resultant trajectory was within the statistically dispersed value of plus-or-minus one sigma.

When I had successfully completed phase 1 of my morning ablutions, I began gathering the energy required to move on to phase 2—an activity I had been looking forward to for a very long time—a nice hot shower.

The wonders of Earth are magnified for an astronaut returning from a long-duration spaceflight. Consider, for example, the joy I felt when I finally maneuvered my body—which felt gargantuan—to the door of the shower stall. There I found a prepositioned chair (thanks to Nurse Cathy) equidistant from everything I would need. It was rapture, but nothing like the rapture of hot water pulsing over my entire body, a temperature-controlled rainstorm of ecstasy. For thirty-seven minutes I languished in this haven of joy. It is beyond my powers of description to tell you how good that shower felt, but the word orgasmic comes to mind.

Next came a trip to the sink for my first Newtonian-controlled shave since launch. I couldn't lift the hand holding the razor without the assistance of the other arm. As I stood naked in front of the bathroom mirror, my earthbound view of the frailty of the human condition was really driven home. My alter ego was skinny, badly shaven, extremely pale, and in desperate need of some food and sunshine.

And he was an astronaut—a flown astronaut!

"Puking: The Sequel" was humorous only after its completion.

Less than three years later, descending the ramp steps to the foot of *Discovery*, I would remember the debacle in full detail.

Again in the osc and again under the watchful eye of Nurse Cathy, I asked if she would please take me to the room where she had witnessed my horizontal puking nakedness in 2007. Nurse Cathy walked me to the place we had shared our intimate moment nearly three short years before.

The room that had appeared so enormous was quite small. I was stunned. Surely this was not the same place. The cavernous room I remembered, with a toilet and sink so carefully placed directly in its center—where had it gone? Nurse Cathy and I smiled and hugged. Apparently, long-duration spaceflight can play tricks with your mind.

18

The Serendipity of Chance

Statistically speaking, life has to be a crapshoot. I often wonder how a person can ever know how things are really going to turn out. I have never been a betting man—as a longtime government employee I work too hard for my paycheck (and a government salary that has always seemed a bit meager), so I can't imagine throwing down huge sums of money at a craps or blackjack table in Las Vegas or making weekly excursions to the horse races like my father used to do back in Nebraska. In all my forays into the underworld of gambling—places like Reno or Las Vegas or Biloxi, Mississippi—I only turned a profit twice: once as a rookie playing Caribbean stud poker in Reno way back in 1991 and then again at the three-card poker table in Vegas in 2008. So my personal experience with the world of statistical-analysis-for-profit is a bit cloudy and highly cynical.

Long before I developed my limited statistical database regarding monetary speculation, and prior to collecting all that good karma from my personal gambling experiences, I initiated the chase of the dream of becoming an astronaut. It was 1998, after fourteen straight years of applications, without a hint of interest from NASA.

In 1998 more than twenty-six hundred applications were received in Houston at NASA's Astronaut Selection Office. One of those was my fifteenth attempt. Of that number, 465 of us were deemed "exceptionally well qualified."

NASA would further pare the number down to 120 hopefuls. These 120 wannabes were broken into six groups of twenty by the selection committee. As in a software line of code with the variable x, the groups were sequentially designated: group x, where $x =$ 1 to 6, next x. Each group was sent in turn to Houston to undergo a busy week of interviews, tours, tests, and poking and prodding from a team of flight surgeons wielding icy cold stethoscopes. Thus, the selection committee would have ample evidence as to who deserved (or did not deserve) to be members of the elite club of NASA's newest astronaut candidates.

The first twenty names were "Group 1." It was rumored—by whom, nobody knows—that veterans of the process say chances for selection are best if you're in the first two or three groups.

In the selection cycle of 1998, I was assigned to Group 1. For the record, I was a member of Group 5 during the 1996 selection campaign. Perhaps it was because they went alphabetically? I probably will never know.

If you were successful statistically in getting selected as a new astronaut, you would then return to Houston with family and belongings in tow to begin a new career as a hopeful spacefarer.

If we pop out our environmentally friendly solar-powered digital calculators and do the math using the 1998 numbers, we find that of the original twenty-six hundred U.S. applicants, the twenty-five selected represents less than 1 percent.

Delving deeper into the realm of spaceflight statistics, let's look at the total number of astronauts selected in our proud nation's history. Add to that cosmonauts from Russia, taikonauts from China, and astronauts from Canada, Japan, and the European Space Agency, which includes Italy, France, Germany, Switzerland, Sweden, Denmark, Netherlands, Belgium, Norway, Spain, and the United Kingdom. Throw in Brazil (then one of our international partners for the space station) and the total number of astronauts throughout history is, depending on your source, approximately 541.

That is akin to winning the lottery, except that the lottery pays a lot better.

According to Rob Navias of the NASA JSC Public Affairs Office, as of September 26, 2014, 541 different people have flown in space. The 51-L *Challenger* veterans who died before reaching orbit are credited with only the missions they survived. The number 541 includes x-15 pilot Joe Walker, who exceeded the internationally recognized altitude of 62.1 statute miles for spaceflight, and all XPRIZE and other commercial space venturers who launched to 62.1 statute miles or above.

Now, let's consider the word *serendipity*. Consulting a thesaurus, we find it is synonymous to *fate, accident, kismet*, and *destiny*. Serendipity is more applicable to me, I think, than destiny.

Let's evaluate the serendipitous nature of my life:

1. I applied to be an astronaut fifteen times (over a fifteen-year period).

2. I was a member of Expedition 15 to the International Space Station.

3. There are fifteen letters in my name: CLAYTON ANDERSON.

4. My second mission, aboard the shuttle *Discovery*, lasted fifteen days.

As luck would have it, there is more.

1. On June 8, 2007, I launched to the ISS onboard the space shuttle *Atlantis* as a member of the crew of STS-117.

2. June 8, 2007, would have been my father's seventy-seventh birthday.

3. My parking space at the Johnson Space Center was E-117.

4. I was selected to be an astronaut in 1998, which was the seventeenth class of United States astronauts chosen in our history.

Still not convinced this is serendipity at work? Well, in true NASA fashion, let's evaluate even more data.

Following a successful eleven-day mission, the crew of STS-117 departed from the International Space Station leaving me on board with my Russian crewmates, Fyodor and Oleg, to begin my five-month stay.

Theirs would not be an easy return. The weather was not favorable for a touchdown at their primary landing site, the Kennedy Space Center. The ability to bring the shuttle back to where she lifted off is a huge savings to the space program and the U.S. tax-payer. The Florida weather continued to persist in its lack of coop-eration. As a result, Mission Control informed the crew that they would be landing at Edwards Air Force Base in the windswept des-ert of southern California. Edwards was the first-priority target of two seldom-used backup landing sites (the other being White Sands Space Harbor in New Mexico).

Though typically blessed with gorgeous weather, Edwards none-theless remained a less-than-optimal landing site because it is three thousand miles from where the space shuttle needs to be and has little of the high-tech equipment required to start pre-paring for the next mission.

Because of that complex decision to change the landing site, the shuttle program would require the orbiter to be mounted on the back of a modified Boeing 747 known as the shuttle carrier air-craft for the flight back to Florida. This continental crossing would cost taxpayers approximately one million dollars. It also necessi-tated that the shuttle carrier stop for fuel midway in their journey. NASA does not readily announce where that stop will be, as their choice is dictated by weather, facilities, and air traffic patterns.

As it happened, the space shuttle, after flying mission STS-117, which had carried Nebraska's first and (so far) only astronaut into outer space, stopped at Offutt Air Force Base in Omaha, Nebraska, twenty minutes from where I grew up. The slow, circu-lar, low-altitude flyover of the Platte Valley provided thousands of Nebraskans with an opportunity never before offered—the chance to see the spaceship that carried one of their own to a place few have ever reached.

Coincidence? You be the judge.

In late October 2007 *Discovery* launched on a mission to deliver a new module—dubbed "Harmony" by a public vote—and a new crewmember to the International Space Station. *Discovery*'s crew moved one of the station's sets of solar arrays (temporarily posi-tioned since its delivery to the ISS with STS-97 in 2000) to its final location on the port side of the station's outboard truss segment.

Perhaps most importantly of all, they returned me to Earth.

We were all aboard *Discovery*, hatches closed and sealed tight, ready for reentry into the Earth's atmosphere. Given that the orbital travel of the shuttle requires her to fly around the globe at a speed of about 17,500 miles per hour and that a successful reentry trajectory can be achieved only when the shuttle has burned off almost all her energy, an effective technique called a "roll reversal" is utilized. Essentially, the shuttle is like a stone being skipped across a lake.

Each time the stone comes in contact with the surface, some of its energy is absorbed by the water. Eventually its speed is sufficiently reduced and it can be "captured," whereupon it sinks beneath the water's surface.

The principle with the shuttle is nearly the same except that instead of skipping across water, we use the Earth's atmospheric layers as a powerful source of friction against her black, silicon-tiled belly. We begin by banking one direction, then swing (roll) the orbiter back in the other. These roll reversals continue until we have decreased our energy enough to be captured by the atmosphere of our planet.

While the two weeks in orbit went well, the mission had been extremely intense. A tear was discovered in the partially unfurled solar array, necessitating an EVA performance from the ground and crew worthy of Apollo 13. Focused solely on mission success, the crew had worked hard and everyone was suffering from fatigue. So much so that Commander Pam "Pambo" Melroy asked if we could have a daylight landing, which would enhance our chances of success. For safety reasons, most pilots would prefer to land in daylight, but our space fliers are trained for night landings as well.

The decision to honor our commander's request required a significant change in our current on-orbit trajectory and flight path. Extra work on Mission Control's end would be required. More than that, the new trajectory would make our atmospheric entry point right over the heartland of the United States. NASA had (purposefully) not done an entry over the continental United States since the *Columbia* tragedy on February 1, 2003.

On November 7, 2007, the planets must have aligned. Special permission was given to Commander Melroy for us to alter our trajectory, enabling us to land in Florida's beautiful midday sunshine. As we initiated our atmospheric entry profile, Commander Melroy keyed the microphone seconds prior to execution of the first of these critical banking maneuvers. In a voice reflecting her years of training and experience, she told ground control, "Houston, this is *Discovery* on air-to-ground 1. We are initiating our first roll reversal over (and she paused briefly for effect) the great state of Nebraska."

Using these specialized maneuvers to slow us down to "entry interface" velocity, we fell toward Earth like a huge stone. Our aerosurfaces performing flawlessly, we made our final turn for the runway at the Kennedy Space Center, and at 12:01 eastern standard time we touched down on runway 15/33. It was November 7, 2007, the fifteenth wedding anniversary of my wife, Susan, and me.

And oh, by the way, did you realize that November 7 can also be written as 11-7 or 117?

Given the data analysis presented herein, I defy anyone to tell me that there isn't a higher power out there orchestrating these things into place so a small-town boy from Nebraska could live his dream. I don't think it could have been scripted any better.

Wait . . . did I mention that my NASA career spanned thirty years; fifteen as an engineer and fifteen as an astronaut?

Serendipitous!

My first trip into space would last at least five months, maybe longer. In those precious few days just before launch, my desire was to have as much private time with Susan as possible (and no, not for what you think). During that time one of the recurring themes running through my life was my undying love for this woman. She had been so supportive of my dream. Susan had sacrificed her own promising NASA career so that she could take care of our family while I was traveling the globe (and eventually *around* the globe). This was her time, too, and I wanted to share as much of the experience as possible with her.

I was really looking forward to seeing Susan at our pad tour. Scheduled to take place a day prior to liftoff, it was another unique opportunity afforded to our family by NASA's family support office. It was going to be a warm day, as *Atlantis* was scheduled to depart Earth during the late afternoon of June 8. It could have been worse—we could have been set to go at noon.

Everyone was excited as we gathered together—spacemen and families—in the astronaut crew quarters facility at Kennedy. Susan looked beautiful (as always) in a pair of khaki shorts with a matching bright red tank top and light sweater emblazoned with our Expedition 15 logo, courtesy of Lands' End Business Outfitters.

I was adorned in my royal blue flight suit and boots, proudly wearing my red Expedition 15 logo baseball cap—the one I hoped to secretly smuggle on board for launch. Our family had chosen red (for "Go Big Red" and Nebraska) as our personal color scheme on launch day in spite of the fact that red is always the crewmember ID color for the mission commander. Officially, my crewmember ID color was burgundy since I was added to the crew so late.

The tour of the pad is specifically designed to be undertaken with one's spouse. Allowances would be made for a significant other or parent if the astronaut was not married.

But my selection of a pad tour partner was a no-brainer. I would have the most beautiful spouse in the history of the astronaut corps at my side.

We boarded the bus that would transport us—using a propulsion system requiring the force of gravity—to a second and more impressive vehicle whose propulsion system was required to defy that same force of gravity.

Upon our arrival at the pad, we quickly assembled for the requisite crew and family photo op before being allowed to begin our painstaking navigation of the launchpad and its towering spaceship. Every turn was precarious, and the utmost care was required to safely move among the pad's hardware, umbilicals, and prepositioned safety stanchions. Eager to get as close as possible to this highly complex machine, we had been prebriefed that touching anything was strictly forbidden.

The marvel of human engineering known as the Space Transportation System stood silently at attention, stretching majestically into the sky over two hundred feet above. Perched atop a circa 1960s belt-driven crawler, the occupant of Pad 39A sent chills up my spine as I imagined the power of the launch soon to come.

As a rookie space flier, I was uncertain of what would transpire over the next days and months. I grasped Susan's hand tightly as we walked past the massive bells of *Atlantis*'s three main engines. We didn't say much, but I truly believe our thoughts were one as we took in the sights, sounds, and smells around us. Our silent prayers for safety occupied our thoughts during what was our final time together for months or, God forbid, perhaps forever.

As we traversed the base of *Atlantis*, her burnt orange foam–covered external tank and gleaming white solid rocket motors appeared to be hugging tightly against her black-tiled belly—as if she were wearing an explosive-laden backpack. Much like teenagers on a first date, Susan and I chose our words carefully, sensitive to the enormous anxiety we were experiencing.

We talked about the magnitude and significance of what we were undertaking together in less than twenty-four hours. We talked of our families and specifically my parents, Alice and John (who was nicknamed Jack but we called him John around the kids to avoid confusion because Susan's father was also named Jack). I casually remarked about how proud my father would have been were he still alive. The simple thought triggered tears to prick my eyes, and it took only seconds before they started to flow fully as I gazed lovingly into Susan's own eyes.

Suddenly we both noticed a small, beautiful butterfly hovering ever so gently above our heads. Almost in unison the moment took hold in our hearts. Our eyes locked again, and I grasped her hands and said, "Hey, maybe that's my dad, coming to tell us that everything will be okay." We smiled and kissed, hoping the moment would somehow last forever. If there was fear in our hearts, we were both fighting hard to hold it at bay.

Eventually we boarded the launchpad's high-speed elevator destined for the 195-foot level. There, the flight-ready crew would soon navigate the narrow gantry way from the orbiter's servicing structure to the small, now quiet "white room." In less than twenty-four hours, we would don our parachutes and harnesses—already hanging there in anticipation of our arrival—for sequential orbiter ingress according to the oft-practiced and well-honed timeline.

The silence was pronounced as we accelerated quickly upward, sensing pressure changes through equalizing "pops" within our inner ears, the result of the rapid rise in our own "mini-launch" sequence. The view of the southeastern Florida coast was spectacular as we emerged through the *Star Trek*–like stainless steel elevator doors, separating quickly and lacking only the audible hiss recognizable from the hit television show of the sixties. It was breathtaking and awe-inspiring at the same time, presenting us with a look that few get the chance to enjoy.

Susan and I followed the emergency evacuation pathway. Shaped like an arrow, the dashed yellow lines painted on the grated floor of the all-metal structure would guide us if there were a major shuttle disaster. The arrows led to the safety system of rescue baskets hanging on the platform's northwest side. They had been used only once by astronauts in a practice exercise in the 1980s. These baskets, reminiscent of an amusement park ride, were designed to carry crew members and pad support personnel down a steel cable to an awaiting concrete bunker on what would truly become known as a very bad day.

With proper crew execution, in the midst of a massive fire-preventing deluge of water, we would move single file, hands on our crewmate's shoulders, following the yellow arrows to reach and occupy the slide wire baskets.

In a true leap of faith, with a desperate slam of the hand onto the baskets' restraint-line cutting device, the gondola ride would begin. Powered only by gravity, the baskets would sail down their zip line to the bunker below, the last hope of safety and survival.

We continued our journey clockwise around the pad and its elevator, moving past the slide wire baskets to stop at another landmark of sorts, the door of the famous 195-foot toilet. Stainless steel with no lid, this metallic commode provides the penultimate chance for ground-based gravity-supported relief. Failure to take advantage of this high-altitude accommodation prior to entering the white room leaves you with the last resort, NASA's maximum absorbency garment, or diaper.

We climbed more stairs enabling us to rise above the level of the white room to reach an even footing with the top of the external tank. Stretching some fifty feet above the orbiter's nose cap, it is the highest point reachable (by humans) on the pad.

Susan and I paused here once again, silently marveling at all God had lain before us. It was only a few seconds until we both noticed we again had a visitor. Our butterfly friend graced us for a second time, both of us remarking that it certainly seemed odd a butterfly would go so high. Our knowledge of butterflies was limited to those seen much closer to ground level and in butterfly exhibits at the zoo. Amid more tears and a hug so firm that it would be remembered for many months, we were indeed one. Our love as strong as ever, we knew that it was my dad. He was right there with us . . . and he approved!

My final moments with Susan would be shared at the beach house. Dubbed as the "kiss and cry" by veteran astronauts, it followed the pad tour, when we assembled for a light lunch and our final walks on the beach. There were no other family members present, just each crewmember and his or her spouse.

As Susan and I departed the pad in our rental car to make our way to the convention center and beach house, I toyed briefly with the idea of finding a secluded road on the KSC wildlife refuge where she and I might be able to share a bit of intimacy for the final time until my return.

But the self-induced pressure I was feeling to meet Commander Sturckow's strict schedule was too much for my first-time flier brain, and I judged it best we arrive at the beach house close to when the others would get there. I would learn later (while in orbit with my ISS replacement Dan Tani) that STS-120 Commander Pam Melroy had provided Dan and his wife, Jane, with a few hours of private time at the beach house before his long-duration flight. Pambo arranged alternate transportation for Dan back to crew quarters, an indication of her thoughtfulness regarding her crew and a stark contrast to the marine corps all-business approach of the man serving as my commander.

Our "kiss and cry" was exactly that, but surprisingly for me it was much more crying than kissing. It was a beautiful moment shared with the love of my life. Our quiet time on the beach—holding hands, hugging, talking, kissing, and crying—would have to hold me over until my return to Earth in the fall. At that moment, November seemed a very long time away.

I needed another appearance by our butterfly.

19

Walking Tall

Winters in Nebraska can be brutal: freezing cold temperatures, mounds of snow, and north winds that can knock you on your ass. I remember those winter mornings as a kid when we wanted to go outside and play in the snow no matter the conditions. Without fail our mother would say, "Please put your boots on before you go outside." Dad would chime in, too, admonishing us: "Put on your hat or you'll catch a cold." They behaved exactly as parents are supposed to, making it their goal to keep us warm and toasty and safe from winter's ills.

Performing a spacewalk outside the space station is not much different from going outside in a Nebraska winter. The space environment is just as brutal as those I encountered as a kid . . . okay, maybe a little bit worse. While it is void of snow, dressing appropriately before heading out the door is just as critical. In space it can mean the difference between life and death.

Our clothing becomes our safe haven in the vacuum of outer space. The suit—the bright white extravehicular mobility unit, or EMU—is our personal spacecraft. It runs on battery power and contains all the oxygen we need to breathe, water to keep our bodies cool, and systems to remove heat and carbon dioxide as we perspire and exhale. It is our life support, micrometeoroid protection, communication, electricity, propulsion, and thermal control, all rolled into one.

The suit contains headlights (which really are near our heads) to help us see when the sun is blocked by Earth, a television camera (giving the control team a bird's-eye view of everything we're doing), and a tool belt. The belt, fastened to the front of the suit and called a mini-workstation, allows us to stow and carry the uniquely designed tools we will need during our time outside.

For an astronaut to be officially assigned to a space station mission, he or she must have already successfully completed a series of tests and an EVA skills training flow, demonstrating they have the capability and aptitude to safely perform a spacewalk.

It is similar to a professional football player who has played quarterback his entire career and has already mastered the skills of passing, performing hand-offs, reading defensive formations, and calling plays and audibles. During a game, those basic skills, coupled with the most recent scouting report on the opponent, allow the quarterback to refine his team's game plan to cover specific situations.

Preparations required of a spacewalking astronaut begin on the ground. First, NASA engineers work closely with the astronaut to get the best EMU suit fit possible to maximize the crewmember's performance during a six-plus-hour spacewalk.

One of the keys to the suit is a good glove fit. Astronauts try on many pairs of pressure gloves previously used by other astronauts in space. Searching for a pair that allows good hand dexterity and fingertip control, with minimal pain, is a tedious and iterative process. Patience and several practice runs are required in order to find the pair that works best for you.

If a good fit is not possible from the inventory, NASA may choose to build a custom-fit pair of gloves. Working with the suit experts at ILC Dover and in Houston is a long, drawn-out, and tremendously expensive process, but it pays great dividends in the long run.

The hard upper torso, or HUT, is another important suit part. It is sized in medium, large, and extra large, and many astronauts struggle to find the perfect fit. Often astronauts squeeze into a size that is smaller than what they might otherwise wear, trading comfort for a tighter fit and an enhanced work envelope. If they can tolerate the snugness for a brief period, the fit becomes more accommodating once the suit is pressurized. An astronaut who demonstrates the ability to wear HUTs of different sizes helps the folks who plan the EVAs. If the suit you usually wear is not available (say, an extra large) because it is broken or not even on board, being able to wear the next smaller size may bail NASA out of a jam when an unexpected failure necessitates an impromptu excursion outside.

The lower portion of a spacewalking suit, known as the lower torso assembly (LTA), is comprised of three major parts. First is the waist assembly (think of it as your briefs), which is connected to the leg assemblies. These are in turn connected to the boots. Achieving the correct length of the LTA is important to your long-term comfort in the suit and is accomplished using various sizing rings, multiple leg lengths, and tiny adjustable leg-restraint cams.

The fit and your personal comfort can be different when performing underwater training sessions than it is working in zero gravity. Underwater, gravity may cause the harder portions of the suit to poke and rub you in places you don't want to be poked or rubbed. When in orbit, your body essentially floats within the surrounding suit, and pressure points can be avoided if your suit sizing is correct. Roughly an inch is added to the lower portion of the suit to compensate for the fact that your spine expands in the absence of gravity. This way, "hotspots" are usually avoided.

Assuming a successful suit fit, astronauts practice spacewalks in the 6.2-million-gallon swimming pool called the Neutral Buoyancy Laboratory in Houston. Dubbed "inner space" by the astronauts, the buoyancy lab is currently the largest indoor pool in the world. It took nineteen hours of continuously pouring concrete to build it, and to fill it with water took over thirty days (due to city water restrictions). The forty-feet-deep, two-hundred-feet-long, and one-hundred-feet-wide body of water is used the same way kids play in the local swimming pool. By taking a huge gulp of air and then letting just enough out, you can keep yourself hovering in the same position underwater. That's almost exactly what we do.

Inside a suit inflated to 4.3 pounds of internal pressure per square inch, you are a simulated balloon on a string. With lead weights inserted into the pockets on the outside of your "spaceship," you can be made neutrally buoyant, neither sinking from nor rising to the surface. It is simulated microgravity.

For a space shuttle mission that had planned spacewalks, ten hours of underwater training were required for each hour spent working outside. Since most shuttle flights were less than two weeks long, everything was precisely choreographed to accomplish many things in a short time. Counting on almost perfect execution, every last detail was "pounded flat" to reduce the chance that something would surprise the on-orbit crew.

For long-duration EVA preparation, the ratio is closer to five hours in the water for each hour in space. This relaxed training template relies on the premise that each astronaut is trained to possess the necessary *general* skills that can be applied to any task they encounter, so it is not necessary to hone highly specific aptitudes. It also makes sense considering the fact that ISS crews are constantly traveling around the globe, making it difficult for crews to train together in the pool. If problems are encountered, the longer ISS missions afford more flexibility to extend the length of the walk or cut it short and come inside. The team can regroup for another try at a later time, since spacewalking ISS astronauts aren't rushing to catch their flight home.

I would spend over 650 hours training in the forty-foot depths of the buoyancy lab pool. Working with one of the most skilled cadres of scuba divers ever assembled and a host of expert spacewalking trainers, this Nebraskan would come to perform six spacewalks, spanning almost forty hours, in his fifteen-year career.

On July 23, 2007, I was poised in the ISS airlock, floating silently above the Earth-facing hatch. Watching the pressure gauge indicator move slowly toward near-vacuum, I was calm. With a "go" from the ground control team, I confirmed the airlock hatch pressure was close to zero and began to manipulate the manual hatch handle. Turning the requisite one-and-a-half turns, the seal separated from the outer ring and the hatch was free to open.

Serving in the coveted slot of lead spacewalker (EV-1), I was heading outside with a Russian cosmonaut. I had never before been on a spacewalk.

Carefully lifting the small welded handle on the hatch's inner frame, I pulled straight up and then pushed forward, folding the hatch's outer edge against the wall and locking it in the open position.

"Houston, EV-1, the hatch is open and locked," I called.

"Copy. Hatch open and locked," came CAPCOM Chris Cassidy's echoing reply.

Awaiting the official call from CAPCOM for egress, I took a few seconds to float over the three-foot opening. Following a curved handrail outlining the hatch circumference with the fingertips of my gloved right hand, I reoriented slightly, positioning myself for a head-first exit. The scene through my new window to the world was a pitch-black canvas.

Having opened the hatch when the sun was shielded by the Earth, it was the blackest black I had ever seen. Tiny ice particles flew from the left, behind my suit, to instantly disappear in the darkness before me. Created by my suit's sublimator (its air conditioning system), the particles originated in the airlock where the pressure was slightly above zero. With the vacuum of space totally void of pressure, the difference pushes the ice from high to low pressure, just as wind blows autumn leaves on the Earth.

Hundreds of thoughts should have been running through my head, but there was only one: "I was born to be here, right now, doing this."

I would perform six spacewalks in my astronaut career, but my first was the most significant.

Fyodor and I spent seven hours and forty-one minutes in the vacuum of outer space, making no errors, accomplishing every single objective on our list.

Key among our tasks was the jettison of two pieces of space hardware. Called Flight Support Equipment (FSE), the first, a Video Stanchion Support Assembly (VSSA)—an aluminum stand that previously held stanchions for mounting cameras and lights—was about the size of a large coffee table. The second, a more formidable piece of soon-to-be space junk, was the Early Ammonia Servicer, or EAS, a storage tank for gaseous ammonia.

Placed on the space station in its early years of construction, the tank provided a source of extra ammonia for the station's external cooling system. On ISS, ammonia serves as Freon, transferring heat from electronic components throughout the station and also near the solar arrays out to the radiators where it is "dumped" to the frigid temperatures of space. This thermal heat exchange brings cool ammonia back to the station, where it repeats the cycle.

The EAS weighed over fourteen hundred pounds. Bigger than a side-by-side refrigerator-freezer, it was no longer needed when the station upgraded to a more effective external cooling system. Rather than bring the heavy and cumbersome tank home on a shuttle, NASA decided to jettison the hardware into space, where it would eventually burn up on reentering Earth's atmosphere.

Fyodor and I worked together on this endeavor. With Russian crewmate Oleg Kotov operating the station's Canadian-built robotic arm—the first time in history that a Russian was to fly the arm solo—I stood anchored to the boot plate of a portable foot restraint installed on top of the robotic arm's grapple mechanism. "Riding the bucket" like a lineman reestablishing power after a hurricane, Oleg delivered me to the EAS and Fyodor, both high on the station's (z1) upper truss.

With a solid grip on the EAS handrails, I gave Fyodor the "go" to release the single bolt holding it in place. With six counterclockwise turns from his pistol-like screwdriver, Fyodor freed the EAS. It literally leaped from the truss toward my suit. Pushing back hard against the massive tank's imbedded force, I was provided with real-time refreshers on the concepts of $F = ma$ and six degrees of freedom.

I verbally guided my Russian crane operator, using mostly English but throwing in an occasional phrase in Russian, while he began flying me toward the hardware's disposal position.

Maneuvering the arm to the appropriate jettison position was tedious. With Oleg operating the Canadian-built manipulator through a combination of computer keyboard and hand controller inputs, the combined mass of me, my spacesuit, and the weighty tank meant our movement would be at the slowest of rates. Moving closer to the time of jettison with each passing minute, we silently bored through the heavens, a continuously writhing snake seeking its optimal striking position.

Our trajectory brought us in over the northwestern United

States on a beautiful daylight pass. Sailing high above the planet, my vantage point seemed Godlike. Tilting the tank down ever so slightly, I could see from Seattle, Washington, all the way to the Great Salt Lake. Moving in a southeasterly direction, the snow-covered Rocky Mountains stretched beneath my boot-clad feet as I fantasized about throwing the EAS away over my home state of Nebraska.

A successful jettison required a trajectory that would deorbit the massive tank safely and not impact anyone on earth. To enhance our chance of success, the control center team had deliberately maneuvered the ISS to fly backward while we slept.

Now, with the station flying a tail-first attitude on its normal flight path, Oleg initiated our final maneuver, turning me upside down on the arm, the EAS still tight within my grasp.

Head pointing to Earth, station flying backwards, I would throw (or push) the tank directly away, as if making a chest pass in a basketball game. Critical to the mission, if I threw it fast enough and directly away from ISS (within a thirty-degree cone emanating from my chest), the effects of orbital mechanics would move the tank into a lower, more retrograde (opposite the direction of station travel) orbit. Objects in lower orbits move faster, resulting in a quicker separation between the station and the tank, alleviating concerns they may crash into one another in subsequent revolutions.

My push required a minimum velocity of about five centimeters per second, but anything greater than twenty centimeters per second would be welcomed. The ground had calculated a toss of that magnitude would guarantee the tank would be on its way to an aluminum-ammonia demise.

They just wouldn't know exactly when or where.

In a manner practiced hundreds of times on an air-bearing floor, in the NBL's huge swimming pool, and with a virtual reality simulator, I rocked back on the end of the arm, holding onto the tank's two vertical handrails.

My sight now totally blocked by the tank's enormous size, I would be throwing it blind. The rehearsed techniques would give me the best shot at imparting ample velocity, in the proper direction, to this now-useless chunk of metal and insulation.

Flexing my lower body to arrest backward movement, then pushing my feet hard against the boot plate to create a heel-to-toe rocking motion, astronaut and massive tank began to inch closer to the jettison point.

Hours of training kept me patient as I held the tank steady, waiting for it to pass the vertical position.

Flushed with adrenaline, I readied myself for release. "Patience, patience," I chanted silently, fighting to keep my arms still, coiled like springs, waiting for the perfect moment.

Forty-five. Sixty-five. Eighty degrees. Vertical! Hesitating slightly, as dictated by hours of rehearsal, now just past vertical, I pushed like hell against the fourteen-hundred-pound mass. Reacting to the combination of forces, the tank moved forward and my body snapped back. The boot plate was the only thing that prevented me from self-launching as I yelled "Jettison!" into my comm-cap assembly microphones.

The tank tumbling away, I studied the direction of its pitching and rolling, calculating rough numbers in degrees per minute. Grabbing a camera from my right-side tool swing arm, I captured its motion against the eerie black background of space.

Fyodor, watching while perched on the station's structure near the lab, excitedly called out in heavily Russian-accented English, "Good jettison!"

Postflight calculations showed I threw the VSSA FSE away at over 140 centimeters per second and the EAS over 40 centimeters per second, far exceeding the premission estimates. Not bad for an old fart!

We had created two new space satellites that day. Our station commander dubbed them "Nebraska 1" and "Nebraska 2." Back inside, relaxing over sips of Russian cognac, forever obliterating the U.S. Space Program's assertion that there is no alcohol aboard the International Space Station, we felt good. The "Three Musketeers in Orbit" had done their jobs, and we had done them well.

The VSSA FSE (Nebraska 1) would reenter Earth's atmosphere in less than a month. The EAS (Nebraska 2), however, took fifteen months to meet its demise, entering the Tasman Sea directly south of the island of Tasmania on November 3, 2008.

I would perform five more spacewalks, two of them with members of the crew of STS-118 while continuing my five months in orbit. Engineer Rick Mastracchio and Canadian medical doctor Davyd (Dave) Williams would each take a turn in venturing outside with the station crew's most seasoned American spacewalker. (That would be me.)

Disappointingly, both of those spacewalks were to be cut short, the first due to a hole in Rick's spacesuit glove and the second because of Hurricane Dean, a Category 5 storm that roared into the Gulf of Mexico bringing with it the fear that is could possibly hit the city of Houston. Shortening the walks by more than one hour each, Mission Control acted reasonably with an edge toward safety. In deference to the STS-118 crew and their families' need to make hurricane preparations, Mission Control also chose to move the crew's undocking and landing earlier by a day, to get them home sooner.

Rick and I would take three more trips outside on the crew of *Discovery* and STS-131. I would become an expert in ammonia operations again, this time aiding in the replacement of the newest ammonia tanks on the station.

Seems like I was in a bit of a rut, but what a rut it was!

According to *Wikipedia*, among the thirty astronauts and cosmonauts who have the most EVA time, the current record (as of January 2015) is held by Russia's Anatoly Solovyev, with eighty-two hours and twenty-two minutes from sixteen EVAS. He is followed by U.S. Astronaut Michael Lopez-Alegria with sixty-seven hours and forty minutes in ten EVAS.

At the end of my career, I had accumulated thirty-eight hours and twenty-eight minutes over six EVAS, ranking me twenty-eighth on the world's list of cumulative spacewalk time. Imagine, twenty-eighth in the history of the *world*, and me, a small-town kid from Nebraska.

That's what I call walking tall.

20

Fame and Fortune

Contrary to popular belief, astronauts don't make a lot of money—at least not when compared to professional athletes, celebrity musicians, or movie stars. We live comfortably for the Houston area, but we are by no means millionaires.

When we arrive in Houston as rookies in the Astronaut Corps and adopt the not-so-complimentary moniker of "ASCAN," we are short on fame and short of fortune.

Each of us is required, if we weren't already, to become an employee of the U.S. government. Military ASCANs are basically on loan to NASA from their respective branch of the service. It is called a "temporary duty station," or TDY, on all the relevant paperwork.

As U.S. Civil Service employees, those of us not in the military are compensated within the guidelines of the federal employee pay scale, which is broken down into "grades" and "steps" based on education levels and/or previous experience.

Prior to becoming an astronaut, I was the manager of Johnson Space Center's Emergency Operations Center. At that point in my career, I had worked for the federal government for fifteen years, steadily climbing the corporate ladder. My 1998 pay level was GS-15 Step 3, or a gross annual salary of about $90,000. Not bad at all. Quite prestigious for a small-town Nebraska boy. It was almost five times what my father was making in 1981, the year I joined NASA as an intern.

My father had been employed by the State of Nebraska for over thirty years when I got my first internship with NASA in 1981, yet my annual pay rate that year topped Dad's by almost $5,000. Appalling.

When I learned of my selection to the Astronaut Corps, I was elated and disappointed at the same time. While anticipating the wonderful opportunities soon to be available, I also learned I was going to receive a demotion.

The head of the Human Resources Directorate at JSC, Harvey Hartman, decreed I accept the demotion. He claimed a precedent had been set with previous astronaut classes. The demotion would not be of the monetary sort—at least not at first. I would be bumped down into a lower *grade* on the pay scale but at a higher *step*. My gross annual income would remain nearly the same. Instead of a GS-15 Step 3, I became a GS-14 Step 10.

What Human Resources didn't point out (and I learned too late) was at the level of GS-14 Step 10, I would be at the highest end of that pay scale versus the lower end of the GS-15 scale.

My "step" salary increases occur after spending time "in grade." In other words, as a low-end GS-15, over the next ten years I would earn five pay raises. At that point I would be topped out and my salary would remain constant unless I moved up a grade.

At the high end of the GS-14 pay scale, I wouldn't get a pay raise for three years. At about $3,500 a year, it would end up costing me about $10,500. Not inconsequential.

But honestly, it was okay . . . after all, I was an astronaut. The most demeaning part of the whole exercise was that I lost my parking space. And man, did I have a good one.

My selection to the Astronaut Corps required me to switch buildings (from Building 30 to Building 4 South) when I reported for duty. I worked to "game" the parking system by contacting my good friend and colleague Steven Elsner.

Elsner, a fellow Mission Operations Directorate teammate, had recently changed jobs, requiring he move from Building 4S to Building 30. We negotiated a deal to swap parking spaces and officially contacted JSC security to make it "legal." With their consent I was to park in the front row of Building 4S, a mere thirty feet from the door. I was living in high cotton!

It was not to be.

Randy Stone, my good friend and former boss when he was directorate chief, lobbied valiantly on my behalf for maintaining my grade level and parking spot. But it was to no avail. Mr. Hartman and NASA's upper management would not budge, reiterating that precedent had already been established. Woe is me.

The life of an astronaut has many more advantages than disadvantages. First and foremost is the obvious opportunity to experience life off our planet, floating, playing, and working in the sway of a near–zero gravity environment.

High on the list of perks is the possibility of meeting distinguished personalities and celebrities. If asked on the street, they wouldn't have a clue as to my identity, but I would certainly know theirs.

I have been fortunate to meet Presidents Bush 41 and Bush 43, Pope Benedict, and a plethora of members from the Senate and the House of Representatives.

I had the privilege of meeting Bill and Melinda Gates, two of the most benevolent people on the planet.

I have refereed NBA basketball scrimmages for the Houston Rockets franchise, calling fouls and violations against All-Stars and future Hall-of-Famers Hakeem Olajuwon, Clyde Drexler, Charles Barkley, and Dikembe Mutumbo.

Being an astronaut has presented marvelous opportunities and led to lasting friendships.

One of the most passionate and space-dedicated people I know, who I now call friend, is Barry Warner. Nicknamed "B-dub" by those who have followed his television and radio broadcasting career, Barry, originally from Buffalo, New York, is a longtime Houston sports authority. He is also a huge fan of NASA. Well versed in her history and a personal friend to many of the "Original Mercury 7" astronauts, Barry has a passion and enthusiasm for our nation's space program that is a wonder to behold. NASA needs more fans like him.

Early in my career as an astronaut, I was honored by the national scholastic honorary Alpha Chi at their convention in Savannah, Georgia. A member of this collegiate honor society while at Hastings College, I was named their Distinguished Alumnus in 2001, following in the footsteps of CBS Evening News anchorman Dan Rather, who received the same honor in 1993.

Flying to an unrelated public appearance just prior to the Alpha Chi convention, I picked up the Southwest Airlines *Spirit* travel magazine from the pocket in front of my seat. Thumbing through its pages, I stopped to read an article about a *New York Times* best-selling author named Nevada Barr. The article contained an excerpt from her latest work, *Blood Lure*.

Nevada, a storyteller of the highest caliber, had authored eight novels prior to this one in 2001. Her protagonist, Anna Pigeon, a park ranger for the National Park Service, had an uncanny knack of stumbling upon, and eventually solving, murders occurring in national parks.

The keynote speaker at the Alpha Chi convention that year was none other than Nevada Barr. We would meet there for the very first time, along with Susan and my family, including four-week-old daughter, Sutton, my four-year-old son, Cole, both of my in-laws, and my mother.

Captivated by her easygoing style and clever wit, I purchased a copy of her book that day, which she autographed: "For Clayton— With Best Wishes and a just little envy. Love, Nevada." She added a short postscript, "I hope our paths cross again. N.B."

Our paths would cross again—in Houston, at a book signing for her next novel, *Hunting Season*.

I arrived early at Murder by the Book, a charming bookstore in Rice Village, hopping in line to purchase a copy of her book and securing my number for the autograph session to follow. Sitting far in the back, away from those eager individuals fully vested in the lore of Anna Pigeon, I stayed quiet. I watched as she regaled a packed audience of adoring fans with lively answers to their star-struck questions.

Following her presentation, a long line formed to meet her. I remained at the back, oblivious to the proper position that my slip of paper guaranteed.

When everyone had gone through, I slowly approached the small table. I had worn my astronaut flight jacket—the drab military-green winter version—hoping its NASA patches would jog her memory. Nevada, head down and her right hand clutching a black fine-point Sharpie, had taken the next book from her stack and opened it to the proper page for signing.

As she looked up and our eyes met, I said, "Hi, remember me?"

She paused for a second and then leaped from her seat, arms outstretched, running around the table and yelling, "My astronaut!"

Our paths had indeed crossed again, and a lasting friendship was the result.

Nebraska football heroes continue to hold a prime spot at the top of my list. As a former athlete and a native Nebraskan, names like Jerry Tagge, Johnny Rodgers, Mike Rozier, Larry Jacobsen, Grant Wistrom, and Jason Peter stir fond memories from my childhood and later years. The fact that I have had opportunities to spend a few moments with these athletic heroes holds a place of significance in my life.

These athletes who performed memorable feats of skill on the gridiron are role models for me, but they pale in comparison to three special men I had the privilege of meeting as an astronaut. When grouped together, these gentlemen present quite a contrast.

Dr. Tom Osborne is a true Nebraska legend. A state icon who is revered by nearly all, he is best known as the longtime head football coach at the University of Nebraska. He put Nebraska football on the national stage and established an institutional tradition that is, arguably, second to none.

I called Coach Osborne for the first time while soaring 215 nautical miles above our planet. He was then serving his state and country as a U.S. congressman (and would later return to the University of Nebraska as athletic director.) During our short conversation, I honored him for his service and the positive impact he has had on our state and our nation. Back on the ground, I would tease him about how he still owed the government for charges from my "collect" call.

And how many astronauts can claim that they are on a first-name basis with the man famous for the phrase "*Git 'r done!*"? Dan Whitney (a.k.a. Larry the Cable Guy) is one of our nation's funniest comedians and a member of the famous Blue Collar Comedy Tour. I am proud to call him my friend.

Susan and I first met Dan and his wife, Cara, on a whim. Noticing in the *Houston Chronicle* that Larry and the Blue Collar Comedy Tour were coming to Houston in January 2010, we contacted our friend Allan Beermann in Nebraska. Beermann, a high-powered and well-connected individual (who served as Nebraska's secretary of state for twenty-four years), seems to know everyone in Nebraska.

After a quick phone call, Allan put us in touch with Dan's agent. Susan and I invited Dan to Houston for a personal tour of the Johnson Space Center on the morning of his show at the Toyota Center.

Much to our delight, Dan accepted our invitation. He flew from Boston to Florida to pick up Cara, whom he declared was an absolute "space nut." Upon their arrival at the space center, our first stop was the world-famous shuttle mission simulator, or SMS. This simulator allows shuttle pilots and commanders to practice realistic ascents into orbit and subsequent landings at airfield sites around the world.

Dan was nervous. He asked if he was going to get motion sickness during the "ride." We assured him all would be well, but his uncertainty was apparent as we introduced him to STS-131 commander Alan "Dex" Poindexter in the lobby of JSC's Building 5.

Cole, now fourteen and tagging along for the day, was pumped, his excitement pronounced as we entered the simulator. For the simulated ride to orbit, Dex took the commander's seat with Dan riding as the pilot. Cole took the mission specialist 1 seat (the same seat I would occupy on *Discovery*'s entry later that April) directly behind "Larry." Cara, positioned in the Mission Specialist 2 chair, was just behind and to the right of Dex, with the best view of the shuttle panels and switches. I rode in the jump seat specifically added for visitors, new trainees, or instructors. Positioned where you really can't see anything, I was the odd man out for our "flight" into space.

Dan, still a bit nervous, listened carefully as Dex gave an orientation briefing. It was evident when he had calmed down because he started to make jokes. Speaking in his normal Dan voice, he asked matter-of-factly, "Dex, is it true you can see the Great Wall of China"—he paused briefly as we anticipated the expected conclusion—"from outer space?"

Instead, he surprised us all. Reverting to his Larry the Cable Guy voice, he added, "and Al Roker from outer space?"

Laughter filled the simulator, and Cole had one of the biggest smiles on his face I had ever seen. This was gonna be fun!

We performed a single-ascent run, with Dex describing important milestones and key data being monitored by the crew on the glowing bright green LED displays in the orbiter's cockpit. When the time came to perform entries and landings, known as "10K's" to astronaut veterans because the runs begin ten thousand feet above the Kennedy Space Center, Dan and Cara's competitive natures came to the fore.

Battling like kids playing video games, each performed their 10K's as if their lives depended on it. With trash talk reminiscent of the NFL's Super Bowl, it was Cara who landed the orbiter *Discovery* with the best technique. When the simulator support team (who all forfeited their day off when they heard who would be flying) came to share the computer printout documenting the results, "Larry" was not a happy camper, and Cara didn't let him hear the end of it.

Meeting Larry the Cable Guy stood in marked contrast to my second meeting with George W. Bush. I had briefly met the president during the *Columbia* memorial service in Houston, but this new opportunity would become a significant event in my family's life. It started in Florida on the day I landed after 152 days in outer space.

After completion of their postflight routines, all the STS-120 astronauts went into Cocoa Beach to spend the night with their families in the NASA-provided condominiums. On the following day, we would enjoy a relaxing time on the beach or at the pool, catching up with our spouses and kids prior to returning to the Cape for a late afternoon flight back to Ellington Field in Houston. All of us had been awake for almost twenty hours, and the standard postlanding data tests and a press conference had left us exhausted.

All? Did I say all? I meant except for Paolo Nespoli and me. As an ISS crewmember with long-duration status, I was the subject of several experiments that required data gathering sessions immediately after landing, and two of those required data the subsequent day, or "L plus 1."

My Italian friend and Penguin classmate, Paolo, would remain in crew quarters as well. The return to Earth's gravitational force after two weeks in space was overwhelming for him. He would need a solid twenty-four hours to recuperate.

I woke on the morning of November 8 ready to stagger—my body still was under the false impression that I was overweight—through NASA's well-thought-out plan for L plus 1. I felt much better than I did on landing day. A good night's sleep, a steaming hot cup of coffee, a solid breakfast (I finally got to eat that steak—only with scrambled eggs instead of a baked potato), and fifteen minutes on an exercise bike energized me physically and mentally.

I was gaunt, pale, and unsteady from the rigors of my space adventure. If I had had any hair I would have been a Tom Petty look-alike. I was already tired of the numerous comments about how pale I was; it didn't seem to matter that I felt pretty good. Everyone else considered me a skeletal member of the walking dead.

No longer required by scientists to serve as a human lab rat (at least not for a few days, anyway), I was looking forward to a day of leisure, lounging by the condominium pool with my family and getting some color back.

Then things changed drastically.

We learned that President Bush, already in Texas for meetings and a fund-raiser, had requested a meeting with the *Discovery* crew. His return to Washington would commence immediately following a short stop for Air Force One at noon on Houston's Ellington Field.

We were told by our commander, Pam Melroy, that NASA management was sending us back to Houston. I could meet briefly with my extended family in crew quarters, but immediately after, Susan, the kids, and I were to report to the nearby Shuttle Landing Facility. There we were to board a NASA business jet to Ellington Field so that when President Bush's motorcade arrived, we would be waiting on the tarmac in front of Air Force One.

President Bush would stop briefly for a "meet and greet," then jump on board for his flight back to Washington.

As the gathered families and crew members waited at the airstrip in Florida, I lay down on the tarmac. Absorbing the amazing warmth from the sun, I was surprised by how much I missed it. Sutton and Cole, my constant companions since our morning reunion in crew quarters, sat next to me, one on each side. No words were spoken as they snuggled close. I sensed their unconditional love through the physical contact, a different kind of warmth they shared with their dad.

Susan, ever present but keeping her distance to allow the kids time to reconnect, smiled broadly as she took in the scene.

Ready to gather our belongings and head to the plane, I struggled to get to my feet. My children were there each time I moved, jumping to their respective positions, Cole on the left and Sutton the right. Serving as steady supports, they were human crutches for their own space alien struggling to readapt to the constant pull of gravity.

Our trio made the slow trek to the foot of the plane's boarding steps like participants in a three-legged race. Joined by Susan, I was soaking it all in, the warmth from the sun and their loving personas.

During the two-hour trip home I mostly slept and held Sutton's hand. She insisted on having the seat next to Daddy. The next thing I knew, we were walking off the business jet and into the massive shadow of Air Force One.

We were early. Commander Melroy ordered me to take a nap until the president's arrival (a totally unnecessary order, I might add) and ordered my crewmates to make notes for their speeches to be given later that afternoon. (Our return ceremony would happen after our meeting with the commander-in-chief, and we needed to be ready to sing the praises of the training and management teams that had prepared us so well.)

When the arrival of the president was imminent, crew and families were directed back out to the tarmac to assume our positions in front of the stairs to Air Force One. Forming a semicircle, we stood patiently, our formation exhibiting the shuttle crew protocol of commander first, then pilot and mission specialists. We arced around the port side of the massive Boeing 747, stretching from her nose to near the leading edge of her massive left wing.

As the "station guy" and an unofficial member of the STS-120 crew, I took my place at the end of the arc. I would be the last to be greeted by the president. Since I was the only long-duration astronaut—the others were the hale and spiffy team that brought me home—they insisted I be given a chair as we waited. Indicative of the perception that I was a blob of humanity, the majority of our welcoming committee felt me incapable of standing on my own after so many months in space.

I held Susan's hand tightly as the waiting was broken by the noise of a motorcade, a parade of black SUVs moving in a serpentine pattern. With the windows tinted black to block the view inside, we had no idea which Suburban held our nation's "top dog."

The screech of rubber tires on asphalt brought me back to reality. I jumped in reaction to the noise, watching with renewed focus as a single SUV departed the governmental congo line and slammed to a stop near the center point of our half circle.

Squinting, I could just make out that someone was inside the vehicle. Arm raised to the back window and exhibiting the familiar, Richard Nixon-like two-finger victory sign, President Bush had arrived.

The door swung open and the president climbed from within. Looking regal and handsome in his finely tailored navy blue suit, pale blue shirt, and red tie, he approached Commander Melroy with the broadest of grins.

He spent considerable time with each crewmember and their family, shaking hands and chatting personably, treating us like normal people just returned from a not-so-normal place. I watched intently, almost studiously, as he completed his quality time with each family and moved in turn ever closer to mine.

As he finished his time with Paolo Nespoli and his beautiful wife, Sasha, his attention turned to me. Our eyes locked solid as he moved to me with purposeful stride, a wide grin on his Texan face.

"Clayton, congratulations on a great mission," he yelled, knowing my name with nary a glance at my flight suit's yellow-trimmed name tag. "But it looks like you lost a little hair while you were up there!"

Cole giggled. Taken aback, I reached out my right hand to meet his extended one. Hands firmly grasped and arms rocking in traditional Texas handshake style, I proudly gave him my smiling reply: "Mr. President, I can't believe you just dissed me about my hair!"

We talked as if old friends, discussing briefly the mission highlights of spacewalks and gorgeous views of earth. He knelt down to Sutton's eye level to speak with her, then six and terribly shy. He shook Cole's hand and talked to him like the solid young man he was. He was gracious and flattering with Susan, giving her a hug and his congratulations on a job well done. Snapping shutters confirmed that his entourage of support staff and photographers captured each moment on their megapixel-display Nikons.

Posing for a final picture with the entire crew complement, he said, "Good job!" and athletically bounded up the lime-green painted staircase, then turned to face the gathered crowd one last time. Presidential in every respect, he smiled and waved with his right arm high, acknowledging our presence and thanking us all. In an instant he was gone, retired to his refuge from the public eye.

It was a proud day for me and a proud day for our family. I was back on Earth after a journey through space and I had met with the President of the United States of America.

I was rich beyond my wildest dreams.

21

Find Us Faithful

Growing up in Ashland, Nebraska, the Anderson family was known throughout town to be faithful and active participants in their church. Disciples of Christ, the First Christian Church of Ashland, was housed in a beautiful red brick building on the corner of Seventeenth and Boyd Streets. It's possible that our family participated in every single aspect of the bustling life within that tiny church. Members of our family sang in the choir, regularly attended church and Sunday school, and served as pianists and organists (as all three of us kids did before heading off to college). In short, we were there, the five of us, with "our prayers, our presence, our gifts, and our service."

A lot of faith was required in my quest to become an astronaut. Having applied fifteen times over fifteen years illustrates that either I did have a very strong faith or I simply didn't know when to quit.

My faith was ultimately rewarded in 1998 with my second trip into the "interview ring." When your number finally does come up and it's accompanied by a request for your presence in Houston, then things truly become exciting. The tension arising from anticipation is alleviated a tiny bit through the selection committee's use of a pre-interview tradition that goes back as far as many can remember. It's called "the question."

Before you sit down with the committee and discuss your life's successes and failures, the committee gives you homework. You are directed to write a response to a question that changes for each astronaut selection. All candidates are given the same question. It can be quite nebulous, perhaps even bordering on meaningless, but the committee is looking for something that makes you stand out from the other 119 wannabes. Their evaluation of your writing and thinking abilities under the pressure of a short deadline gives them a head start on the interview process. Perhaps it's their way of generating appropriate questions to throw at you—or maybe, just maybe, it's hazing.

The question posed to those of us in the NASA Road One Quality Inn in January 1998 was "What do you have to offer the U.S. Space Program?" My response is provided here in part, illustrating precisely how faith is an important part of my belief system. I began by referring to a song entitled "Find Us Faithful," whose lyrics refer to difficult journeys and how those who undertake them first can help lead our way.

> These ideas form the initial verse to a popular contemporary Christian song I have sung many times. Penned by Jon Mohr and recorded by Steve Green, they parallel the human desire to explore. This journey is not just about technical achievements; it is about people. It is about our planet; it is about the future of the entire human race. What began from an era of competition, fueled by the launch of Sputnik forty years ago, has now become the ultimate challenge of cooperation and teamwork. We must continue the journey, for that is where our future lies. This is what we owe our children and all future generations. I want to help "line the way"!

After outlining my technical background and diverse skill set and experience, I emphasized how these characteristics helped me to understand what it means to undertake new and difficult programs. I explained how my leadership skills and my ability to develop and nurture successful partnerships—all critical aspects to the future of human space exploration—would serve me well in the position of U.S. astronaut. My essay ended as follows:

> Our children have big dreams. We must pursue the exploration of space; we cannot take their dreams away. They find themselves in such a complex world, a world full of questionable role models. I want to be a positive role model for them. I want to help teach them the importance of commitment to someone or something, commitment

to a relationship or a dream. I can visualize myself as a United States astronaut speaking to the youth of America about how they too can succeed. I may sound trite, but the truth is I want to make a difference in their lives and the future of America. I want them to know that if a boy from a tiny town in the state of Nebraska can succeed, so can they. I want to be an astronaut and share in that responsibility because I reach for my dreams . . . and I hold firmly to my dream to become a United States astronaut.

Astronauts are constantly asked to respond to questions, many of which are repetitive in nature. For example, I have often been asked about whether my time in space did anything to change me or my spirituality. Each time my answer is the same. My time in space was truly spiritual and it did nothing but strengthen my faith in God.

Sailing around planet Earth at 17,500 miles per hour and watching her beauty unfold with every passing second was inspiring, moving, and surreal. The time spent gazing earthward through an ISS window, multiple panes of glass the only thing separating me from the deadly vacuum of outer space, was an honor and a privilege. It was a time of reflection, a time to turn to God and thank him for the tremendous blessings he has provided me throughout my lifetime.

Within the Astronaut Office, faith and religion can be funny things. Not funny ha-ha, but funny unique, funny strange. Not all astronauts carry a religious faith. Some are true Christians, ready to provide you with anything you need. Others appear to use faith to their advantage, calling upon it when it provides a "Hallmark moment" (e.g., the first time two Jewish astronauts flew together in space). Others are atheists and proud of it. Faith is a personal choice, and the diversity within the Astronaut Corps clearly reflects that fact.

This diversity was driven home to me early in our basic training as astronaut candidates.

Not a single American member of the Penguin class of 1998—twenty-five rookie astronauts all told—had flown in space when I returned in August 2002 from the National Outdoor Leadership School experience in the Wind River Range of Wyoming. After eight days of trudging through the mountains, experiencing the natural beauty of that rugged landscape along with Catherine "Cady" Coleman, Tracy "T.C." Caldwell, Greg "Box" Johnson, Koichi Wakata (JAXA), Ken "Hock" Ham, and the crew of STS-107 and *Columbia*, my appreciation of God's majesty had risen exponentially.

The Penguins had gathered at the home of classmate Mike Foreman and his wife, Lorrie, for an autumnal get-together celebrating nothing more than the fact that we were all still astronauts. In a chair overlooking the Foremans' pool, relaxing with a glass of Cabernet, one of my classmates asked me how our trip to Wyoming went. My exact words escape me, but my response was reflective: "I can't imagine how someone can spend time living in the gorgeous beauty of a place like that and not believe in God."

Illustrating our class diversity, astronaut Stan Love (a brilliant man with a PhD in planetary science), who was sitting on my left, offered his contradictory response. His reply was classic Dr. Love: well thought out, clear and concise, and directly to the point. His slightly condescending tone hinted at a lack of respect for anything godly and told me this was a battle I didn't want to fight. It's not that I was ashamed of my faith—far from it. It's just that knowing him as I did, I decided it was a fight I would never win.

My faith was tested constantly from the first moment I became an astronaut. Yet it's entirely possible that it was tested no more or no less than it would have been otherwise. It's just that as an astronaut, those times seemed magnified. From the minor episode of a torn ACL on the ballfield to the monumental struggle of *Columbia*, my faith was pushed to its limit like never before.

In late 2006, having just been assigned to the STS-118 mission, I had only recently moved into our new office. Shuttle crews beginning the training flow moved into shared office space in one big room with a conference table in the center. Sitting together as a crew was viewed as a simple and effective way to enhance crew camaraderie and maximize communication and mentoring opportunities during the typical nine-month training flow. It also enhanced the crew and training team's abilities to conduct meetings, last-minute classes, and informational exchanges pertinent to the mission's objectives.

I was working in our office one morning, along with STS-118 commander Scott Kelly, when my phone rang. Our secretary, Suzanne Singleton, informed me that my sister, Lorie, was on the line. Thinking she was calling to find out when my next trip to Nebraska might be, I punched the button on the telephone console, ready to chat about small-town life in Nebraska. Calls from Lorie typically began with a bubbly voice saying, "Hi, this is your sister." There was none of that this time; it was just serious elder sister delivering information that I already knew was not going to be good.

"Mom has a spot on her lung," she began. The words that followed were what you might expect from a family member delivering bad news. She never actually said the word cancer, choosing instead to relate how encouraging the doctor was, how he had said it was very early in the process and he couldn't really be sure of how things were going to play out. At her words, tears immediately welled up and I fought to keep them at bay. My steely-eyed astronaut persona would not allow me to cry in front of my shuttle commander, who I stereotypically perceived would consider it a sign of weakness. I shifted my body position and lowered my voice to shield my predicament from what I assumed were his curious eyes and straining ears. Continuing to fight off a flood of emotion, I pushed to end the conversation quickly so that I could exit the office and deal with my fears in privacy.

When a subsequent phone call confirmed a positive biopsy result, reality was driven home. My heart swelled with fear and uncertainty. Our mom was fighting for her life against lung cancer. The news was devastating. I prayed to God to spare her life and to not take her from me as Dad had been taken almost twenty-two years earlier.

Coping with the news of my mother's looming battle brought unneeded stress to my training, diverting my focus from the technical aspects of a space shuttle mission. Living so far away and having no travel flexibility given our training flow, I constantly searched in my mind for ways to help her.

While my assignment to the STS-118 space shuttle crew due to fly to the station was well known within the Astronaut Office, NASA was withholding the official press release announcing my triumph to the world until the international community could come to agreement on the actual names of the assigned crew and the manifest schedule.

Having a press release didn't really matter to me personally (although my ego would have enjoyed it immensely). I had a crew, I had a patch, and I had a mission. It was my mother I was worried about.

To help my mother fighting a battle for her life against cancer, I wanted to be able to give her something she could hang on to, something she could look forward to and use as an incentive to fight as hard as possible and see it through: her son's first spaceflight.

After a "local" T-38 flight I decided to reach out to STS-118 commander Kelly. His rarely used informal call sign, "Grumpy," born of his gruff exterior, diminutive stature, and typically brief, no-nonsense conversations, was a misnomer for this decorated navy fighter pilot with a warm sense of humor and an engaging laugh. We were returning to the office in his well-worn half-ton pickup truck when I decided it was a perfect time for me to bring up the subject that had been eating away at me. I told him the story and asked if there was anything he could do to push for the press release because it was important to me that some kind of official notice came soon. Scott, his brow furrowed with concentration, continued to look straight ahead, and promising nothing, agreed to try.

Whatever clout Scott had with our leadership team manifested itself a few months later with a formal announcement of our impending spaceflight. My stress level dropped considerably, knowing that there were now dates associated with the upcoming journey of the space shuttle *Endeavor* and STS-118.

Like Houston and its unpredictable summertime weather, there was more uncertainty lurking in the shadows, this time on launch-pad 39A.

The STS-117 crew—led by U.S. marine colonel and veteran shuttle commander Frederick "C.J." Sturckow—had been busily preparing for a March 15, 2007, launch date. With their shuttle, *Atlantis*, poised and ready on Kennedy Space Center's launchpad 39A, they approached their terminal countdown test on launch minus thirty days. The all-male crew, limited to six to offset the massive weight of their solar array cargo, was ready.

A hailstorm had other ideas. It hit the east coast of Florida, pelting the foam insulation of the stack's external fuel tank, rendering it unsafe for launch.

The delay threw off NASA's entire launch schedule. Suni Williams, already living aboard the ISS, was to return home with the STS-118 crew. The hail-induced launch delays would impact both STS-117 and STS-118 and Suni's return to Earth, putting her precariously close to her radiation flight limit, thereby increasing the risk that she would lose the chance to fly again.

The STS-117's new flight date would be based on the tank repair schedule. Encouraged by the engineers' progress, NASA set a launch date of June 8, 2007. NASA's weight, balance, and center of gravity calculations showed that a margin did exist for them to carry an additional passenger. This put me in position to potentially become Suni's "knight in shining armor." If I were reassigned to the *Atlantis* crew, I could swap places with Suni so she could return home.

Heisenberg's uncertainty principle was now in full control of my life. My mid-August launch date—moved up to June—threw my family's plans into an uproar.

While my wife fought with hotels and caterers to change room dates and redirect deposit money, I was engulfed in a new and more urgent training flow.

I had little time to train with my new crewmates. I found myself thrust into the fixed-base portion of the shuttle mission simulator (it doesn't move like its hydraulically driven counterpart), where they were well into their final eight-hour simulation, focused on activities performed immediately after reaching orbit. I worked feverishly looking for ways to contribute. I approached every STS-117 alpha-male crewmember with the offer "What can I do to help you?" They would all reply, "Thanks, but I've got it," leaving me to huddle near the food hydration station of the shuttle's middeck, adding four ounces of hot water to crinkly packages of green bean casserole and macaroni and cheese, accepting my newfound role as spaceflight lunch caterer.

But all was not totally chaotic. Mom had faithfully completed her five rounds of chemotherapy, and just weeks before launch had been given a clean bill of health. The relief my family and I felt from this God-given news charged us with renewed confidence and energy as we moved toward the event that would define our lives forever.

In no time at all, I was seated in astronaut crew quarters in Houston with our pastor from Webster Presbyterian Church, the Reverend Mark Cooper. At my request, we had gathered to take communion and pray together one last time before I would depart (temporarily) from Earth.

My faith, although I felt it was strong, was clearly being challenged with all that had transpired, and I found myself on edge as Pastor Mark carefully removed the elements from the felt-lined case that protected its hallowed contents. Nervous energy pulsed through my body as we sat on the foot of my bed, but as we prayed together, I experienced a new sense of calm. As Pastor Mark asked God to protect me on this perilous journey, I knew this was the right place for me, that it was my destiny to head into this potentially deadly and intriguing frontier.

After three days in Houston watching "crew-bonding" movies— *Smokey and the Bandit, My Cousin Vinnie,* and *A Few Good Men* (what marine colonel and shuttle commander could resist that one?)—and being quarantined so we wouldn't launch sick, I found myself climbing the blue metal ladder to strap myself into the back seat of a T-38 for a trip to Spaceport USA.

My pilot that day was rookie astronaut Kevin Ford (who would serve as the ISS commander in January 2013), a man I had come to know well during his tenure as our director of operations in Star City, Russia. We arrived at the Shuttle Landing Facility within minutes of my crewmates, who had already disembarked and were assembling in front of the symmetrical formation of now-quiet jets.

We had a press conference on the tarmac. Commander Sturckow had informed us beforehand that we would be "keeping it brief," hinting that we make the same remarks we did at the Terminal Countdown Demonstration Test (TCDT). Having not participated in their TCDT, I didn't know what I would say, but I knew it would be brief! Afterward we were off to crew quarters to spend the three days prior to launch.

With all preflight preparations and training complete, my focus during quarantine was on my family and the length of time I would be away. Fear had been trained out of me, but I did have anxiety about the separation looming on the horizon.

Two days before launch we had the second-to-last get-together with family. The first, held at the KSC Resort and Conference Center (called the beach house) where President John F. Kennedy was purported to have spent some quality time with Marilyn Monroe in the sixties, was the traditional crew dinner with spouses and up to four special guests.

I had been to the beach house before, first on an orientation trip with my fellow Penguins in 1998 and then as a family escort for the *Columbia* crew. It was considered an astronaut sanctuary on the beach, the place where astronauts and their loved ones assembled one final time before launch.

This time my experience in the beach house was different. I recalled how I had been only a small part of the gathering of the *Columbia* crew a few short years before. Commander Rick Husband had embraced the moment in a leadership gesture. He opened the night with a loving prayer and then took the opportunity to introduce each of his crewmembers and relate something unique and special about their contribution to the mission and crew.

Now, experiencing my own launch party, I realized I had been given a precious gift that night with the STS-107 *Columbia* crew. I had had a glimpse into the true camaraderie of a close-knit crew led by a man of deep faith, a glimpse that allowed me to see the pride and the love they had for their families and friends, all gathered together, harboring the same excitement and the same fears.

Our festivities stood in stark contrast to those of *Columbia*. Commander Sturckow was a marine, a businesslike, no-nonsense leader but no less an effective commander. There was no prayer, no formal introductions of his crew. It seemed he considered this simply another mission distraction, one of a long list of social events that had to be tolerated and completed.

It wasn't that way for me.

My entourage included Susan, Mom, Lorie, Kirby, and Cole. Having my son there was a pleasant surprise—NASA had recently changed the rules to allow any child over the age of ten full access to the beach house event—*if* they received a clean bill of health from the mission's flight surgeon. The only negative in having Cole there was the fact that his six-year-old sister was not.

The weather was cloudy and spitting rain. I had been praying hard for the rain to let up because Cole had brought his baseball glove and catcher's mitt, hoping to pitch and catch with his dad on the beach. With Cole's selection to League City's Little League All-Star Team, his coach, Ali Velasco, had agreed to "allow" him to come to launch as long as he vowed to keep his arm tuned up for the tournament that lay ahead.

When the drizzle finally abated, I found myself down on the beach with Cole, marking off the forty-six feet required of a Little League pitcher and his battery mate. Cole's catcher's mitt on my left hand clearly identified me as the receiving end of the battery.

With Susan watching tearfully and my brother, Kirby, filming Cole humming strikes to his old man, it was a moment I had dreamed about for a long time. When our time reached an end, I walked slowly to my son, wishing that this moment would never end. I hugged him tightly while attempting to tell him through my tears how much I loved him and how proud I was of my tiny All-Star.

I didn't want to let him go, but darkness was beginning to fall and our ever-punctual commander was sending clear signals that it was time to wrap up what seemed to him to be a colossal waste of time.

The next day would prove even harder for me.

The day before launch, or L minus 1, is packed with activities. First and foremost is the pad tour with your spouse, followed by the "wave across the ditch" and, finally, lunch with your spouse, the final time to be together until landing day.

The day was fraught with emotion, as evidenced by our butterfly visit during the pad tour. But nothing could have prepared me for the emotion of the wave across the ditch.

The wave was another space shuttle tradition. Because quarantine is necessary, an astronaut has only a single chance to see all of his or her specially invited guests. Separated by nearly fifty feet of what was once a grass-lined ditch but is now a paved road, the crewmembers and their spouses stand with the shuttle and launchpad to their backs, waving and talking to the excited guests packed several rows deep on the other side of the road.

It was here that my heart was ripped from my body. It was easy to pick out my brother, Kirby, and brother-in-law, Jay, as they stood tall above the rest. I saw Dad's brother, my uncle Jim, wearing his ever-present *Atlantis* ball cap, waving at me with tears flooding his eyes. Hanging far to the back was my Iowa State roommate, Todd Reiher, with his family, quiet as usual, taking everything in. But when I saw my mother with my two children, the flood of emotion was overwhelming. Mom, having shed the albatross oxygen tank dictated by years of smoking, wore her ever-present Expedition 15 pin, positioned smartly at the top of a red, white, and blue ribbon. Her oversized sunglasses, like virtual reality goggles on the head of an elementary school kid, covered her eyes and then some. Not far away stood ten-year-old Cole, his cousin Brice at his side, looking just as he did when we played catch on the beach. Ball cap firmly in place, he was grinning, his teeth gleaming in the sunlight.

And finally, I could see her. Pushed to the front by well-meaning relatives, my daughter, Sutton Marie, appeared, riding firmly on her aunt Lorie's hip.

The fifty feet of asphalt could just as well have been the Grand Canyon. I wanted to walk across that small stretch of pavement and hold them all once again. The pain of not being able to touch my baby girl was almost more than I could bear. Family members were yelling for her to "wave to Mommy and Daddy." She was surrounded by loving family, but to me she looked utterly alone; she needed her daddy.

The tears came hard and I squeezed Susan's hand, moving toward the road to be as close as possible without violating the unwritten law of distance. "I love you, Sweet Pea," I choked out. Tears clouded my vision. I would not see them or touch them for at least five months. I needed God now, perhaps more than ever. I prayed that I would hold them all again.

The last few days of an astronaut's launch preparation have an intangible quality that is hard to describe in words. I experienced a quiet sense of excitement and growing anticipation; isolation gave the days a quality bordering on surreal. The entire final week before launch is a period of quarantine for the crew. We are physically housed in astronaut crew quarters; these facilities exist both at Johnson Space Center and at Kennedy Space Center. Building 27 and Building M-7355, respectively, offer many of the comforts of home and are part of an overall effort to launch us safely to orbit in top health. So much so that crew contact is limited to only those few key personnel who are closely involved with the crew. All others must undergo a physical and be pronounced fit and healthy—free of "bugs"—before limited contact with crew-members is allowed.

Heading off on my first and possibly only spaceflight, I was often alone with my thoughts during my quarantine, especially at Kennedy. The original STS-117 crew was well trained and ready to go, full of hard-charging type A personalities. Led by their intrepid marine commander, who was competent and very set in his ways, they exhibited considerable camaraderie, a result of the hundreds if not thousands of hours spent training together. As the "station guy" assigned at the last minute, I found myself alone in the KSC crew quarters' computer pit just days prior to launch while my crewmates took off on their daily run, not having notified me of the time and place so I might join them. While that was only a single incident, I was alone and I felt it.

Bolstered by the knowledge that my entire family would be present for launch, I was still feeling considerable angst about what was going to happen in the next few days. Although Mom's battle with cancer appeared to be going well—the spot on her lung was gone and she no longer required supplemental oxygen—I still felt a gnawing uncertainty.

The feeling was not fear. Detailed training had taken that from the equation. It was more of a constant ache, like a blister on your heel. Aware of the inherent risk of spaceflight and the uncertain outcome of our mission, I felt a tremendous need to communicate my feelings to my family. I wrote them a letter, with the thought in my mind that a tragedy like *Challenger* or *Columbia* could happen, and that I might not return alive.

I was in nearly the same situation three years later while preparing to launch with the crew of STS-131, facing the boredom and monotony of days in crew quarantine. But this time, to my surprise, I felt different. Again I was restless and uneasy, but I wasn't thinking about an accident. I was second-guessing my decision to become a member of this crew in the first place. My thoughts centered on death and mortality, and I was struggling with feelings of selfishness and doubt. Was I trying to cheat death one too many times? Was I risking my family's stable life just so I could chase a dream I was already fortunate enough to have fulfilled? It was a tough time for me, and I prayed for God's guidance. Trapped in quarantine, I penned a second letter, based on the letter I'd written the last time but altered slightly to include words for my older and much more aware children.

MARCH 25, 2010

My dearest Susan, Cole, and Sutton:

I am so sorry that you have to read this. I am writing this letter to you on Thursday, March 25, just a short time before I must enter into quarantine. I decided that I need to say some things to you all in the event of a tragedy during our space shuttle launch or mission. I hoped and prayed that you would never have to read this note, but now, you must know that I am ready for whatever God has planned for me and for us.

I love you all so very, very much! I never dreamed how much I could love someone until I met you, Susan. I couldn't even imagine the joy that you, Cole and Sutton, have given me. We have a beautiful family and a life that I am sure many people envy. I am so very proud of you, Susan; so beautiful, strong, intelligent, and independent. You are a wonderful wife and the best of mothers to Cole and Sutton. I thank God every day for the time that I have spent with you and the joy that entered my life way back in 1989.

Cole, you have grown into a fine young man. My memories of you will always be some of the favorite times of my life. Playing catch on the beach in Florida before I went to Station; watching your confidence level grow with each passing year; seeing you and your strength of mind and character, coupled with your warm and sincere heart. I am so proud of you and I love you so very much, son!

Sutton, you are my precious "Sweet Pea." The love between a father and daughter is nothing short of amazing. Your energy and smile are riveting for me and I will always remember our "wrestling matches" on the living room floor . . . when you put your hands on your hips and said, "Daddy, get down on the floor, right now!" You are so beautiful . . . just like your mother. I love you and I am very proud of you, too.

To be reading this . . . something must have happened to our shuttle crew or to me. Please, please know that life must go on. You all will adapt and become stronger because of the loss. I know that you are in good hands with our friends and families. And our church family will be there as well. Be strong, my loves, and continue to live proudly and in God's glory. Know that I died doing what I had dreamed of doing for my entire life. Something that I always thought was possible, but unlikely. I was able to live my dream and do it with all of you by my side!

I wish I had more time to pen this letter to you . . . to think about the words to write and make them perfectly clear and poetic at the same time. I wrote songs for Cole and for Sutton and had always planned to write a song for you, too, Susan. I started it but was not able to get it finished. I chose the title for your song, "I See God's Love in Your Eyes," which seems so appropriate for you and for us. I thought that I would finish it one day . . . such that I could sing it to you; sorry that things got in the way! But don't worry . . . we will be together again, with our kids, in a place that is more beautiful than one could ever imagine. I will sing for you then.

I love you with all of my heart and soul. Thank you for being my family.

Clayton

Neither letter was ever intended to be read, and thank God their planned purpose never materialized. To read them now is important, for if you learn nothing else from reading this book, it is how much my entire family needed tremendous faith in God.

The importance that I place on family was also manifested from orbit when, near the end of my five-month odyssey in space, I used my on-orbit journal to send down "A Note to My Family":

> This journal chapter will be my final one from orbit. It is a very special chapter for me as my time in this wonderful place is coming to an end. There are so many things that I just didn't get done . . . time has passed so quickly! But today, in these words, I hope to complete a task that I consider extremely important, and that is why this chapter is for my family. To all of you out there who have been following this adventure, you are welcome to read along and I hope that you enjoy it . . . but it is truly meant for my family: Susan, Cole, and Sutton.
>
> To my beautiful and intelligent wife, my strong, tall son, and my energetic and playful daughter, I must say that it has taken me far too long to pen these words. But I think that now is the right time. I have been thinking about how I might "cap off" my on orbit journal in a unique way. What could I say; what should I say to convey my feelings for you? How will it make you feel? I want it to be right and I want it to make you feel special. I want you to understand how important our family is to me. My time here in space has been my dream come true, yet it is quickly drawing to a close. So it is time for me now to share with you some of my reflections.
>
> First and foremost, I must simply tell you, thanks. Thank you for letting me pursue my dream. Thank you for putting up with the travel and my time away from home, my crankiness when I was tired after long days at work and for missing all of those practices, games, and first days of school. Believe it or not, there are people in this world who would not let a loved one do something like this. Their thoughts would have been more focused on themselves, about how it might

change their lives in some way, how it could adversely impact what they were trying to accomplish. But not the three of you. You have given to me a gift that I may never be able to fully repay. You have given me the gift of love, the gift of trust and support, the gift of family. You have all sacrificed for me in a way that is truly remarkable by staying strong and focused, and by working together to assume the responsibilities that previously fell to me.

My dearest Susan, you have been a mother and father, a chauffeur, an accountant, a landscaper and wife, all while continuing to perform at the highest level in your job. Cole and Sutton, you have grown up more quickly perhaps than I wanted you to, but you have learned a great deal. You have continued to mature in positive ways and I pray that you now understand better what it means to give to, and sacrifice for, others. I am sorry for all of your events that I have missed over the years; I truly wanted to be there for you. I will be there now.

I have missed you all deeply. There has not been a day that goes by where I did not think of you, pray for you, and smile because of you. I so looked forward to our weekend video visits over the airwaves and our chats on the telephone. It meant so much to me to be able to see your faces as well as hear your voices. It brought me home for just a while and helped carry me through the days. You mean everything to me and I am so proud of you. We have done this together as a family and we are stronger because of it.

If all goes well, I will be home soon. We will be a family once again and I can't wait!

I love you all!

I flew twice and I survived twice. Perhaps that "I" ought to be changed to a "we."

In July 2007, just the second month of my time on the space station, I called Susan on the Internet Protocol (IP) phone. It was eerily similar to the phone conversation with my sister in my JSC office that day, only differing by the location of my "office."

Susan's tone was somber, her words measured. "The spot is back," she said. Four simple words left me speechless. My thoughts went quickly to unavoidable anger, with the realization that God was testing my faith yet again.

"This time she'll require both chemo and radiation," Susan continued. "It's going to be a tough fight."

Mom and I would share many loving conversations over the IP phone in the next several months. Each time I would counsel her on the need to do exactly what the doctors said. "I need you to be strong," I would tell her, while ending every single conversation with "I love you and I'll see you at landing." I prayed continuously for the remainder of my increment, hoping my two-hundred-plus-mile advantage in altitude would push Mom and me toward the top of God's priority list.

On November 7, 2007, as the space shuttle *Discovery*'s onboard computers used their ones and zeroes to target a landing at the Kennedy Space Center, I was tightly strapped into the center seat on the shuttle's middeck. Resting comfortably on my back, I took everything in as the shuttle initiated her energy-reducing roll reversals—the first having occurred directly over Nebraska—on her way to Florida. We were coming home!

My 152-day journey in space, which began with a thunderous launch of the space shuttle *Atlantis* on what would have been my father's seventy-seventh birthday, had come to an end as we touched down not so gently on Runway 15/33 and rolled to a stop. That monumental day marked not only the completion of 151 days, 18 hours, 23 minutes, and 14 seconds for me in space but also the fifteenth wedding anniversary for Susan and me.

Less than twenty-four hours later, I was gingerly navigating the confined space of my private room in the astronaut crew quarters at KSC to enjoy my first hot shower in over five months. After spending ample time with the water pelting me, I slowly dressed myself in my NASA astronaut flight suit, feeling like I weighed much more than my two hundred pounds. I was back in the gripping confines of Earth's gravity.

Having grunted and groaned, stretched and tugged to get my flight boots on, I carefully rose from my chair and eventually emerged from my room to begin a slow, deliberate walk down the hallway, aided by the wall.

Moving with a determination bolstered by five months in outer space and keeping my head steady so the world wouldn't start spinning again, I closed the distance between me and the main lounge area, prepared to fulfill one of the greatest days of my lifetime.

As I entered the room I was reunited with my wonderful family—not just my wife and children but my brother and sister and their families, my in-laws, and my uncle Jim. And there in the back, sitting quietly in a chair and wearing her oversized sunglasses, sat my mom, Alice. The smile on her face stretched across the room and I am certain was matched only by the identical one on my face. My heart swelled with a pride and love that only a son can have. I had dreamed of this moment since before launch and I had prayed that she would be strong enough to be there when I returned to Earth.

I approached her with all the speed a recently earthbound astronaut could muster. She slowly rose from her chair as I reached to her outstretched hand. I pulled her toward me ever so gently. We held each other tightly, no words being said. When it seemed the right time, I relaxed my embrace, holding her at arm's length to tell her I loved her. She looked deeply into my eyes with a mother's love and said that she was "better now." She told me that what she really wanted was to touch me and hold my hand, and that in doing so, she would know that I was real to her again and back safely upon the Earth.

Mom lost her fight with cancer on December 13, 2007, just a little more than a month after we saw each other for what turned out to be the final time.

She was seventy-seven years old. We did not really know what she died of; perhaps it was the cancer. But we knew in our hearts that whatever the cause, she was just tired . . . tired of chemotherapy and radiation, tired of fighting to stay strong enough to follow our family's adventure as I journeyed into space and back home. Together, my sister and brother and I took great comfort in the fact she was able to be a part of the journey and we were all able to reunite as a family at the Kennedy Space Center on the day after the landing of STS-120.

Our mom was a gracious, loving, and giving person who taught us that we could be and do whatever we dreamed. She loved her family and her church, and she understood what it means to instill solid values and a keen sense of responsibility in her children. The world needs more moms like her.

Mom was a beacon of faith, and her presence that day helped to solidify mine.

There have been many times since her death when I simply needed to talk to my mom. Fortunately, I can listen to the phone message she left me a few days after our meeting in Florida. She had just called to say "Hello, this is your mother. Welcome back."

Thanks, Mom, for everything. I miss you.

22

Impacts

At ten years old I became a huge fan of the NBA's Milwaukee Bucks and their star rookie center, Ferdinand Lewis Alcindor Jr. A graduate of UCLA and the undisputed leader of the college's three-time NCAA basketball champion Bruins, Alcindor would become an icon for those who grew up witnessing the epic battles between professional basketball big men such as the Los Angeles Lakers' Wilt Chamberlain and the Boston Celtics' Bill Russell. Alcindor, who would later convert to Islam and change his name to Kareem Abdul-Jabbar, was my first autograph. I didn't get one in person. I had to write to the Bucks' home office in Milwaukee. Several weeks later, a four-by-six black-and-white photo arrived in the mail. It was Alcindor in his forest green jersey trimmed in white and red, emblazoned with the number 33, throwing one of his famous "skyhooks." I was in heaven. "Big Lew" became my idol and role model.

The job of role model is a very serious one. I believe my actions as a United States astronaut set an example for people both young and old. While a huge responsibility, it is a critical part of the astronaut job description. Our behavior must be above reproach because we never know when we may touch the life of another human being.

Speaking to a crowd of over five hundred at the 2008 Governor's Premiere of the Nebraska Educational Telecommunications documentary movie *Homemade Astronaut: The Clay Anderson Story*, I discussed the importance of being a role model.

"I want you to know how honored I am to be in this position," I began.

I want you all to know that I am simply a man, a man who loves his God, who loves his family, and who loves his country. And as a United States astronaut, I really *love* the United States part. I take my position as a role model so very, very seriously. I have NEVER cheated on my taxes; I have NEVER cheated on my wife; I have NEVER spit on an umpire; I have NEVER charged into the stands at an event and fought with a patron. I have NEVER run a Ponzi scheme and I have NEVER taken steroids. But I'm here to tell you tonight that I have NEVER been more proud to be a Nebraskan!

Throughout my fifteen-year career as an astronaut, I have participated in hundreds of public appearances. In each and every one, I hoped that I could positively affect those in the audience.

Or even perhaps just one.

It started with the receipt of a letter in the mail in the spring of 2006.

Delivered by our steadfast but often maligned U.S. Postal Service, the envelope arrived at our home address in League City, Texas. Though it was from Hastings, Nebraska, the return address was unfamiliar.

It was a handwritten note from a worried grandmother. Her grandson Thomas needed to be fitted with a palatal expander. This would be followed by ugly, unmanageable headgear and, ultimately, braces. According to her, Thomas was afraid of how he would look and whether it would hurt, both normal concerns for any young person facing orthodontia. His parents were fearful that he wouldn't follow the orthodontist's instructions, thereby risking failure of the doctor's plan.

"Grandma" had a simple request of Nebraska's astronaut. She politely asked if it would be possible for me to write Thomas a letter to let him know that everything would be okay and that he had nothing to be worried about.

As I read the sincere and touching letter, I had conflicting thoughts about how to deal with this request. Normally I would sit down and write him a letter, just as his grandmother had asked. Yet to do it properly would require that it be put on NASA letterhead, addressed from me within the astronaut office, and sent in a NASA envelope. Those efforts would require more energy than I wanted to expend. It would also involve bothering one of our NASA secretaries to type up the draft letter and prepare it for mailing.

But the lad was, after all, from Hastings, Nebraska, and I really should honor the request. It was the right thing to do; it was part of my responsibility as a U.S. astronaut. It would be considerably easier if I just called him on the phone. Wouldn't that be just as good, maybe even better?

I didn't have the youngster's phone number, but I did have his name and I knew he lived in or near Hastings.

I called Joan Primrose, secretary to the president of Hastings College, to ask if she could possibly locate the family. Joan, as expected, came through like a champ, mostly because there was only one family with that name in her phonebook.

That evening, shortly after dinner, I dialed the number of the Michael Harling family of Hastings, Nebraska.

Thomas himself answered the phone.

"Hello, this is Clayton Anderson, the astronaut from Nebraska. Is this Thomas Harling?" I asked.

"Yes . . ." was his tentative reply.

We proceeded to become better acquainted and were enjoying a pleasant two-way conversation when I heard a loud voice: "Thomas, who are you talking to?"

"Astronaut Clayton Anderson," came Thomas's matter-of-fact reply.

"Thomas, c'mon," his father, Mike, said skeptically. "Who is it really?"

"Astronaut Clayton Anderson," Thomas reiterated more forcefully.

"Give me the phone," his father demanded, obviously thinking Thomas had been hoodwinked by someone who was simply jerking his chain.

It took me almost two minutes of explanation and quoting of space station factoids before his dad finally believed I was who I purported to be.

In a changed tone of voice, Michael said, "Oh, this is just an honor, sir!"

Now the problem was he wouldn't give the phone back to Thomas! He pummeled me with questions and comments for twenty minutes. After some gentle verbal nudging on my part, he reluctantly returned the phone to his son.

I didn't think much more about Thomas Harling and his braces for quite some time. I had a mission to prepare for and many more important things on my mind.

Thomas and I would cross paths again at the *Homemade Astronaut* movie premier. In the spring of 2008 the Nebraska Educational Telecommunications (net) network, then led by general manager Rod Bates, and producer Sue Maryott released a documentary about my life and career, after a premier gala at the Strategic Air and Space Museum in my hometown of Ashland.

Thomas Harling came with his father. He presented me with a picture of us together from a previous event. In the photo I was kneeling in my royal blue flight suit, leaning over Thomas's shoulder. We both had broad smiles on our faces. On the back he had written of his dream to one day go into space.

I tucked the cherished keepsake into the breast pocket of my suit coat and promised Thomas that I would take his picture with me into space one day, should I be lucky enough to receive another such opportunity.

When the time came for me to begin training with the crew of sts-131, I remembered to put all my photos, including the one from Thomas, into one of the plastic sleeves that the Flight Data File folks had glued (at my request) to the inside covers of my official crew notebook. On April 5, 2010, it would journey with me the eight-and-one-half minutes to space in a notebook precariously affixed to my left thigh.

On Flight Day 10, all our spacewalks were completed and the mission was winding down. Smiling at the memory of the impromptu phone call and my friendship with Thomas, I removed the picture of him and me from the plastic envelope. A Nikon d2s camera with a manual release cable, fastened securely to a Bogen bracket arm on a station handrail, stood at the ready.

As the weightless photo floated inches from the station's cupola window, with the docked space shuttle *Discovery* and the vacuum of space serving as the background, I mashed the plunger of the manual release and captured a digital image of me and my friend Thomas.

After landing, while going through the thousands of on-orbit photos, I came across the one of Thomas and me. Grinning, I emailed my friends in the jsc photo lab to please provide me with a color eight-by-ten print of our smiling mug shot. Pushing "send," I experienced a tremendously warm feeling inside my chest. I would take Thomas's original photo, along with an eight-by-ten of the photo I had taken in space, and have our sts-131 crew secretary, Suzanne Singleton, provide us with an official nasa "flown item" certificate. The certificate would say in part:

This photo was flown for my friend Thomas Harling aboard the United States Space Shuttle *Discovery* to the International Space Station. *Discovery* launched at 6:21 a.m. edt on April 5, 2010, from Pad 39a at the Kennedy Space Center, Florida. At 9:08 a.m. edt on April 20, 2010, *Discovery* landed on Runway 33 at Kennedy Space Center's Shuttle Landing Facility having traveled 238 Earth orbits.

Discovery reached an altitude of 221 miles and a speed of 17,500 miles per hour. The flight duration lasted 15 days, 2 hours, 47 minutes, 10 seconds covering a total distance of 6,232,235 statute miles.

When the print from jsc's Building 8 photo lab arrived at my desk, I grabbed one of my fine-point black Sharpies. The beautiful blue sea and white cloud background of Earth blended perfectly with the orbiter's starboard orbital maneuvering system pod making the ideal spot for a dedication. On its upper left-hand corner I inscribed: "*Thomas—I keep my promises!*" Then I signed my name above *Discovery's* port wing, making sure not to block the part of the photo depicting the logistics module in the payload bay, and added the words "sts-131" below my signature. I didn't know whether Thomas had received this package from nasa until August 2010, when my good friend Jack Dunn invited me to make a public appearance in Nebraska.

The afternoon I was to speak at the University of Nebraska's Morrill Hall and Mueller Planetarium, I got an email on my Facebook account that someone had tagged me in a picture. Not yet an avid and committed Facebook user, I rarely would receive an email notice and then actually *do* something about it. For some reason, on this day I did. It was another picture of Thomas Harling. This time he stood poised and proud in front of a poster from the NET *Homemade Astronaut* movie, holding in his hands the authenticity certificate, the eight-by-ten photo, and the original shot of him and me that started this whole thing.

The smile on his face was HUGE! I quickly broke another one of my astronaut rules about "What Not to Do on Facebook" and posted a comment letting his mother—it was she who tagged me—know how pleased I was that they had received the memorabilia.

That night the Harlings were surprising Thomas with a trip to the museum to see me. He arrived with his little brother, Scott, and their mom and dad. The two boys were identically dressed in brown shirts with white lithograph images of the space shuttle in flight. Even though I was in a bit of a hurry to set up my audio-visual equipment for the presentation, and there were Lincoln media folks waiting to film interviews before the show, I made sure to swing by Thomas.

"Don't I know you?" I asked.

He grinned.

"Thomas . . . right?" I winked at him, grinned at his mother and headed on my way to set up.

Thomas's mother, Tracy, would later write to me: "Not only are you Thomas's hero and little brother Scott's, but Mike's now too. We are very proud that Thomas and Scott have you as their HERO and role model. There are so many bad influences in this day and age, so I am very grateful Thomas chose you, and that you have taken the time to make the boys feel special. The things you have done will never be forgotten by us."

I made an impact—a good one—on Thomas and his family, like Ferdinand Lewis Alcindor Jr. long ago had on me.

I first met Devlin at the Johnson Space Center prior to embarking on my long-duration mission in 2007. A mere eight years old, Devlin and I bonded with a simple handshake and became fast friends. During my time in orbit, I was able to establish a critical "long distance" relationship with Devlin through the efforts of my wife and her colleague in the public affairs office, Jeannie Aquino. Jeannie served as the family's point of contact at JSC and as my liaison during my five-month stay.

Devlin had cancer.

Jeannie's updates provided word from Devlin's father, Paul, that his battle against the cancerous brain tumor seemed to be going well. "We have been having check-ups with different doctors and they continue to be pleased with Devlin's recovery," his father wrote. "His hair is really starting to grow back now and before long he will need a haircut." His proud father speculated that when enough of Devlin's hair had grown back, no one would ever know he even had a tumor.

The good news continued with a report from Devlin's radiation oncologist, who thought that the grade of the tumor possibly could be lowered, the best news the family had received in quite some time.

Jeannie and her colleagues in the public affairs office kept Devlin's spirits high by sending him "cool NASA stuff." Jeannie wrote me that a memorabilia package that even contained a few astronaut autographs allowed Devlin and his family to "re-live the excitement of the day" of their JSC visit. According to his mom, "Devlin and the other boys (and, of course, Dad) are especially excited about all the patches, stickers, pictures and everything you put in the collection!"

Paul wrote back on a positive note: "Thank you, [Jeannie] and everyone at NASA, for all that has been done for Devlin. I know as he gets older he will look back on this experience and be amazed at the special privilege that was given to him."

In the midst of Devlin's battle, NASA at JSC was experiencing troubles of its own. Waging their own war with the unknown, Devlin's parents found the strength to acknowledge the tragedy inside of the space center's gates: "I was very sorry and sad to hear about the tragic events from the last few weeks everywhere in the USA but especially at NASA. I hope everyone is coping well (I am not sure what to say; I suppose this is how everyone feels when talking to us)." (Devlin's father was referring to a shooting incident that took place on the grounds of JSC, where a NASA contract employee, struggling with his employment situation and his own personal chaos, brought a concealed weapon on site. He shot and killed one person before committing suicide.)

As NASA slowly recovered, the news from Australia took a tragic turn. Paul Russell reported: "I am sorry it has been so long since an update and I am even sorrier that this update is bringing bad news."

"Devlin has suffered a significant turn for the worse; he can no longer walk unaided and keeps falling asleep (the tumour is pressing on the sleep center of the brain). We have him at home and he is comfortable and not in any pain. We probably do not have much time left."

They were ominous words.

Paul wrote: "We continue to fight the good fight. Devlin is more awake these days but still cannot walk unaided or use his left side, and his right eye is permanently closed." Devlin's unconstrained child's heart was still evident: "He is watching heaps of TV, but is very alert and talks heaps and keeps us both on our toes."

The acknowledgment from Jeannie that Devlin was aware of my mission brought comfort to me. Devlin's father wrote: "It is exciting to see familiar names such as Clayton up on the ISS when I am reading the Space.com web page. I keep Devlin up to date on any of these events that I find."

As Paul signed off from his latest update, his tone said it all. "Talk to you again soon, hopefully with a miracle!" When I read that, the wheels in my brain started to turn.

It was time for me to see if I could provide some encouragement to this young man fighting for his life.

A quick email to the ground and Jeannie provided me with Devlin's contact information. Flying over the Great Barrier Reef of Australia, I sent him his first cyberspace note: "Hello, Devlin, from 215 miles above the earth! I am soaring around the earth at five miles every single second. Today I flew over the northeast coast of Australia and saw the Great Barrier Reef. Pretty cool if you ask me! I saw the most beautiful blues and turquoise colors I have ever seen. I just wondered if there were lots of sharks down there."

"Keep fighting, strong young man! You have a good friend in outer space!"

"All the best to you and your family."

As I hit the "send" key, I couldn't help but wonder if my efforts would have any impact.

Devlin, his condition worsening, was still excited by my note.

His father conveyed his reply. "Hi, Clayton, thanks for the e-mail. We are very impressed and honoured that you would send an e-mail to us from the iss. Devlin's response to your e-mail, especially the speed you are going, was 'Holey moley!' It made us laugh. . . . I can only imagine how beautiful the reef would look as well as the other amazing sights you would see."

I was touched by the level of courage displayed by this tough little boy who "despite his setbacks . . . continues to amaze all the doctors at how well he has done and how long and well he has been fighting."

Paul closed his latest report: "Not too many people can really say they do have someone looking down and looking out for them."

While I was getting only snippets about Devlin through the notes from his father, they were confirmation that I was touching his life. In the midst of the situation, Jeannie Aquino affirmed my influence: "I know you have lots of important work that you're doing on the iss, but I just wanted to tell you how absolutely wonderful I think it is that you're taking the time to send a few notes to Devlin. I'm sure Devlin is beside himself when he gets them, and I know that his parents are extremely grateful that you are interested in making his last days so special. Once again, it goes to show what a really great guy you are!"

As promised, my shark scouting expeditions continued for Devlin.

"Devlin: Just as promised . . . I looked for you on the reef yesterday. Didn't see you there, but I didn't see any sharks either! That's probably a good thing, huh?"

"Check out my pictures! Keep looking up!"

Before leaving my keyboard, I had an epiphany of sorts. Wrestling mentally about how I could better help this lad, I came up with what I thought was a unique and potentially therapeutic idea that I could implement from outer space.

And all I would need was a little help from the ground.

I keyed the handheld microphone and called the Mission Control Center. Reaching the on-duty CAPCOM, I told them my message was aimed at the biomedical engineer, Karin Gast, who was dutifully working the Orbit 1 shift from 11:00 p.m. to 7:00 a.m.

I explained that I wanted to send Devlin a personal message. In space station terms, sending a message meant I had recorded something on board and wanted it "delivered" to the intended recipient. This is where Karin's skills were required.

Through the magic of electronic media, Karin would work with the television and media folks to have my words transferred from the space-to-ground audio loops, sent to the experts in Building 8, and packaged for shipping via a trip through the ether back to Karin.

Jeannie would then work with Karin to get the message to Devlin and his family.

Jeannie's excitement was conveyed in her words to Devlin: "In my e-mail this morning was a very special audio file to you from Clay Anderson on the International Space Station. It is my honor to pass it along to you. Next time I see you, looks like I'll need to ask you for your autograph!"

The message I recorded for my friend was short and simple. The transcription does not come close to relating the emotion contained in my voice as I delivered the words I had pored over so long.

CLAY: Houston, ISS on 2 for general favor.

CHRIS CASSIDY (CAPCOM): Go ahead, Clay.

CLAY: Yeah, I wanted to tell the folks on the ground that last summer I had the opportunity before I launched to tour a young lad from Australia. His name was Devlin—Devlin Russell.

Devlin was quite a young man; he's very bright and very energetic—he had a really good head on his shoulders and he asked really good questions and I was very proud to be able to give him a tour when he was down in Houston, so—I would just like to say "hello" to Devlin from the International Space Station, and I would like to make him an honorary crew member of Expedition 15 if I could . . . and with all the rights and privileges thereof.

So I would like to wish my earthbound crewmate Devlin of Australia a very wonderful summer, and keep lookin' up, Devlin. Hang tough, buddy. You've got some friends in outer space!

And Chris, if you would see that that gets to Jeannie Aquino, please.

CASSIDY: Will do, Clay. Thanks for the nice words.

CLAY: You bet! Thanks.

Conferring the rank of honorary Expedition 15 crewmember upon Devlin turned out to be easier than I anticipated, mostly because I followed the age-old advice to beg forgiveness later rather than ask for permission.

Devlin's response was penned by his parents, as expected, but to hear of his trials was tough on my heart: "Devlin would like to send his appreciation and thanks for the kind words and for making him a member of the crew. Even though Devlin is currently going through a very tough patch he still keeps Trina and I on our toes. He asks most days for us to take him to school to see his classmates. When we go in on Monday we will be taking your message and playing it to his class."

The father's emotion was evident in his further words:

I have always been very excited about the things NASA does with space exploration and development, but I think that will now have to come a distant second to the obvious kindness and generosity that is in the hearts and souls of every person there. Perhaps it is in the nature of all people that want great things for this planet and all those who share it to see the big picture but not to forget the little people. Keep up the great work, everyone.

I would not hear from my crewmate Devlin again.

On Thursday, August 23, 2007, Devlin Russell lost his battle with cancer.

Almost as if in answer to my question of whether I had made a difference, Paul wrote that Devlin's younger brother Casey "informed me last week that he would like to become an astronaut."

When I learned of Devlin's death, I flew into my sleep station and closed its doors. I cried that day. I cried for a little boy who didn't deserve the burden that had been placed upon his tiny shoulders. I cried for a family that just lost a loved one and who would now have to deal with a huge emptiness in their lives that I simply could not comprehend. And I cried for an astronaut who was blessed in countless ways with a life he could have never imagined but who on this day felt helpless and alone. For in this instance, he wished he could have done more . . . much, much more.

There is an old saying that says if you touch one child's life, you will be blessed for a lifetime.

Impacts, indeed.

23

The End Becomes the Beginning

During fourth-grade recess at Ashland's elementary school, we were playing pickup basketball. The court was on a concrete surface beside a gravel playground with equipment badly in need of repair.

My drive to the hoop was met with a hard, cutting hack across my arm from Bobby Jordan. I cried foul. He claimed innocence. We began a shouting match.

Local bully Pat Keckler, who was older because he was held back a year, stepped in to assume the role of referee. "Finish this after school," Pat ordered.

Those were the only words he spoke, and they portended my doom. My name had just been entered onto the after-school fight card.

I spent the rest of the day sucking up to Bobby Jordan. Having never even been close to being in a fight, I was doing my damnedest to not start now. Lacking confidence in my ability to survive—let alone win—a fistfight, I talked to him nicely, asking him questions about his favorite hobbies and TV shows. I offered him candy and chewing gum that I didn't even have.

My pitiful efforts to avoid the fight were in vain. As the school day ended, I emerged from the exit doors and found Bobby waiting at the bottom of the steps. His entourage of about forty students would ensure that the impromptu fracas during recess would come to its conclusion.

Slowly descending the steps, I wondered how this would go down. The crowd began to enclose Bobby and me in the circle of a classic playground fight.

Eyes glaring over tightly balled up fists, held just below and in front our noses, we circled each other for what seemed like an hour. With the crowd shouting encouragement, Bobby made his move, coming directly toward me with his arms flailing. Avoiding his advance, I spun quickly as he flew past, and then I wrapped my arms tightly around his chest. Gaining the advantage, I threw him hard to the ground while wrapping my legs around his waist and holding on for dear life.

On the offensive, I tucked my right arm under his chin. Pulling tightly toward my chest, I increased the pressure against his throat, calmly telling him to give up.

He uttered some noise, unintelligible from lack of air. His words were clarified with the help of the crowd. I was engulfed in a mass of elementary school kids yelling, "He gives up! He gives up!"

Just as on that playground in the fourth grade when I had no idea how to have a fistfight, I had no idea how to work for NASA when I started as a summer intern, and I had no idea as to what kind of journey I had begun.

Now, after thirty years with NASA, I can look back on a career that brings me an enormous amount of pride. And through it all I am still not sure I knew what I was doing.

I am now a retired astronaut. Not a former astronaut, but a retired astronaut. When I returned to the planet Earth after the STS-131 mission, I was on top of the world—literally and figuratively. As a crew, we accomplished every objective for which our mission was tasked. Now that the space shuttle program is "in the books," with shuttles mounted on concrete pillars across the country, I am proud of our contributions to this nation's space program and grateful to be a part of U.S. history.

But leaving certainly wasn't easy.

My final two years in the astronaut office was a difficult time. Astronaut chief Peggy Whitson believed I did not have the temperament for another long-duration spaceflight. She claimed that she had "much better choices to fly in space than me." With no more short-duration shuttle missions on the horizon, my flying career was over and I was left staring at a future of considerable uncertainty.

Without active astronaut status, I was moved into management. I was frustrated, angry, hugely disappointed, and jealous of those deemed worthy of continued mission assignments. It was obvious that just as when I was a young neophyte fistfighter, I didn't know how to deal with this either.

It would take a big leap of faith.

As an astronaut, there was no one prouder to don that royal blue flight suit than me, no one more honored to serve his country and risk his life in the vastness of outer space than me. There was no one more humbled to have his name recorded alongside the greatest space pioneers in history than me. There was no one more privileged to speak with people around the globe and share the wonders of my life and journey than me. And there was no one more grateful to have experienced the power and majesty of our Almighty God than me.

The end of my time as an astronaut has become the beginning of my next journey. Like writing this memoir, everything is new and challenging again. The journey is still in its infancy—my family and I have no idea where it might lead. But we have faith, and we pray it will be as rewarding and challenging as the years I spent representing the Astronaut Corps and the United States of America.

It was fun being famous. When I returned to Nebraska it was cool to have people recognize me in restaurants and on the streets. It was an honor when they asked me to pose for a picture or sign an autograph. It was wonderful to see the excitement of children when they asked me questions or stood shyly by while their parents explained, "Little Joey just *loves* outer space!" Remember . . . I had influence.

And I still do!

The fame and notoriety can be difficult. Good or bad, there are "space groupies" out there. It takes a strong love of God and family to withstand the temptations. For me, having met Susan was critical, both for my life and for my career. Being able to share this ride with her has made it even more special. Her love and patience are boundless . . . just like our universe.

These days, I am sometimes introduced as a "former" astronaut. That just seems so weird. I know other "formers" do public appearances, entering an auditorium in their blue flight suit, ready to dazzle the audience with stories from their astronaut past, and that seems normal enough. But it makes me feel a wee bit awkward.

The workday pace and corresponding job duties change drastically in the mundane world of the "management" astronaut. There is no more flying in the T-38. No more training simulations or Russian language classes. Shifts are available in the Mission Control Center as the ISS CAPCOM, and that can be a great deal of fun. Sitting back at the console, having actually lived on board, gave me the feeling of being tremendously useful. But even then, the shifts didn't hold the aura of excitement they once did.

A plausible analogy is that of a professional baseball player nearing the twilight of his career. Imagine having been the starting shortstop or third baseman for a major league baseball team. It's game day and you've arrived at the ballpark. Just as you've done hundreds of times before, you suit up, you stretch, you become engrossed in warm-up tosses, fielding reps, batting practice, and maybe even an interview or two with the local media. Then the game begins and you must apply your skills—developed through years of training and hard work—for the good of your organization and those who pay your salary. The game ends and it's on to the next contest. You have competed at the highest level within your profession.

But on this day you don't even get in the game.

I participated at the highest level (220 miles high) of my profession. I lived in outer space for a total of 167 days. I performed six spacewalks, totaling thirty-eight hours and twenty-eight minutes crawling around in the vacuum of outer space. I circled the Earth once every ninety minutes, and I pooped in four different spaceships! As many astronauts like to paraphrase, "I was livin' the dream baby!"

It was out of this world and I miss it . . . I miss it a lot.

Yet in order to be honest with myself, I have to admit that it was my own irreverence that sent me into the "astronaut penalty box" and off of flight status. And I take full responsibility.

The cancellation of the shuttle program, first suggested by President George W. Bush and then carried out by President Obama, dealt severe blows to the aerospace job market. With the retirement of the space shuttle, NASA was left with an excess of both contractor support and civil servants. For the contractors it spelled layoffs. For NASA and U.S. government employees, efforts were made to provide transfers. But there were a considerable number of former shuttle workers and managers. Many at the top of the government service pay scale would be difficult to place in other organizations.

Fortunately for me, the Johnson Space Center was able to convince the Office of Personnel Management that a voluntary early retirement allotment (VERA) was in order. Providing retirement options to those not yet at their official retirement date might convince some to leave early, alleviating (ever so slightly) the problem of having more people than viable job opportunities.

After putting my name into the hat for the VERA, it was time to seriously seek my next opportunity.

"What do you want to do now? What is your dream job?" were the questions everybody asked.

Now that's a difficult question to answer. I had already lived my dream job. Nothing could top those experiences. What other job application asks for someone with experience in the areas of spacewalking, flying robotic arms, speaking the Russian language, operating a complex space vehicle, and learning the ins and outs of life in zero gravity?

My next adventure needs to be exactly that, an adventure. I must be passionate about what I do, ready to throw my heart and soul into it, like I did when I was selected as an astronaut.

Another astronaut myth is out there that says you can only play the astronaut card once. That may be totally true, but whatever my next endeavor turns out to be, I do not want to simply assume the role of former astronaut, new office "potted plant."

I have a loving family—a beautiful wife and two incredible children—and a legacy career. I hope to be remembered as a compassionate leader, someone of strong character, striving to do the right thing whenever possible.

On January 31, 2013, I would write my final government email. It would be sent to the astronaut office's lead secretary to be formally distributed to everyone supporting the organization known as CB–the Astronaut Office). It looked like this:

From: Graham, Kelli (JSC-CB111)
Sent: Thursday, January 31, 2013 12:07 PM
To: JSC-DL-FCOD-VITT-CB4S
Subject: "See Ya Later" from Clay Anderson
From: Anderson, Clayton C. (JSC-CB611)
Sent: Thursday, January 31, 2013 11:51 AM
All:

The time has come. Today will be my final day as a NASA Civil Servant, but not as a United States Astronaut. I didn't think I would ever reach this point, but the planets have aligned (do you like the space reference?) and it is right for me to move on to my next adventure.

As many have already said, this is the best job in the universe. I agree wholeheartedly and have diligently tried to leave this a better place. You here in CB are, without question, one of the most talented groups ever assembled and I am proud, honored, and humbled to be considered a small part of that legacy.

Best wishes to all of you . . . it's been one helluva ride! Please keep in touch and continue to study those "Famous Cities from Nebraska!" There may be a quiz. Go Big Red!

Sincerely,

Clay

"May the Force be with you." It's always been with me.